Photographs by *Lynn Houston*
Additional photographs by *Femmy DeLyser*

JANE FONDA'S
NEW PREGNANCY WORKOUT
AND TOTAL BIRTH PROGRAM

by FEMMY DeLYSER

VIKING

VIKING

Published by the Penguin Group
27 Wrights Lane, London W8 5TZ, England
Viking Penguin Inc., 40 West 23rd Street, New York, New York 10010, USA
Penguin Books Australia Ltd, Ringwood, Victoria, Australia
Penguin Books Canada Ltd, 2801 John Street, Markham, Ontario, Canada L3R 1B4
Penguin Books (NZ) Ltd, 182–190 Wairau Road, Auckland 10, New Zealand

Penguin Books Ltd, Registered Offices: Harmondsworth, Middlesex, England

First published in the USA by Simon and Schuster 1989

First published in Great Britain by Viking 1990

Printed and bound in Great Britain by
Butler & Tanner Ltd, Frome and London

A CIP catalogue record for this book is available from the British Library

ISBN 0–670–83226–X

About the Illustrations

PHOTO on title page, from left to right: Janie Gates, Wendie Jo Sperber, Sandi Wildman Padnos, Cola Smith, Sandra Macat, Monica May, Pia Vai, Kirsten Frantzich, Beth Collins, Anne-Marie Crighton, Martha Coolidge, Jillie Mack, Kathryn Gimbel, Teri Herron and Elaine Balden.

ILLUSTRATIONS on page 140 and pages 173 to 224 by Michael Speaker, on pages 231 to 232 by Sam Gimbel, on page 201 by Steve Beebee.

THE ILLUSTRATIONS by Michael Speaker and Steve Beebee were reprinted from *Childbirth in the Modern World* by Femmy DeLyser, Los Angeles chapter of the American Society for Psychoprophylaxis in Obstetrics, 1977, with kind permission of L.A. ASPO.

PHOTO on page 32 by John Toll, on page 193 (bottom right) by Clint Allen, on page 295 (left) by Jim Balden, on page 298 by John B. Cahoon, III.

PHOTOS on pages 29, 34 (bottom), 35, 36, 54, 56, 57, 61, 73, 91 (top), 144, 146, 147, 153, 154, 155, 158, 159, 162, 163, 164, 168, 169, 182 (top), 184 (top and right), 185 (top), 186, 187, 195, 196, 207, 210, 211, 217 (right), 220, 221, 227, 228, 229, 231, 232, 234, 237 (top), 242, 243, 245, 248, 249, 250, 256, 258, 269 (top right and bottom), 270, 272, 273, 275, 276, 277, 278, 279, 282, 284, 289, 291, 292, 293, 297, 299, 300, 301, 308 (top) and 309 by Femmy DeLyser.

PHOTOS were developed and printed at Focus photo lab.

PHOTO on page 130 reprinted from *Bloemen van het Heelal*, Alit Veldhuisen-Djajasoebrata, Sijthoff, Amsterdam and the Museum voor Land-en Volkenkunde, Rotterdam, 1984, with kind permission of Alit Veldhuisen-Djajasoebrata and the Museum voor Land-en Volkenkunde, Rotterdam, Holland.

PHOTO on page 134 reprinted from *The Natural Childbirth Primer* by Grantly Dick-Read, Harper & Row, New York, 1955, with kind permission of Harper & Row, Publishers.

All other photos by Lynn Houston.

The instructions and advice in this book are in no way intended as a substitute for medical counseling. We advise a pregnant women to consult with her doctor before beginning this or any regimen of exercise. The author and the publisher disclaim any liability or loss, personal or otherwise, resulting from the procedures in this book.

Acknowledgments

Like others who have studied one subject for years, I am indebted to hundreds of people for sharing their knowledge and insights or for giving me feedback. I thank every one of them, especially Milton Erickson, M.D.; Virginia Satir, M.S.W.; Alexandra Levine, M.D.; Paul Fleiss, M.D.; Audrey Naylor, M.D.; Ruth Wester, R.N.; Ellen Silbergeld, Ph.D.; Vern Katz, M.D.; Daniel Kosich, Ph.D.; Barry S. Schifrin, M.D.; Jane Davis, M.D.; Uzzis Reiss, M.D.; Jim Varga, M.D.; Patsy Jones, R.N.; Jo Friedman, R.N.; Wendy Haldeman, R.N.; Corky Harvey, R.N.; Pat Clinton, R.N.; Leslie Stewart, C.N.M.; Sandra Steffes, M.S.; Rikie Prins, M.S.; Dutch midwives Beatrÿs Smulders and Astrid Limburg; and all my students. I thank Jane Fonda for her trust in my work, Eileen Davis for years of assistance with the Pregnancy, Birth, and Recovery Program at the Jane Fonda Workout Studio, Deborah Rothman and Mindy Odegard for helping me organize panel discussions in many cities on issues related to birth and new parenthood, Chrys Atwood for her support, and Debra Winger for being a source of inspiration and love and for patiently reading and rereading every draft. I thank the members of the medical profession who allowed me to photograph them at work, photographer Lynn Houston for her dedication, and Focus photo lab for their assistance. I thank artists Michael Speaker, Sam Gimbel, and Steve Beebee for their artwork, and at Simon and Schuster I thank Fred Hills, Ursula Obst, Eve Metz, Judith Lee, Leslie Ellen, and Kimberly Ruhe for their assistance with the text and with placing the illustrations. Above all, I thank the natural teachers in my life: my parents, Jan Booy and Fem Veuger, and my children, Dydia and Roland DeLyser.

For my students and
their babies

Contents

Foreword

by

JANE FONDA

There is perhaps no experience in our lives that quite equals that of becoming a mother. I have loved that role (I have two children, Vanessa and Troy), and it is always a pleasure to see other mothers, whether they are expecting or already caring for their infants. Fortunately, I have been able to meet many mother/baby couples because of a program at my workout studio especially designed to help women with pregnancy, birth, and new motherhood. The woman responsible for this program is Femmy DeLyser.

I first met Femmy DeLyser in 1973, in her sun-drenched living room in Santa Monica, where I had come with my husband to begin a series of classes in preparation for the birth of my second child. Femmy's voice, tinged with her soft Dutch accent, seemed to carry in its warmth a link to all women of all times who have shared this experience. She spoke to us not only of the profound changes our bodies were going through but of the history of childbirth and how the customs surrounding it have changed through time and vary from culture to culture. In her discussion of labor she did not promise freedom from pain, but she explained that if we fully understood the birth process and applied the techniques she would teach us, we would be better able to ride on top of the pain, not be submerged helplessly in it.

I had given birth to my first child five years earlier without such preparation, although I had very much wanted to experience natural childbirth. I had felt somehow that birthing would be a defining experience, one that would prove me to myself, but to hedge my bets I went to a teacher of the Lamaze method, which, it was implied, could make labor relatively painless. Her lessons consisted exclusively of breathing exercises, and when I found nothing about those little panting breaths that seemed likely to help me overcome pain, I gave up. When my labor started, I was not equipped with techniques and insights that would help me handle the contractions. Overwhelmed by the pain, I panicked. The doctor had wanted to conform to traditional rules—no husband in the delivery room—and I felt alone in that unfamiliar clinical environment. As a result, I was so heavily medicated that I was unconscious when my daughter was born.

Femmy gave my husband and me a comprehensive understanding of the changes my body would be going through during labor, and within that broad context of knowledge she helped us practice the techniques that had helped other women with their contractions. This time, when labor came there was no panic and no loneliness. Tom and Femmy were with me, and in spite of the pain, I felt in control. I also felt free to ask for pain relief when it became too much. The baby came before any drugs could take effect, and I did experience an unmedicated birth.

Beth Collins reenacts the birth of Rachel (in my arms).

During both pregnancies, accustomed though I was to regular and strenuous exercise, I stopped for nine months for fear of harming the fetus. I grew puffier and more sluggish than I needed to be. With both pregnancies I found myself confronting the greatest physical challenge of my life feeling like a sack of overripe tomatoes. That is why six years later, when I was about to open my first workout studio, I wanted to include a program of exercises for pregnant women, the kind of class I wish I'd had during my pregnancies. Because of the quality of my experience with Femmy during the birth of my son, it was natural that I turned to her for help.

Frankly, I was thinking mainly in terms of exercises to maintain circulation and to keep women from gaining too much weight. But Femmy said, "Why stop there? Why not offer a total program of exercises, skills, and information, not just for pregnancy but for birth, recovery, and infant care as well?" I liked that idea a lot, so when the Workout opened half a year later, we offered the Pregnancy, Birth, and Recovery Program as an integral part of our curriculum. And what a wonderful thing it has been to watch!

It did not surprise me that exercising helped the women who went through the program to feel better, gain less weight, recover faster, feel more energetic, become more aware of their bodies, and look more beautiful. What I had not anticipated was the value

of the social interaction—the sharing. Some of our new mothers come back to Workout within two weeks after their babies are born, to exercise but more especially to tell their still-pregnant peers what they learned and to show off their babies.

Though we don't always admit it, many of us are not at all certain how we will hold up in labor, how "brave" we'll be, or how competent we'll be as new mothers. (Endless questions nag at us: Will breast-feeding hurt? What do other women do to prepare their nipples, and how will I know whether my baby gets enough milk? If I take the baby into bed with me, could I roll on it in my sleep? Will it get spoiled if I hold it all the time and nurse it when it asks for it? What is the best way to help a baby with colic? Is it really better to labor without drugs for the pain? What about the epidural; does that affect the baby? And if I have one, will I still be able to push?) How wonderful to share these worries and questions and to learn from firsthand reports by women who just went through the experience—especially when the discussion is under the guidance of a nurse with expertise in the field of parent/child health (Femmy did her nursing training in her native country, the Netherlands, before we met).

Soon we began to get letters from women who had read about our program or seen reports about it on television. And when the letters kept coming Femmy said, "Maybe I should write a book based on our program." "If you write the book, I'll write the Foreword," I answered, and that is how our first pregnancy, birth, and recovery book came to be.

It is now eight years and a few thousand babies later—we sometimes have the pleasure of announcing seven new babies in one week. The exercise classes are going strong, and I love watching the students come and go—the mothers with their babies, getting their figures back, and the pregnant women with their steadily growing bellies, all so proud of themselves. The program has been expanded with talks on topics ranging from how to prepare for a pregnancy to injury prevention and first aid for new parents. On Sunday afternoons, after the last exercise class, the Workout transforms from an exercise studio into a place for expectant and new parents.

The exercises have changed too. There is more emphasis on cardiovascular fitness. Most of our pregnant women like to use resistance—weights or rubber bands—to strengthen their upper body. And the stretches that are part of the cool-down are done in positions that can be used during labor and birth.

Femmy has grown with the program. The international success of the first book enabled her to look at childbirth in many countries and to study with experts in a variety of fields related to helping people prepare for birth and new parenthood. Thus, it

came as no surprise when she wanted to redo the pregnancy book based on new research and many years of testing the program. And I am more than proud to lend it my name once more. Doing so gives me hope that more expectant parents will benefit from its content. I have always believed Femmy to be a kind of philosopher and healer, a woman who knows how to nurture with skills that go beyond knowledge and mere technique. She has managed to bring many of her special insights and her humanity, feminism, medical knowledge, and sensuality to every page of this book. In my opinion there is no other book like it; it is the definitive compilation of all you need to know from planning a baby through new parenthood. It is truly the Total Birth Program.

Speaking of
Pregnancy

THE FOUR "TRIMESTERS"

Between conception and the day when a baby begins to shed the
need for around-the-clock care lies approximately one year. This
year of phenomenal growth is commonly divided into four
segments: the three trimesters of pregnancy and the newborn pe-

riod, which—to imply that the need of a baby for constant accessibility to its mother does not end at birth—has been called the fourth trimester.

Each trimester tends to place new and different demands on the mother, and, if the parents are close, on the father as well. And no two pregnancies are alike. I have known women who felt sick within days of conception and women who did not realize they were pregnant until they were nearly seven months into their term. And, occasionally, I meet a baby who gives up the need for night feedings within a week after birth. Each mother and father has a unique tale to tell. The following overview is based on thousands of such stories.

The First Trimester

The embryo's nestling into the uterine wall and its rapid growth can cause quite an upheaval in the mother. A number of women feel tired, prone to headaches, and more vulnerable, and many notice more sensitivity of the breasts. Some experience an increased frequency in the urge to urinate, and quite a few do feel nauseated. Some, especially those who did a lot of soul-searching about their readiness to become a mother, experience self-doubt, which becomes exaggerated when their doctor or books imply that nausea or headaches might be psychosomatic. This is not true, even when these symptoms can be relieved with hypnosis. The most likely cause of nausea is the hormone secreted by the emerging placenta, human chorionic gonadotropin, and how abundant this secretion is may depend in part on the baby's genes; the amount of nausea a woman experiences often varies with different pregnancies. In the case of headaches, the culprit might be a new level of the already familiar hormones progesterone and estrogen.

Some nutritionists think that low levels of certain nutrients contribute to queasiness. A drop in blood sugar can definitely cause headaches. Small frequent meals and a variety of snacks have been reported to help. Among the latter are bananas, oranges, dried fruit and nuts, apricot nectar, baked potatoes, crackers, and ginseng tea. Some nutritionists say foods high in B vitamins, especially B6, should be tried; of these, breast of turkey is usually best, because it is lean, relatively odorless, and mild in flavor. They also get good results when doses of 25 milligrams of vitamin B6 are taken in tablet form six times per day. In addition, they suggest that women eat whenever they feel least nauseated.

On the positive side, a good case of nausea may indicate a pregnancy with a low risk of miscarriage. Women whose morning sickness lasted well into the second trimester often report a great pregnancy, a healthy baby, and a good recovery. Don't worry about not being able to eat enough. A body that is well nourished before conception does appear to have the reserves to supply the min-uscule embryo with the nutrients it needs in order to develop. During this initial growth period, eating lots of nutrient-packed food seems less important than avoiding harmful substances such as recreational drugs, alcohol, cigarettes, over-the-counter drugs, and toxic chemicals. Since nausea warns women that they are pregnant and often gives them an aversion to what they should not ingest, it is for some a blessing (in an unpleasant disguise).

About 40 to 50 percent of women experience bleeding in the first trimester. Frightening and worrisome as this can be, quite a bit of first-trimester bleeding seems related to one's menstrual cycle, and most of the women who experience it go on to have fine and healthy babies. The reason for the bleeding is not always clear even to the best diagnostician, and mothers continue to wonder what might be wrong until they hold their baby and can check it over. Reassurance can keep such worry in bounds, but it does not take it away. It is in the nature of motherhood to care deeply and feel responsible.

While the mother struggles and rejoices with new emotions and sensations, the baby builds the foundation on which to grow for the rest of its life. During this period saunas and hot tubs are best avoided or used for no more than fifteen minutes, the time it takes for the mother's core temperature to rise, because there are some studies that indicate that the fetal nervous system can be dam-aged by too great an increase in the mother's temperature. Heavy physical labor, including strenuous exercise, is better avoided too, especially in a humid atmosphere, since the body's ability to cool itself through perspiration is greatly reduced when there is a lot of moisture in the air. It might also be wise to forgo regular, lengthy sunbathing when the sun is high in the sky. Such exposure temporarily reduces one's immune response, and it does expose one to radiation at a time when the rapidly dividing cells inside are very susceptible to damage. For the mother, it increases the chances that the changing pigmentation of her skin will cause dark spots to appear on her face, the so-called mask of pregnancy.

A good piece of general advice for women at the start of this exciting journey is to listen to your body. Don't push yourself to prove that nothing has changed. Do what feels good, and be cautious with physically demanding activities that you have not done before.

The Second Trimester

Most women enjoy the second trimester. The pregnancy becomes visible without getting in the way. The baby's movements become strong enough for the mother to feel. The uterus has grown out of the lower pelvis and now causes less pressure on the bladder. The extreme fatigue lessens and, often, so does the nausea.

Now comes the next challenge, accepting the weight gain.

Women usually have no problem with the fact that their bellies get rounder and their waists disappear. This they were prepared for. It's the rounding of the thighs, the broadening of the buttocks, and the increased fullness of the upper arms, the shoulders, and the face that they object to. In a time when feminine beauty is equated with thinness, this increase in dimension is almost threatening. Yet these fatty pads are the body's response to new hormone levels. Some say it is nature's way of establishing a food reserve, thus protecting infants from a possible famine.

In the eyes of the man whose child she carries his partner is often more rather than less attractive. The new life within adds a dimension to an intimate relationship, and it tends to make the woman who carries it a deeper person. These qualities bring more to love and romance than matchstick-thin thighs. It helps to remind oneself of this at a time when the need to feel loved by one's partner tends to become so pronounced that it could be called a subjective sign of pregnancy.

In some this need to feel loved combines with the greater sensitivity of the breasts and the genital region and expresses itself in increased sexual desire. Health-care providers can give you the latest data on the effect of sexual intercourse and an assessment of any risk to you in particular. Women in good health for whom conception came naturally usually do not need to abstain.

Whether sexual intercourse has an effect on the baby is not known. Hormones of love and pleasure probably pass the placenta, and the uterine contractions of an orgasm might be noticed by its occupant. This does not mean the baby knows what brought them on, and even if it did know, it probably wouldn't mind. Women who notice pain in the lower abdomen and/or the lower back and some cramping after an orgasm might ask their health-care provider if they can continue lovemaking if they avoid climax. That way they and their partners can still enjoy this fine exchange of feelings, yet lessen the risk of a premature onset of labor.

Other women feel less interested in sex than before they conceived. Some men's interest in sex may diminish too, although they have the same loving feelings toward their pregnant partners. Don't be afraid of such changes. Often the quality of personal communication improves when one is forced to make changes in established patterns.

Because of the danger of sexually transmitted diseases to the child within, people who continue sexual intercourse during pregnancy are well advised to be monogamous. Practicing good personal hygiene in general, taking a shower or bath before sex, and emptying the bladder after intercourse can reduce the risk of vaginal and bladder infections, two problems to which pregnancy makes women more prone and which can lead to premature labor. Bacteria that feed on the now more abundant secretions of the vagina do not like air. Wearing cotton underwear or, sometimes, no underwear at all can lessen these problems too.

Once the nausea is gone, eating can be a great pleasure. To keep the fear of weight gain from interfering with that pleasure, empty calories and fatty foods should be kept at a *tolerable* minimum (Katharine Hepburn once told Jane Fonda that a woman should have a piece of chocolate every day). Gone are the days of constantly weighing a pregnant woman and scolding her whenever she gains one pound more than what doctors have decided upon as ideal. Obstetricians have realized that metabolism is an individual matter, and when there are two individuals involved, as in pregnancy, allowance must be made for more rather than less variation. A healthy weight gain for pregnancy ranges from fifteen to as much as fifty pounds. Many mothers shed the extra pounds without much effort shortly after delivery, and those who don't can put their minds to losing them in the year following birth.

The weight and size of the rapidly expanding uterus may begin to challenge the neuromuscular and vascular systems. Aches and pains develop depending on where there are weaknesses. Exercise, physical therapy, chiropractic adjustments, acupuncture, and massage can all be helpful.

Headaches usually taper off during the second trimester. If they persist, they might be caused by the change in posture. As the pelvis tilts forward, the upper body is thrust backward for balance and the chin is tilted up. This position of the head can cause muscle tension, which in turn interferes with the flow of blood to and from the brain. A gentle adjustment of the neck vertebrae by a chiropractor or an osteopath, or a few treatments by a physical therapist to rid the muscles of their chronic tension combined with instructions on how to correct posture, might bring relief.

Women who have not exercised in years are now often moti-

vated to start. Novices should probably begin slowly to avoid too great a biochemical upheaval. Experienced exercisers have usually learned how to listen to their bodies, and they can safely continue their familiar fitness program for as long as it feels right. Pregnancy, when all is well, is a healthy state. The body only appears to be more sluggish. For example, the digestive and vascular systems are both relaxed by the pregnancy hormones, sometimes leading to constipation or varicosities, yet on a molecular level these systems are capable of doing more work than before. The bowels are able to absorb more nutrients, and the cardiovascular system pumps a greater volume of blood a longer way through a denser network of tiny blood vessels.

The estrogen-induced increase in vascularity may manifest itself in little spiderwebs of capillaries. Those in the face and on the breasts usually disappear after the baby is born, and those on the legs usually become less pronounced. Some say that bioflavonoids with rutin, found in orange and grapefruit peels (pregnant women very often crave the white of an orange peel), help the body heal the bluish spots that result when tiny capillaries break. The white of one orange or grapefruit should provide the necessary amount. If no organically grown citrus fruit is available, an alternative is bioflavonoid in tablet form. If you wish to take this, ask your health-care provider if it is okay for you to take about 500 milligrams per day.

The heart functions primarily as a pump, not as a suction machine. It will have no trouble getting blood to the lower pelvis and the legs, but the pressure of the enlarged uterus on softened vein walls may make return to the heart a bit sluggish. The resulting distension in the veins can cause varicosities, sometimes around the vagina, sometimes in the legs. Movement helps the veins empty themselves. Other preventive measures are to avoid sitting with crossed legs; to move the legs regularly while sitting and put them up at regular intervals; to get up, stretch, and walk around every once in a while; to stand with the knees slightly bent rather than locked; and, if forced to stand for a long period, to step in place off and on. Supportive hose can be helpful for women at risk on account of their job and/or their predisposition. They work best if put on before getting up, when the veins have not had to work against gravity for a while. Also, if possible, they should be taken off for a few minutes every couple of hours and the legs should be elevated. Varicosities around the vagina seem to go away more completely once the pregnancy is over than those in the legs.

Don't get scared by the thought that some signs of pregnancy may never quite disappear. Being true to one's nature and fully alive and able to love are more important than physical perfection, and those essential characteristics tend to grow stronger with motherhood.

Increased softness and bleeding of the gums are not uncommon, nor is a change in the mucous membranes, noticeable by an increase in the secretions from the vagina and by stuffiness in the sinuses and the nose, much as with a head cold. Some women get nosebleeds. A vaporizer, especially when the air inside is dry, does seem to bring relief. If used, it should be cleaned regularly to avoid mold formation. For nosebleeds, a little Vaseline on the inside of the nostrils seems to help too.

Low blood pressure, often associated with the first two trimesters and probably one cause of first-trimester headaches, can now cause dizziness. To avoid lightheadedness when getting up from a supine position, turn on your side first, raise the upper body, pause, and then rise to your feet. This is also easier for the large muscle between the pubic bone and the rib cage, the rectus ab-

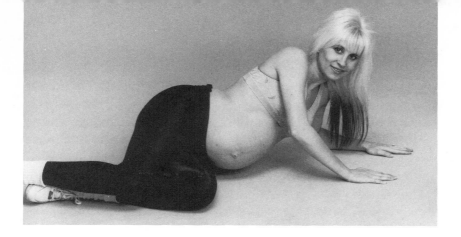

dominus, which loses some of its strength as it is stretched by the growing uterus.

Quick movements also increase the chance of straining the round ligaments that anchor the uterus to the pubic bone. The growing uterus stretches these ligaments upward, making them prone to spasm, which causes pain in the groin region. For relief, lie on your side, bend your knees, and bring your thighs close to your abdomen. To avoid pulling these ligaments, move more slowly. Place your body in the direction of movement instead of turning quickly or twisting.

Leg cramps may occur, usually in the calves and often at night. Their exact cause is not always clear, but the calf muscles do singularly bear the extra weight of pregnancy. Like any muscle forced to do extra work, they need a lot of careful stretching. In addition, it may help to reevaluate your diet and perhaps rebalance the ratio of your calcium and phosphorous intake. Some women report that taking more magnesium brings relief; others find that wearing leg warmers to bed lessens cramps during the night. Sometimes leg cramps are caused by the enlarged uterus pressing the sciatic nerve against the pelvic brim during sleep. See if you have fewer cramps when you lie on your side, with lots of pillows to prevent turning on your back, during sleep. If so, check with a chiropractor or an osteopath because an adjustment could help. To relieve the immediate pain, straighten your knee and pull your toes toward your shinbone. Activating the muscles in the front of the leg helps the ones in the back to relax, especially when the cramping muscle is massaged firmly at the same time.

Many women notice a change in their body thermostat. Rooms that are comfortable to others seem too warm, and they perspire more easily. The skin becomes more of an organ of excretion; it also commonly undergoes pigmentation changes. A dark line on the belly is common, as is an increase in the size and coloration of the nipples and the areolae. These colorations, including those that occasionally occur on the face, usually completely disappear not long after delivery.

Quite a few women say that their hair changes, from curly to straight, for instance. Good hairdressers usually advise against hair coloring or a perm, not only because the materials used can be toxic to the fetus, but because experience has taught them that the hair can react unpredictably now.

The breasts become full and firm. A properly fitted supportive bra is probably a good investment. Many experts feel that good support while the breasts are enlarged may prevent some stretching of the breast tissue. Since the breasts will not get much larger, even when they fill with milk, a bra bought now can be worn while nursing too. A regular bra can easily be changed into a nursing bra with Velcro. When choosing a bra, look for one made of cotton for better ventilation, with wide shoulder straps to help carry the weight, a chest circumference that can be adjusted after the baby is born, and cups that support the whole breast without applying localized pressure. For large breasts, bras that close in the front might distribute support more evenly than those with flaps.

The Third Trimester

Now the baby might be able to live were it expelled from the womb. This means it has gotten quite large, reminding its mother almost constantly of its presence and of the fact that it is getting ready to emerge. What was done in the second trimester to strengthen muscular weaknesses and improve posture will now pay off, because the large localized weight gain of the third trimester taxes everyone. Physically it is harder for short women and those with poor muscle tone than for tall women and those in good condition. Emotionally it seems hardest on those whose livelihood depends in part on physical beauty—models, actresses, and others frequently in the public eye—and easiest for those who can keep a sense of humor and perspective. It might help to

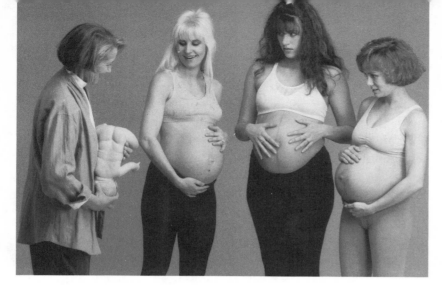

The baby doll approximates an eight-pound baby. However, as the doll lacks a newborn's softness and flexibility, it appears disproportionately large.

bear in mind that in China, a traditional compliment to women is "You look white and fat"—"white" meaning that one does not have to work in the fields and "fat" indicating that one has enough to eat.

The rapid expansion of the belly causes many women to underestimate their size and makes them prone to loss of balance. It also makes most women wish that they could put their baby next to them on the couch or bed for a few minutes every once in a while. Some women massage their stretched skin with warm oil to help it feel less itchy from stretching. Such massage may or may not prevent stretch marks. If they appear, remember that they will become much less visible when the belly returns to normal.

Now even those women who always needed a sweater or suffered cold feet feel warm most of the time. Two complaints of the last trimester have so far escaped everyone's effort at a cure. They are heartburn and lower-uterine ligament pain. For the latter, women have tried corsets, worn a strapless top of stretchy material over their bellies, or used a supportive contraption made especially to help carry the weight. For heartburn, taking frequent small meals of low-fat foods, separating food and fluid intake, wearing nonrestrictive clothes, staying upright after food intake, and having chiropractic adjustments have been reported as helpful. Antacids help too, but their use can interfere with iron absorption. If you must take one, choose a kind without aluminum or large amounts of sodium, and double-check with your health-care provider to make sure it is safe.

Edema, or swelling, especially of the ankles and feet, occurs frequently and is hard to combat too. Wearing a bigger pair of shoes is a better remedy than ingesting medications or herbs to eliminate the excess fluid. Such diuretics reduce the circulating fluid and may lessen the supply of blood to the uterus. Edema results not from too much circulating fluid, but from fluid seeping out of the cells. Exercise, through its stimulation of the cardiovascular system and its milking action on the lymphatic system, will help the cells reabsorb some of it, but immersion underwater is even more effective; the hydrostatic force of the water pushes the fluid back into the cells. Therefore, the deeper the body of water, the greater the result; a swimming pool will work better than a bathtub. Experts say that a twenty-minute immersion every other day will significantly reduce pregnancy edema, since fluid seeps back out of the cells only gradually. Vitamin B6, familiar already as a remedy for nausea, has also been found helpful in combating edema. Determine the correct dosage in consultation with your health-care provider and/or a nutritionist. Resting on the left side, the position in which there is the least amount of pressure on the vena cava (the vein that returns the blood to the heart) and therefore the best blood circulation, three times a day for half an hour or so can alleviate some of the swelling too.

Some women complain of a tingling sensation in the fingers of one or both hands. This is caused by pressure on the ulnar nerve, which goes through a narrow passage, the carpal tunnel, at the wrist. Water retention makes this tunnel smaller. Rest sometimes helps. Diuretics should not be used. If the tingling develops into complete numbness, splints that hold the hand in the position of least pressure might be in order. This usually necessitates a consultation with an orthopedist.

Occasionally women break out with itchiness. If it is accompanied by little red spots, it is an immune response of the mother to some of the baby's secretions. Hydrocortisone ointment of ½ or 1 percent strength seems to be safe and gives relief in most cases. If the skin shows no change, the itching is probably caused by an increase in bile salts, which have stagnated in the skin. Cholestyramine, a complex compound that binds the salts, sometimes helps. Also, cool showers and cold cloths on the itchy areas can provide a little relief. Both of these immensely irritating conditions are relieved with delivery.

The growing uterus begins to press against and displace the bowels, interfering in some with regular emptying. Fiber- and fluid-rich diets, exercise, and a regular toilet time may help. Some women say placing their feet on two stacks of books or on a footstool while sitting on the toilet helps them. If it doesn't, a laxative approved by your health-care provider is probably in order. Some women complain about pain under the ribs on the right. Sometimes stretching up and then over to the left side relieves it; sometimes getting on the hands and knees and rocking the pelvis helps. It may be caused by gas trapped in the ascending colon, which turns a rather sharp corner in this area, or by pressure of the baby against the liver.

Quite a few women complain of shortness of breath, and some experience brief spells where they feel as if they can't get any air. The enlarged uterus makes deep breathing more difficult, and the body's mechanism for regulating the ratio of carbon dioxide to oxygen has become more sensitive, sometimes dictating a different rate of breathing. Whenever you feel that you can't breathe, exhale slowly, then slowly inhale; allow for a slight pause, exhale, pause, and inhale while imagining that the upper chest is expanding and while letting the shoulders move up (this is easier when the arms are raised over the head). Exhale with a sense of relief. Continue breathing this way for a few more breaths.

Standing ceramic figure, Nayarit, West Mexico, 100 B.C.–300 A.D.

Mood swings are common. Hormones and a changing self-image are contributing causes, but so is concern for the child within. Women agree that positive feedback about the baby and its coming into the world makes them ecstatic, whereas anything that threatens their belief that this pregnancy is good, that the birth will go well, and that the world will be a good place for their baby makes them want to cry. Exposure to news from all over the world makes it more difficult than ever to steer a stable course. Yet if the problems come from human beings, the answers can come from them too. We are an evolving species characterized by a great need to experiment, learn, and create. Each new baby brings with it the hope that it will help us see new ways of thinking.

Also common is the inability to sleep through the night. The fluid that had seeped between cells during the day reenters the circulation at night and is quickly steered to the kidneys, where it is filtered out as urine and sent to the bladder. And of course the bladder, with a new neighbor constricting its space, cannot hold quite as much as before. Relaxing back into sleep is harder when one worries that tossing and turning will awaken a sleeping partner. Sometimes it is better to sleep at least part of the night in separate beds. A fairly firm mattress seems best for the back, but it can make your hip hurt when you sleep on your side. A washable lambskin (great later for the baby) placed under the hip region might relieve some of the discomfort, and lots of pillows, including one to put under the belly and one or two to place between the legs when sleeping on the side, help. Some women make or buy a firm backrest and sleep part of the night in a semi-sitting position, with the knees bent and supported by pillows. Women with a waterbed say it allows them to sleep on their stomachs well into the last month.

The knowledge that the mother's circulation after the fifth month of pregnancy is best when she lies on her left side and worst when she lies on her back makes many women afraid to rest in any other position. While it is probably very important for the mother, and consequently the baby, to have optimal circulation during labor, during exercise, and under other physically demanding circumstances, this seems a lot less essential during sleep. When the body is at rest, its metabolism is different. Also, if the uterus were to place too much pressure on the vena cava (which is on the right of the vertebral column), the mother would probably turn in her sleep or wake up and change positions. The artery that takes blood away from the heart is on the left. Veins are more easily compressed than arteries, which is why it is better to let the weight of the uterus fall toward the left. The ideal position would be facedown on a waterbed or on the beach with the belly resting in a little hole, dug for that purpose. Getting some sleep by letting the body find comfort naturally in a variety of positions seems more important than forcing oneself to stay in the same position all night for the unproven benefit of optimal circulation.

Some women say their inability to sleep was remedied by increasing calcium intake or by eating a light protein snack or drinking some warm low- or nonfat milk. Some take tryptophan, the amino acid that makes milk a sleep remedy. Be very careful with this because there is some evidence that tryptophan taken in a higher dose than naturally occurs in food can irritate the fetal liver. Check with your health-care provider as to what dose might be safe for you. Some relax by playing music they enjoy. Newborns often respond positively to the music their mothers enjoyed during pregnancy. The sounds in the womb seem to be mostly of a low-frequency, pulsating kind (the mother's heart and circulatory system), along with some rumbling (air and food moving through the mother's bowels). Some say that babies prefer high-pitched sounds. Others claim that babies prefer Mozart and hate rock. I don't know how they know.

If these simple measures fail, look at the problem philosophically. Maybe this is nature's way of preparing expectant mothers for the around-the-clock care their babies will need after they are born. Napping during the day seems a good idea. Women with full-time jobs could pack a lunch and squeeze in a short nap during the lunch break and another one when they return home from work. Learning to get rest from a few short naps is a good way to prepare for the fourth trimester.

Many women say that they dream more frequently and more vividly during the third trimester. Some keep a diary of their dreams and note recurrent themes often revealing of the psyche's preparation for motherhood. Quite a few women are pleasantly surprised with erotic dreams. Sexual intercourse can still be enjoyed if all is well. Women now usually prefer tender rather than vigorous stimulation. This is better since with vigorous thrusting movements the tip of the penis can touch the now soft and blood-rich cervix and cause some spotting. Should a little spotting occur shortly after intercourse, it does not warrant a trip to an emergency room in the middle of the night. If it continues, a checkup is necessary.

Close to the due date the hormones begin to fluctuate again. In some this brings back occasional nausea; in others it causes general fatigue and sometimes depression. Here the company of other pregnant women is the best remedy, because while some women lose their sense of self-esteem, others find a new sense of dignity and purpose as they feel their child getting ready to be born. Also, among pregnant peers the feeling of ungainliness, so common in the presence of husband or colleagues, is replaced with pride. At our studio, where women continue to work out in leotards all through their pregnancies, I see women stroke each other's bellies and compete to see who has the biggest one.

The last month, with its fluctuations between eager anticipation and spells of worry, fatigue from the constant burden, and moments of supreme bliss, makes it seem as if pregnancy lasts eight normal months and one month that is like a year.

Labor and Birth

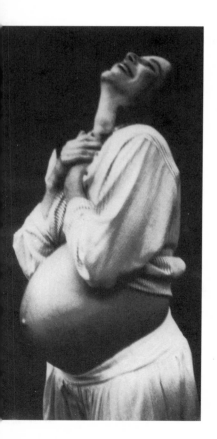

Somewhere toward the end of the third trimester, usually and preferably between thirty-eight and forty-one weeks of gestation, baby and mother agree, through the interactions of hormones and enzymes in the placenta, that it is time for birth. The womb, which has been contracting off and on since conception, perhaps to improve the exchange of nutrients and waste between mother and baby, and to help the muscle fibers stretch and strengthen, now produces contractions that progressively become longer, stronger, and closer together and that will not cease until the baby is born. This process, called labor, consists of three distinctly different stages.

During the first, the dilatation stage, each uterine contraction tries to produce cervical retraction. This stage ends when the cervix is fully opened over the baby's head. The continuing contractions now expel the baby out of the womb and through the vagina. This, the expulsion stage, ends when the baby is born. While the baby discovers its mother's breasts by nuzzling against them and perhaps suckling a bit, the womb from which it was just expelled contracts even more strongly. These contractions shorten the uterine wall, thus helping the placenta detach. The third, or placental, stage ends when this complex organ, with the sac that encompassed the baby and the cord that was once the baby's lifeline, is expelled through the vagina.

The process is relatively short (six to twelve hours) and painless for 15 to 20 percent of Western women. No one has been able to predict with accuracy who will fall into that category. Nor can it be foreseen who will fall into the middle group of 50 or so percent for whom labor is longer and more difficult, or who will be one of the growing number of women who need a cesarean section.

Some experts claim that labor is easier and faster in cultures with less technology. It is generally assumed that the ease with which one gives birth is primarily genetically determined but is also affected by the mother's current state of health and by the genes of the baby (for example, those for size) and the baby's position during labor. The mother's position during labor must have some influence too. In the past, before forceps and cesarean sections, women knelt on all fours, stood, squatted, or walked up and down stairs to help labor progress. A woman's labor proceeds best when she feels at ease in her surroundings. Contractions can become less effective or stop altogether when mistrust, self-doubt, or fear set in. Labor pains can be accompanied by the exhilarating feeling that the body is working well or by the desperate notion that nothing is happening and the baby is not coming. Thus, feedback from one's birth attendant has an impact. And while it seems too much to ascribe long labors without progress to the mother's fear of hospitals or of birth technology or to her busy professional schedule, in which there is no time for the baby, emotions do play their part. Birth is a physical, emotional, social, and spiritual event.

The effect of the mother's age on length of labor is not known, nor is it known how physical fitness or lack thereof affects a woman's ability to cope with the birth process. Our students say that their physical strength and endurance, along with the willpower they derived from exercising regularly, were very helpful. Quite a few of our students have been over the age of thirty-five, and some of the shortest labors reported to us were those of women over forty.

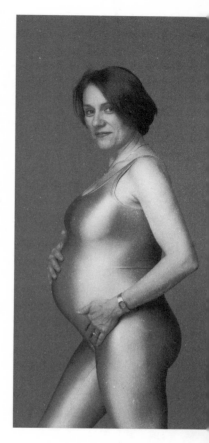

Statistically, babies born to such mothers have a harder time getting conceived and being carried to term, but once born, these babies are lucky, because mature women make great mothers. The process is the hardest on babies born to mothers under eighteen.

The Fourth Trimester

Within moments after the dramatic separation of birth, both mother and baby seem eager to meet each other. Even babies who

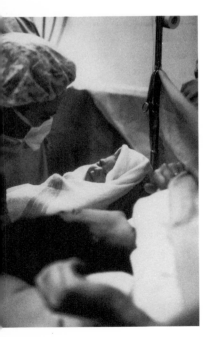

cry vigorously at the light, cold, and other unwelcome sensations that are part of many modern births will stop when placed on their mother's bare abdomen or chest, especially if they are covered with a warm blanket. I remember with fondness how one young mother's baby, after a difficult birth, broke out in a smile at the sight of her breasts. The increase in pigmentation of the nipple and the areola probably helps the baby see the breast. Babies often look up toward their mother's face when they hear her voice. If the father was close to the mother during the pregnancy, the baby will show signs of recognizing his voice too. One baby, born by cesarean section, whose parents sang a song to him all through the pregnancy showed clear signs of appeasement and delight when they sang the same song in the operating room while the father held him close to his and his partner's face.

There are two kinds of mammals, according to biologists. Among one kind the babies feed intermittently (the northern fur seal nurses only a few times per week); among the other, babies are continuous feeders. Human babies fall into the second category. With them the urge to suckle arises very frequently at first, slowly tapering off during the first two to four months of extrauterine life, as the organs mature and the brain grows. Chimpanzee babies (we share 99 percent of our genetic material with the chimp) nurse every hour for a few minutes during their first year. Perhaps we should see the mother's arms and breasts as a temporary pouch out of which the baby is slowly weaned during the fourth trimester, while the mother's body and mind adjust to the hormonal upheaval following birth and to the intense feelings of new motherhood.

While the interaction between mother and baby is primarily intuitive and spontaneous, rather like the responses of two people who have just fallen in love, some knowledge of babies and how to care for them comes in handy. Then the fine task of mothering can consist of applying what is known about infants in general to one's own unique baby.

Carrying a baby in the arms or in a sling is easier for women who strengthened their upper body during pregnancy. Exercise during pregnancy has another payoff now: better posture, fewer backaches, and a quicker return to the configurations of the non-pregnant body. With a bit of discipline in continuing the exercise habit, new mothers can look as good as, or better than, they did before conception. To prevent bladder and lower-back problems, the muscles weakened by pregnancy and birth should be rebuilt by regular exercise in the year following birth.

If women could redesign their bodies, they would probably ask for a special sling of muscles to hold up the uterus during the last weeks of pregnancy, for a cervix that opens easily during labor, for a pelvis that widens painlessly with each contraction until the baby can slide through, and for an extra pair of arms to hold the baby close to their breasts those first three months. The hairless chest of human mothers makes it hard for the baby to hold on by itself. Lacking control over biological design, women turn to their culture for help and guidance. Pregnancy and new motherhood tend to make women more eager to learn, and less independent.

As for the father, anthropologists tell us about the couvade, a series of duties and prescribed behaviors found in many cultures and intended to help the less direct participant realize his importance. According to Margaret Mead, on some Pacific islands the father had to wade out into the ocean and stand with his lips just above the rising tide for the duration of his wife's travail. On Bali the father's job was to keep the demon who favored birthing rooms away from his wife.

Ceramic figure, Jalisco, West Mexico, 100 B.C.–300 A.D.

Ceramic figurine, Quimbaya region of Colombia, 1200–1400 A.D.

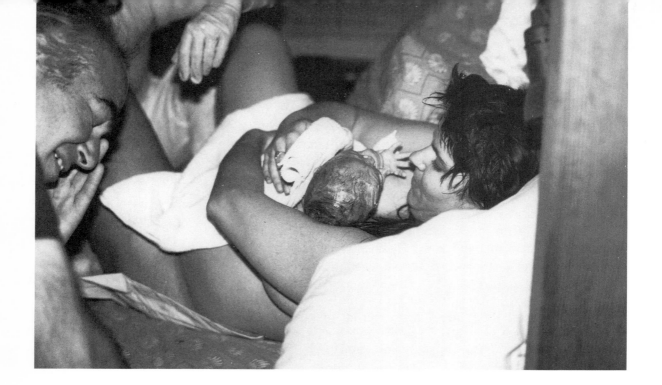

Factual understanding of, and a new degree of control over, conception is changing the way men approach parenthood. Men who choose to have a baby seem more eager to help their women carry the burdens and share the joys, including those of labor and birth. They often take the time to learn how to help their partner through her travail. Women thus supported often acknowledge, "I couldn't have done it without him." For many men, helping their child be born is a humbling and moving experience.

More and more new fathers also try to share equally in the day-to-day care of their small infants. In Sweden it has become customary to give mother and father a paid leave from work so that they can take turns caring for their child during the first six months to a year. Increasingly many men take classes in infant care with their partners, and those who did not grow up with nurturing fathers often make a conscious effort to give their child what they missed.

The number of childless women is decreasing, but so is the number of babies each woman wants to bear. More women postpone pregnancy until they are ready. Then, when they get pregnant, they approach motherhood with a new attitude. If they are in a close relationship with the child's father, this new approach is amplified by the power of two who are one in their innermost hearts.

Of course, the prevalence of this "new attitude" does not mean a clean break with ancient feelings and traditions. Nature, when she forms something new, builds on existing structures. For example, when the embryo is forming, three sets of kidneys appear in rapid succession. The structure of the first set is not discarded when it is replaced; instead it gives rise to the ovaries or the testicles. A similar phenomenon probably happens with cultural developments. The feelings and hopes with which modern parents approach parenthood are built on ancient and familiar ones.

I was born on a river barge in Holland. Barge people were sturdy and practical, and, at that time, they lived the way most of the world still lives, without running water, electricity, or gas, and without any health education or prenatal care. Seeing a doctor because you were pregnant was an absurd notion. When my mother, who gave birth to ten children, felt her time to be near, she consulted a midwife in whatever town the boat happened to be in. If the midwife agreed that the baby was soon due, the boat was tied up and the last days of waiting began. When her labor was well under way, my father would go to get the midwife. I particularly remember one who was German. My mother could not understand a word she said, but the barge, loaded with cargo for the Upper Rhine, was near the small town of Boppard when her labor started, and she had no choice. The midwife usually stayed for an hour or so after my father had shown us our new baby and came back once or twice in the next few days. When she declared mother and baby sufficiently well, the boat, with an aunt or a cousin who had come aboard earlier to help with the household, resumed its course. Children pitched in very early in life: Ten-year-old girls often ran the household during the birth of siblings, and boys, from the age of eight, had to help on deck. It was more or less assumed that the children would earn their livelihood the way their parents did, and parents relied on their offspring for support in old age. I remember wondering, as a child overhearing adults talk, why people had so many babies. They loved them after they were born, but they often had to make quite an adjustment during the pregnancy. A woman praised her husband as a good man if he did not get angry when she became pregnant again.

I have only two children, and I have spent the last twenty years observing and teaching parents who carefully plan their pregnancies. We do not expect our children merely to fit in, but believe it is our task to help each child develop its own inner self and find its particular calling. For me, raising children was a very different experience from what it was for my mother. My students' dedication to parenting, as well as the many resources now available to new parents—prenatal care, health education, child-development education, and family counseling—makes me wonder if we might not be at a special point in our history. Evolution does sometimes take a sudden leap. Maybe aspects of human nature that were only occasionally able to flower under the circumstances of other times will now burst into full bloom.

PLANNING BEFORE CONCEPTION

With the ability to postpone conception until one is ready comes the opportunity for pre-conception planning. Absurd or unnecessary as this may seem to our grandparents and maybe even our parents, such planning has many merits. Geneticists believe that infant-mortality rates will improve not with better birth technology but with pre-pregnancy planning, including, where necessary, genetic counseling. Nutritionists say that nutritional planning for pregnancy should ideally begin about half a year before conception. And, as a pregnancy-health educator, I know that fitness is more easily maintained than built from scratch during pregnancy. Here too it helps to plan ahead.

Of course, people have long known that a clean, healthy, and fit body is a better start for a new life. The health laws set forth in many old religious texts suggest an awareness that a woman's body is the gate to health for her offspring. But we have learned only recently that a man's sperm is an important determinant too, and that his occupational and recreational exposure to toxins and drugs can affect not only his ability to impregnate but the health of the child he sires.

Since what both parents were exposed to before the pregnancy matters a great deal, it is clear that existing workplace restrictions for pregnant women are not sufficient. (It is a sobering fact that the United States ranks only eleventh in environmental safety in the workplace.) Inability to conceive is sometimes remedied when the male partner changes jobs or personal habits. Sperm counts go up, and the ability of the sperm to reach the egg improves when the environment is less toxic or less warm. The common increase in births nine months after a cold spell is probably not due to people snuggling up and making love more often but to the fact that cold weather makes a man more fertile. A sedentary job in a centrally heated office, the habit of wearing tight underwear that keeps the testicles close to the body, or daily saunas can interfere with fertility, as can repeated exposure to a relatively low level of environmental toxins. Something as simple as training less hard can increase the sperm count in men who are on a heavy exercise schedule.

While moderate exercise is beneficial for a woman's appearance, for her ability to carry a baby without too many aches and pains, and for her long-term health, heavy training can stop ovulation. Also, a woman's body needs a bit of fat (about 20 percent) in order to accept a pregnancy. Nature seems to want some insurance that the calories needed to complete the process are going to be there. Body fat probably influences hormone production as well.

I often hear parents say that the thought of being responsible for a new life was an inspiration for them to take their own health more seriously. Some act on that inspiration right away; in others it lies dormant until the reality of a pregnancy or a new baby spurs them into action. Start when you can, and don't expect that you will be willing or able to change everything at once. When we demand too much of ourselves too soon, we become overwhelmed and depressed, and inaction follows. Making lasting changes takes time and thought.

IMPROVING YOUR NEST

A good place to start creating a healthier environment is at home. Home is where you have the most control and where you participate in health-promoting activities such as food preparation, eating, bathing, relaxing, and sleeping. Experts say that the air inside many homes is often six to ten times less healthy than the air on a smoggy day in downtown Los Angeles. Radon, asbestos, formaldehyde, cigarette smoke, pesticides, dry-cleaning fluids, lead, cleaning products, oxides of nitrogen, aerosol propellants, and cosmetics all contribute hazardous molecules to the old and familiar indoor pollutants, such as dust, molds, and incomplete combustion, to create an invisible and almost odorless "soup" of bad air. The more insulated the home, the thicker the soup. Thus a first step to a healthier home is regularly opening a window, especially in the bedroom.

If you have, until now, more or less ignored reports about indoor air pollution, do not panic upon reading the long list of toxins present in modern homes. Toxins have always been present in the air. Whether or not they are harmful depends on the quantity and the combination; some grow more toxic in each other's company. Cigarette smoke, for instance, makes radon and asbestos more dangerous. And the dangers of petrochemical solvents increase when there are four or more different ones in the air—a mixture, experts say, quite common in modern homes. Also, reactions to toxins are, like everything else about us, quite individual. Substances that at minute levels make one person unable to function can, at ten times that level, go unnoticed by someone else. Unborn babies and small children, however, are likely to be more sensitive than their parents.

Ridding your shelves of chemicals you never use is a good idea, since, unless hermetically sealed, even closed containers can add toxic molecules to the air. Moreover, whatever you get rid of now cannot get into the hands and the mouth of your child later. Be especially aware of the danger improperly labeled cans and bottles pose. Never keep a poisonous substance in an empty Coke bottle. And do not throw poisons away with the trash. If it is not illegal to do so in your state, it should be, because such disposal increases the risk of groundwater contamination and other serious threats to everyone's health. Call the recycling or trash-collection department of your town and ask where and how you should dispose of what you have collected. While you have an informed government official on the line, you might also ask if your town has a place where you can deposit your dead batteries. As batteries disintegrate, they release heavy metals such as lead (already too prevalent everywhere), mercury (which can be broken down by bacteria into the very toxic and easily absorbed methyl mercury), and cadmium (another metal for which our body has no use and no efficient mechanism of detoxification). These three heavy metals will probably go down in history as the main contributors to mental retardation and the crowding of mental hospitals in the twentieth century. Next, promise that you will not use such serious offenders as aerosol-propelled pesticides. Both the propellant and the content are toxic, and the very small droplets will stay in the air for a while, penetrating deep into the lungs and saturating things you did not intend to contaminate.

Do not let relatives or friends discourage you from the task of making your house a safer nest. Some mothers may say to their pregnant daughters, "I didn't do that when I was pregnant with you." At that time pollution was less pervasive, and we did not know that toxins could cause sterility and miscarriage or that exposure in the womb could cause learning problems or cancer. Set aside your fears and the feeling that you have already been exposed to too much. If you have just finished redoing an old house, you probably did get some lead in your system. But your body can tolerate some, and so can that of an unborn baby. The human body has a tremendous capacity to heal itself, and this capacity is even greater in the embryo. The rapidly dividing cells of a developing embryo are both more susceptible to damage and more able to recover if the assault stops in time. Once you lessen the amount of toxins you are exposed to, your body will clean and repair itself. The same seems to be true of our rivers and streams: Once we stop polluting them, their ability to sustain a variety of life returns with amazing speed. That is why even though serious, the state of pollution is not hopeless.

Water, our planetary solvent, supports us, as well as organisms that can kill us, without discrimination. That is why better sanitation and the filtration and chlorination of water have probably saved more people from an early death than all the advances in medicine combined (except perhaps for immunization). Unfortunately, when a big stride forward is made and recognized as such, further progress is often impaired because complacency sets in. For instance, there must be a better way to rid water of harmful microorganisms than with chlorine, which seems to contribute to chronic diseases such as breast cancer. Until a replacement is found, chlorine is necessary to get clean water to our homes. Once there, it can be filtered out before the water is used for drinking, cooking, or bathing. Depending on where you live, filtering the water might be a good idea for yet another reason: the steadily increasing pollution of groundwater with agricultural and industrial chemicals.

Municipal water companies are rapidly discovering the need for extensive testing but some have not kept up with the emerging necessity of extensive filtration. Clusters of childhood cancers such as have been documented in California's San Joaquin and Silicon Valleys are serious lessons. Perhaps of even more serious concern are household water pipes that have copper or galvanized iron joints sealed with lead solder. This lead leeches into the water, especially in areas where the water is "aggressive" or "hard," that is, of low pH and low mineral content. Proper correction of this problem has to be done by the water supplier. Also, be aware that at this time bottled water is generally tested less thoroughly than water from municipal water companies. Even though it is more expensive, it is not necessarily safer. For more information and for organizations you can call for assistance, see Resources for New Parents, pages 324 to 329.

CHECKING YOUR WORKPLACE

Like the home, commercial buildings, including hospitals, often contain a number of indoor air pollutants, and the presence of more materials and more people adds to the risk of contamination. Air-conditioning creates two problems. First, it makes the air dry, and dry air causes discomfort to the mucous membranes of the nose and throat and impairs their ability to fight off infections; second, a space that relies solely on air-conditioning usually has an abundance of positive ions. One of the reasons why the air just before a rainstorm feels so great is the surge of negative ions in the atmosphere. A predominance of negative ions in the air is invigorating; an excess of positive ions makes us irritable and tense. If the windows in your office are constructed so that they cannot be opened, and you often feel more tired and irritable at work, consider getting together with colleagues to have the air analyzed. If necessary, ask for a restructuring so that the windows can be opened. A simple remedy for air that is occasionally too dry is to use a vaporizer.

Do not conclude that your workplace is safe simply because it is the kind of place one would expect to be fine. The National Institute for Occupational Safety and Health says that as many as 15 million American workers may be exposed to substances known to cause birth defects and cancer. Often these workers have no idea that the products they are working with are toxic. In an office, be especially aware of copying machines in a poorly ventilated area, and avoid reading large amounts of freshly copied papers in a small office with the windows closed. Small companies and people working at home usually escape inspection and guidelines from public health officials. Hairdressers, for instance, usually have no idea that they are at risk for upper-respiratory problems and lung cancer, especially if they work in a salon where nail care is also offered. Apparently the combination of aerosol-propelled hair sprays with solvents and dust from nail care is quite hard on the bodies of those who are continuously exposed. Recovery room nurses may not realize that the anesthetic gases exhaled by their patients can cause miscarriage in the nurses who are constantly exposed. Artists too are often unaware of the toxicity of the materials they use. These problems are not new. Goya, the famed Spanish painter, died of lead poisoning. Remember the saying "mad as a hatter"? It dates from the time when felt-workers used mercury to prepare the felt. Today we have more toxins, but we are also fortunate to possess a greater awareness of their danger than people who lived before us.

PREPARING YOUR BODY

Part of what makes reactions to toxins so individual is genetic makeup, but lifestyle also plays an important role. Well-nourished, fit people who spend some of their daylight time outdoors handle toxins, including such serious ones as lead, much better. So make friends with good nutrition, aerobic activity, and daylight.

In the realm of nutrition, be wary of "experts" who give specific dietary advice, especially concerning quantities, without knowing you. Counting slices of bread and glasses of milk makes eating a bore; we probably get more out of our food when we enjoy it and when we trust our system to take what it needs and no more. Nutritionists, allergists, and toxicologists agree that there are no required foods, only required nutrients, and the exact amounts in which these are needed is individual. Consuming moderate amounts of a great variety of foods is the best way to ensure that nutritional needs are fully met and that there is no overexposure to a particular allergen or toxin. Learning to let one's body steer one to certain foods is more likely to lead to a balanced intake of required nutrients than following specific recommendations from a book.

Even though a lot of important nutrients have been identified, this does not mean all nutrients necessary for proper functioning have been discovered. Laboratory rats raised on a precise synthetic diet still fail to grow or reproduce and are more likely to contract cancer. Therefore, when possible, get foods in their natural state. Refined foods with added nutrients do not have the nourishing quality of unrefined foods.

If you are exposed to a lot of toxins, make sure you get plenty of vitamins A, E, and C. Laboratory research suggests that these three vitamins can stop the type of cell division that otherwise would lead to cancer. Interestingly, vitamin A seems to work better when the body gets it from nutrients rather than from pills. It is also toxic in high amounts. Of course, this is true of everything; even the best substances can be toxic when taken in excess, and what is too much for one is not enough for another. In general, it seems best to rely on foods for these important vitamins (yellow and dark green vegetables and fruits are high in beta carotene, the precursor of vitamin A; grains are high in vitamin E; and vitamin C is in all fresh fruit and vegetables, especially citrus fruits and cabbage). On a particularly stressful day, however, vitamin tablets (take them with a meal or snack to ensure that they are absorbed) or a couple of glasses of carrot juice and a handful of seeds and nuts may give the body the extra dose it needs, especially to handle the stress of environmental toxins. Zinc (found in grains, seeds, and meat) and calcium (found in dark, leafy vegetables, figs, and dairy products) seem to help the body cope with metals such as lead, mercury compounds, and cadmium.

Wash all fresh fruits and vegetables thoroughly to rid them as much as possible of lead and pesticides. Food grown near a highway tends to contain more lead, and for the same reason produce bought at a roadside fruit stand should be washed with extra care. In terms of pesticides, be especially careful with foods grown in third-world countries. Pesticides banned in the United States for their toxicity can be sold to other countries, where they are often used by people who cannot read the instructions. Foods imported from these countries are not very well tested for toxic residues.

Even the pesticides commonly used in the United States are not as carefully analyzed as they should be. The agencies responsible for testing lack the funds to keep up with the many new products that come on the market, and their manufacturers are powerful. Unfortunately, when we buy our food, we often have no idea what pesticide, fertilizer, or fumigant was used and when. And even though many supermarkets list the pesticide residues in the produce they offer, we would need a handbook of toxicology (mine is two thousand pages long, and it still does not list everything) to do our grocery shopping. Pesticides kill insects by their effect on the transmission of nerve impulses or on cellular energy metabolism. Since they have not been tested for their impact on the fast-growing and highly sensitive brain and rapidly multiplying cells of a developing baby, I suggest that everyone planning or starting a pregnancy ask the manager of their supermarket to carry organically grown produce. Shoppers in Sacramento got a Safeway store to carry organic produce by asking for it!

Organically grown grains, legumes, root vegetables, and coffee beans are often available in bulk at health-food stores or by mail order. There is good reason for going to the extra trouble and expense. Grains can have residues of mercury compounds, legumes tend to accumulate heavy metals, carrots absorb and even concentrate the toxins from the soil in which they grow, and coffee beans are almost always grown in third-world countries. Many of these foods can be stored for a long time, and it might be worth your while to stock up.

Dairy products will carry fewer toxins when their fat content is reduced. Since the American diet tends to be disproportionally high in fat, nonfat milk or, if that is too unappealing, low-fat milk diluted with steadily increasing amounts of nonfat milk will help you cut down on fat without giving up important nutrients.

Very innocent-looking foods such as commercially prepared cakes and cookies can be quite high in fat. So can the foods that we eat for their protein value. Let's take cheese as an example. A sample one-ounce serving of cheddar cheese contains 110 calories, seven grams of protein, one gram of carbohydrate, and nine grams of fat. Since one gram of fat provides nine calories and one gram of protein or carbohydrate provides four, the 110 calories in this ounce of cheese break down into 81 calories of fat and only 28 calories of protein.

Fat is nature's storage capsule. Plants contain some, but dairy products and meat usually have more. Meat also has protein and, properly prepared, is delicious. There is no need to give it up, but it is not necessary to consume a big piece every day. It is also not necessary to eat everything on your plate. If you grew up with a rule like that, a rule that intrudes on your ability to choose what and how much you need, see if you can change it. This might not be easy, because when we learned this kind of behavior we were small and dependent, and survival became associated with obeying the basic rules of our family. Gradually change each rule you no longer need. If you still believe you must always eat everything on your plate, see how you feel when you say, "I can sometimes leave something on my plate," and, when you can do that, say, "I am free to eat from my plate what I need." Next, as your sense of how your body functions increases, experiment with changes in what you put on your plate.

It is true that protein is essential for growth and repair, but our bodies can get it from grains, vegetables, legumes, fruits, nuts, and seeds as well as from animal products. Less meat and more vegetables might be a healthy change. An abundance of animal proteins tends to be hard on the kidneys, which are already challenged in pregnancy. This does not mean that it is better to give up meats entirely. They are an excellent source of many nutrients. Iron is absorbed more easily from meats than from vegetables, and iron is especially important to women in their reproductive years and to small children.

In selecting your meat, be aware that both antibiotics and growth hormones fed to farm animals stay in the meat and affect the health of people who eat it. While the use of growth hormones has been banned in the United States, they are still used illegally, especially on chicken farms, and are legal in South American countries, which export a lot of beef. Fortunately, many supermarkets carry organically raised chickens and turkeys, and some also offer organic beef and pork.

Even organically raised animals retain toxins in their tissue from the air, the water, and the food on which they were raised. These toxins collect in the liver, the organ so often recommended to pregnant women because of its superior nutritional value. Until the world has rid itself of the current heavy load of toxic chemicals, avoid liver and other organ meats, particularly from animals high in the food chain.

Fish, even those low in the food chain, have not escaped environmental toxins. Deep-water fish tend to be cleanest, eel and mussels dirtiest. Fish from the Great Lakes are heavily polluted. When preparing for a pregnancy, be especially cautious of PCBs, a byproduct of many industrial processes, because they accumulate in the fatty tissue of the breast and pass to the baby through the mother's milk. During pregnancy, the pollutant of greatest concern is methyl mercury. Prevalent in fish, it passes the placenta readily and accumulates in the fetus, where it can cause nervous-system disorders. Fish shops ought to tell you where the fish were caught and display a water-pollution map of the world. Until that happens, consider avoiding fish that generally swim in polluted waters: carp, catfish, lake trout, whitefish, bluefish, and striped bass. The highest concentration of mercury is found in predatory fish near the top of the food chain. Avoid swordfish and eat no more than one-half pound of tuna, halibut, bass, burbot, perch, pike, or sheepshead per week. Salmon and sardines swim in very deep water and are relatively clean. If you eat them canned with the bones, they will also give you a lot of calcium. Do not store them in an opened can, since the air may oxidize the metal, a hazard especially with lead-soldered cans.

Vegetables and fruits secrete toxins when they begin to rot. According to the widely used and highly respected Ames test, bruised celery is more carcinogenic than some of the substances commonly labeled as such. However, organic substances do not accumulate in our fatty tissue, as many of the new petrochemical substances do.

Another and more serious example of nature's aptitude for chemical warfare is a mold that secretes aflatoxins, one of the most potent carcinogens known. This mold is quite fond of peanuts and grains. Fats, once they are removed from their natural state inside living cells, turn rancid easily, thus increasing their carcinogenic potential. Therefore, store oils, shelled nuts, cereals without preservatives, other grains, and peanut butter, along with your vegetables, in a cool place. Try to make room for them in the refrigerator. One way to do this is by taking out some of your soft drinks. Easing up on your intake of carbonated beverages helps your body's calcium/phosphorous ratio, which is particularly important if you spend most of your days indoors without daylight and without much walking or other weight-bearing activity.

What you drink during meals affects your body's ability to absorb nutrients. Taking coffee or tea with meals drastically reduces the body's ability to absorb vitamin C. Since this is one of the three important vitamins that protect the body against cancer, as well a key aid in helping connective tissue (the cells that hold the body together) stay strong, it might be a good idea to practice the European custom of serving coffee after a meal rather than before or during it. Vitamin C greatly enhances the body's ability to absorb iron from food, especially grains. Thus, a glass of orange juice makes a great appetizer for a vegetarian meal, and with breakfast it helps us get iron from cereal and bread.

How you prepare your food makes a difference too. Cooking in cast-iron pots adds quite a bit of iron to your food, especially when you are preparing tomato-based sauces, soups, or stews. Cooking with fluoridated water in an aluminum pot increases the amount of aluminum released into the food and should be avoided. Barbecuing adds unhealthy fumes to the unhealthful composition of charred foods, particularly if a starter fluid is used. This might be fine once a week but not every day. Smoked foods are not good on a regular basis either. People in parts of the world where smoked foods are a main staple seem more susceptible to cancer of the nasopharynx and the stomach.

Equally important to eating well is giving the nutrients a chance to get to where they are needed. Aerobic activity helps in this respect. When the heart and the circulatory system are stimulated into good performance, healthier organs, stronger connective tissue, and denser bones are built or maintained. Also, aerobic activity of the proper type, intensity, duration, and frequency, combined with a diet composed mostly of complex carbohydrates (unrefined grains, vegetables, fruits, and legumes), is the best way to eliminate stored toxins, including DDT and PCBs. Rhesus monkeys with the same level of PCBs as is common in people have a hard time carrying a pregnancy to term. Many environmental toxins are similar in structure to estrogen and might well interfere with the body's natural hormonal interaction and timetable. Do not attempt detoxification through weight loss when already pregnant or while nursing, because the toxins will be released through the placenta or into the breast milk in larger amounts than if they were left alone.

While trying to improve your cardiovascular fitness, don't worry that you might not be able to assess whether or not you are working at the correct intensity. Your heart will get exercised safely and effectively when you work at a tempo that invigorates you but does not make you feel breathless. To choose a proper activity, just keep in mind that anything that moves the large muscle groups (the arms and the legs) simultaneously in a rhythmic fashion will do: walking, running, ballroom dancing or aerobic dance in an exercise studio, rowing (in a boat or on a machine), cycling out in the open or on a stationary bike (preferably one with movable handlebars that you pull), etc. You don't have to choose one or the other; variety increases the chances that all muscles will get worked and reduces the risk of imbalance or injury from overworking one particular muscle group. However, since daylight is a stimulus for many hormonal activities, especially those that govern metabolic functions, it is wise to do some of your aerobic exercise out of doors. Something as simple as a good brisk walk about three times a week for half an hour enhances the body's ability to handle toxins and improves calcium metabolism. This simple rule will help you decide on the proper duration: Working the heart muscle harder than normal for fifteen minutes or more will strengthen it; anything shorter will still help but is less effective. And finally, in terms of frequency, while the heart will get stronger from an aerobic workout three times a week, if the aim is to burn more fat, five or six times a week is better.

Optimal burning of fat occurs with sustained activity that causes your heart to work harder than normal but does not impair your ability to breathe. You should always be able to talk. For some people, drinking a cup of coffee about an hour before aerobic activity seems to mobilize the fatty acids so that they are more readily available as a fuel—one cup does the job; two or three cups are *not* better. Swimming seems less effective as a fat-burning activity than other forms of exercise that involve large muscle groups, perhaps because immersion in cool water prevents the body from perspiring and attaining a sufficiently high core temperature.

Fat accumulation is more of a problem among sedentary people. The body has a mechanism that prevents us from eating more than is needed. The less physically active a person is, the less well this mechanism works. Refined foods and growth hormones in meats are thought by some to interfere with the body's "enough is enough" sensor. If you are sedentary and somewhat overweight, take encouragement from the fact that your body, when you ask it clearly to burn fat, will increase its level of fat-burning enzymes, which will enable you to burn more fat with every workout. To give your body the kind of unequivocal message to which it can respond, you must be disciplined about the way you ask. Start a routine of seven or so minutes of aerobic activity six times per week and do not let up.

If you are completely out of shape, it is safest and best to start calmly with an activity you don't dislike too much. Work up to longer and more intense sessions slowly. Once you get stronger, branch out to other activities, especially ones that look like fun.

While aerobic activity is phenomenally important in terms of health, it is only one of the four components of fitness. The other three are strength, flexibility, and a proper percentage of body fat. When getting ready for a pregnancy it is a good idea to give all four some attention. A fit body is much more able to handle stress, much better equipped to cope with an endurance activity like labor, and much better at returning to its former shape after the baby is born.

Muscles grow stronger when they must resist the movement they are designed to make. Lifting weights, pulling rubber bands, squeezing beach balls, and working out on resistance machines all increase the gain from muscle-strengthening exercise. Doing such exercises once a week will improve muscle tone slightly, but twice a week will yield more visible results, and seeing the improvements increases the chances that you will stay with your exercise program.

In preparation for a pregnancy, pay special attention to the muscles that might be weakened by your particular lifestyle. In women with desk jobs, the muscles in front of the chest have often lost flexibility from not being stretched, while those of the upper back are weak from not being used, creating the hunched-forward look so characteristic of people who are out of shape. This particular posture contributes to upper-back aches in pregnancy and may worsen as the mother carries her baby in her arms, nurses, and bends over to change diapers and render other care. Working the muscles of the upper body, front and back, in their full range of motion will restore their length in the front and their strength front and back, and it will make carrying the baby a lot easier and more becoming. For a full set of upper-body exercises and stretches, turn to the pregnancy workout on pages 92 to 101. For two quick-to-do and easy-to-learn exercises, see exercises 5 and 6 on pages 263 and 264.

Another set of antagonistic muscles (muscles that cooperate by having opposing functions) to which you should pay attention as you prepare for pregnancy are those of the abdomen and the lower back. The abdominal muscles usually need strengthening, while those of the lower back need protection from overstretching, which can occur when bending forward to stretch, especially in those with tight hamstring muscles. The abdomen is commonly strengthened with curl-ups, but these seem more effective for the upper segments of the rectus abdominus than for the lower ones. Since strength in the lower abdomen is a great asset in pregnancy, try curl-ups with a five-pound weight placed on the chest once regular curl-ups have become easy. You will feel the lower abdomen kick in a lot more. For regular curl-ups, it also helps to visualize the separate segments of this muscle and emphasize tightening the lower part. (See pages 261–62.)

The lower back is at increased risk for overstretching if the hamstrings and calf muscles are short. Wearing heels shortens these muscles. Heels are great for cocktail parties and ballroom dancing, but in daily life a flat shoe is much better for the body's alignment.

Lack of flexibility is so common we don't even see it as such. Compare yourself for a moment with women of cultures where it is customary to sit in a squatting position for such work as weaving or painting as well as during meals and while engaged in conversation. Imagine how different the pull of the hamstring and calf muscles on the lower back is among such women, compared to the pull of those muscles in people who only sit in chairs and get around in cars. Sitting in chairs also shortens the invisible but very important hip-flexor muscles, which help us stand upright. This contributes to lower-back problems. For a set of safe stretches for these muscle groups, see the pregnancy workout on pages 82 to 86. Stretching is safer and more effective when the muscles are warm, such as after aerobic activity.

If you have not done any form of exercise in years, the hardest part may be getting started. Once you begin and hang in there until your body gets the message, you won't want to stop, because you will have discovered the key to youth, health, and vitality and will be on your way to getting in touch with long-lost sensitivities. Exercise activates dormant neurons and enables all neurons to relay messages more quickly and accurately. It also increases the secretion of hormones that make you feel better. Gradually, all the measures you take for better health become a pleasure rather than a struggle.

Once you have gotten your exercise program under way, look at some of your other habits. If your diet and physical activity are up to par, moderate and occasional use of drugs, alcohol, or cigarettes is not quite as bad for the body as it could be. The trouble is that most people who use addictive substances overindulge in them and forget about nutrition and exercise. Another problem is that none of these substances are pure anymore. Wine and beer contain all kinds of chemicals, tobacco and marijuana have often been sprayed with dangerous pesticides, and it's anyone's guess what profit-hungry dealers have used to cut their cocaine. Your body is already exposed to so much you cannot control no matter how health-conscious you are; the least you can do is to rid yourself of any substance dependencies so that you will be able to abstain totally during your pregnancy.

This may not be easy. Living in a materialistic world provides us with many comforts and securities, but it is hard on our spirit and soul. Momentary release from the ordinary tedium of life is as necessary for our nonanatomical selves as nutrients are for our bodies. Fortunately, there are mind-expanding techniques that can help you satisfy that need. What will work for you is a matter of predisposition. Trust that your intuition will lead you to what is right for you. When someone you know manages to give up bad habits or acquires a superior consciousness, regard it as an affirmation that it can be done rather than as an example of how it should be done. Our journey through life loses meaning when we forget that each of us has a personal path and that the compass we need for it is not man-made.

CHOOSING PREGNANCY HEALTH CARE

Taking good care of yourself can be much easier and more effective when you work in cooperation with a health-care professional. Such an expert can give you inspiration as well as feedback on where you might have particular weaknesses. During pre-pregnancy planning, for example, it is important to check your immunity to viral infections such as rubella (a common and innocent infection in children, but one that can be devastating for the fetus if contracted during pregnancy) and toxoplasmosis (transmitted by pets) and to make sure you do not have a case of chlamydia. You can be vaccinated against rubella, and you can be taught how to avoid the toxoplasmosis virus if you are not immune to it—there is no vaccine against it yet, and it can harm a pregnancy. Chlamydia, a sexually transmitted disease, is much more common than toxoplasmosis, often produces no obvious symptoms, and can cause miscarriage. Once diagnosed, however, it is easily treated.

You will need your health-care provider to be available and able to answer all your health-related questions. If you already have a sound relationship with a gynecologist who is a good obstetrician, you may be set. However, if the relationship suffers from flaws in communication, or if the doctor practices at a hospital where the labor and delivery department does not provide the kind of care you want, give yourself a chance to meet some others. Pregnancy often becomes a time of growth, and your health-care provider can be a support or a hindrance in your development. Try to see the search for the person to whom you will entrust your prenatal care as an exciting part of your overall preparation.

For a woman in good health, the ancient and universal fear of childbirth—among some forest peoples of Borneo, the courage of men going head-hunting was considered equal to that of women facing birth—is no longer quite justified. The pain can be relieved, either by skills the mother acquires or with drugs; problems can be detected and remedied; and loss of life (mother's or baby's) is becoming extremely rare among healthy, well-nourished women in the developed world.

Numerous advances of the last hundred years have contributed to this unprecedented security: better sanitation, improved nutrition, greater understanding of the birth process and better training of birth attendants, improvements in surgical techniques, in-depth understanding of newborn physiology and needs, increased availability of good medical care, and—last but not least

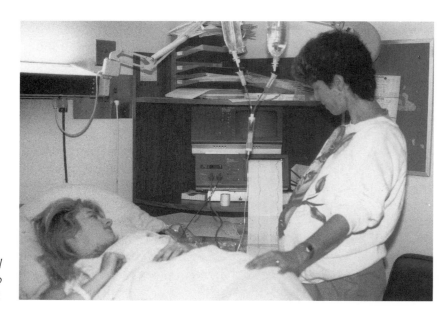

Many health-care professionals bring personal experience as well as professional expertise to the care of women in labor.

—better education, especially of women. As is often the case with complex developments, we tend to ascribe the improved safety of childbirth to a single, visible cause: the move from home to hospital of giving birth. Yet, in Holland, a country long envied for its low infant-mortality rates, more than 40 percent of births take place at home, and those families that do opt for birth outside of the home often choose a small birthing center close to a well-equipped medical center rather than the medical center itself.

The switch from midwives to physicians, another development of this century, does not deserve credit for lowering birth risks to mother and baby either. All northern European countries use midwives in conjunction with physicians and have good safety records. Midwives give prenatal care and attend to women in labor. The doctor's expertise and skill are called upon only when necessary. This keeps the cost of birth down, and it also seems to keep the cesarean-section rate from escalating unnecessarily.

In the United States women have a choice of three different types of practitioners: an obstetrician-gynecologist, a family practitioner, or a nurse-midwife. Which one is best for you depends on your health and on what type of care you need and/or prefer. For instance, if twins run in your family, if there are reasons to suspect that a pregnancy might be hard on your health (if you suffer from diabetes or high blood pressure, for example), or if you have had a previous problem pregnancy, you might look for an obstetrician who specializes in problems similar to yours or one who specializes in high-risk obstetrics. If you are in good health and want a doctor who can provide both you and, later, your baby with health care, you might prefer a family practitioner. And if you see pregnancy and birth as a natural, nonmedical event, you might like the idea of a midwife. Midwives are trained to attend to birth in both home and hospital settings, whereas the training of family practitioners and obstetricians usually excludes experiences with home birth.*

To an American woman whose mother, mother-in-law, aunts, sisters, and friends all gave birth under a doctor's care in a hospital, the idea that a midwife and or a home birth can, under the right circumstances, be quite safe probably seems outrageous.

---

* For organizations that can provide you with references, see the list in "Resources for New Parents," page 329.

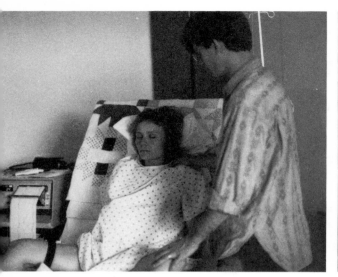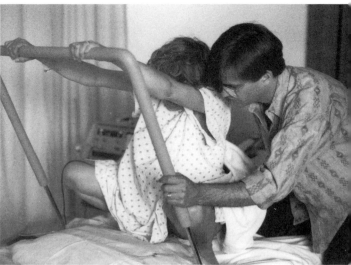

Usually, in the course of growing up we form an image of what constitutes an appropriate setting for a safe birth. This image is not easy to change. Respect your own beliefs when you make your choices. Going against them will create inner turmoil and doubt, and this will lower your ability to cope with labor; building on them will make you stronger.

Thus, if one of your friends had a successful home birth but the thought of it frightens you, trust your intuition and consider instead a well-equipped, well-staffed medical center, one with a lab, a blood bank, ultrasound equipment, an operating room, and a neonatal nursery, all staffed around the clock. A freestanding birth center without such facilities is useful when your home is too far from a hospital with lifesaving equipment, and you prefer a relaxed, nonmedical atmosphere. If you choose such a center or a home birth, you may want to check out the hospital that your care provider uses in case of problems.

Never select a hospital for the champagne it serves with dinner. More important than the wallpaper and the rocking chair are the staff and the labor beds. An obstetrical anesthesiologist who is available around the clock is a great asset, and so is one well-trained nurse per woman in labor. The first guarantees you the most effective and safest pain relief when you need it, which is especially important in case of a long labor or a sudden complication; the second increases your chances that you will have a compassionate professional at your side. While having your part-

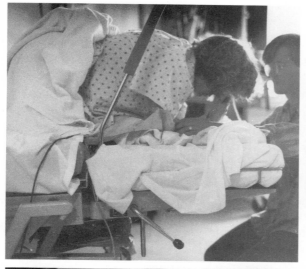

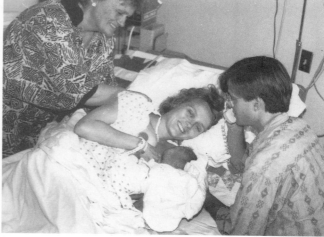

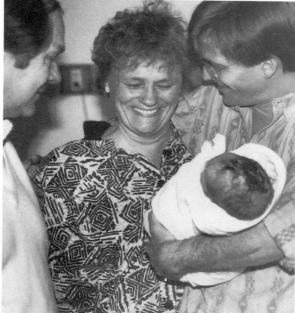

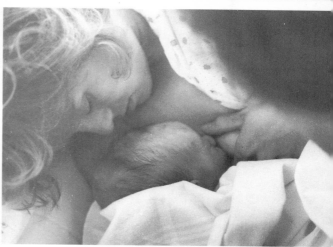

A modern labor bed allows the mother to assume any position of choice, including one for rest after the baby is born.

ner there as a helper can be nice, he, like you, may be new at this, and all the tips learned beforehand are sometimes forgotten unless a skilled attendant helps you both remember.

A labor bed that at the touch of a button can be changed into a birth stool or a platform on which to get into a squatting position is useful, especially if it is in a room in which you spend the hours of your labor, give birth, and recover. Such rooms are called LDRPs (for Labor, Delivery, Recovery, and Postpartum) or LDRs (for Labor, Delivery, and Recovery), and they are better than a setup that requires you to move from labor room to delivery room to recovery room to postpartum room. Separate rooms are useful only when the more elaborate equipment of a delivery room or the closer supervision of a recovery room proves necessary because of complications.

Less important than the staff and the beds, yet worthy of some consideration if you are choosing between two facilities that have the above-mentioned essentials, are the other characteristics of the rooms: Labor rooms with windows tend to be more cheerful and help one stay in touch with the cycles of light and dark. Windows that open increase the availability of fresh air, with the proper ratio of negative to positive ions. Rooms that rely solely on air-conditioning often have an abundance of positive ions, and these make relaxation and a pleasant state of mind more difficult to achieve; also, such rooms are often on the cool side. Women's bodies function better when the room in which they labor is cozy and warm but not stuffy, and newborn babies like warm rooms better too. Having a shower or a large tub in the room is a plus. Women who have warm water available to them during labor almost always opt to use it, sitting under it or in it, or applying it to their bodies in the form of compresses.

Some birth centers allow women to stay in the tub during the baby's expulsion. During labor, submersion in warm water seems to lessen the pain for quite a few women. The idea of underwater birth started in Moscow. When I went there to see how it was done and why, I was surprised to hear the reason its originator, Igor Tcharkovski, gave. Two practical ones had come to my mind—less pain for the mother and less immediate pressure change on the baby's head at birth—but the translator told me that Mr. Tcharkovski believes "that human beings are very close to dolphins and that this closeness is greatest while in the womb. Dolphins will come close to shore when a pregnant woman calls them from the beach, because they sense the fetus. Babies born underwater maintain this contact more easily, and with such interspecies communication they are more likely to remain harmonious with nature and natural processes." Doctors in the Los Angeles area who practice underwater birth say that the benefits are mostly for the mother and that it is best to let the baby surface as soon as possible. Naturally, it is also important that the tub, the water, and the mother's body be clean.

While a neonatal nursery supervised by a doctor with expertise in newborns is great if a baby needs extra care or if a mother needs rest, a healthy baby and mother are much better off when this facility is not forced on them by outdated hospital routines. Newborns like their mother's smell, voice, skin, heartbeat, and breasts. They like their father's presence, too, if he made himself familiar during the pregnancy. Therefore, a hospital that does not separate you from your baby unless there is a medical reason or you need a rest is preferable to one that sends all babies, or every baby delivered by cesarean section, to the neonatal nursery for the first few hours after birth. A new mother may need some rest from her baby later, but that should not deprive her of those first hours with her newborn. Unless the new mother wishes differently, her baby should also be allowed to stay with her during visiting hours and during the night.

One other factor to check into when you look at the hospitals in your area is the kind of staff on the postpartum floor. Do they have nurses who are trained as breast-feeding experts and as parent educators? A first baby can be quite puzzling to its parents—there is so much at stake, and the baby looks so vulnerable. And breast-feeding, while a natural function of the new mother's body, can be somewhat bewildering the first few days.

If you live in an area where there is only one hospital and the facilities leave you unimpressed, talk with the head of the maternity department about what you do not like. Hospitals are very eager to please their clients. You might be able to bring some friends, flowers, your own pillow, a hot-water bottle, a vaporizer to moisten the air in a dry room. Decide what you need to make the hospital labor room a more attractive place for your baby's birth, and discuss it with the person in charge.

If you choose a home birth, ask your birth attendant to recommend a pediatrician or lactation consultant who will come to your house. Also plan on lining up someone who will look after you for a few days while you recover and take care of your baby.

Opting for a home birth does not always mean having one. First there is a screening to rule out all risk factors for the known complications of pregnancy and parturition. Then there is a 10 percent chance you may have to be moved to a hospital during labor. Don't fear this too much. The most common reason for a transfer is a labor that does not progress, and this is not an emergency. Actually, most labor troubles, including a baby's inability to cope with the contractions, are usually detected before emergency measures are needed. Those problems that do need immediate attention—compression of the umbilical cord or bleeding after the baby is born—can usually be remedied temporarily: Placing the mother in a position where the baby falls away from the cord relieves compression, and giving her intravenous fluids and medications to make the uterus contract can stop postpartum bleeding.

Thus, a woman who chooses a home birth does not put herself or her baby at risk if proper conditions (including quick and easy access to a well-staffed, well-equipped medical center with twenty-four-hour anesthesia) are met. The one exception is the small but serious possibility of uncontrollable bleeding. However, this might occur in a hospital too, and in a small hospital the time lost waiting for one's doctor and anesthesiologist to arrive would probably equal the time lost in being moved from home to hospital. The one other risk at home is lack of extensive resuscitation equipment should the baby experience difficulties immediately after birth. No matter how great modern medicine's ability to screen is, not all problems with birth or newborns can be predicted. Some babies do need immediate expert assistance and equipment.

A freestanding birth center or a home birth assures one of a staff that believes in birth with the least amount of intervention. This leads us back to how we want to be cared for during labor and birth. One way is not necessarily better than another. What matters is that you feel comfortable and secure. If, when picturing yourself in labor, you worry most about the pain, you should be in a hospital with obstetrical anesthesia staffing around the clock, and an obstetrician might be a better choice than a midwife.

Of course, choosing a midwife does not mean rejecting technology. Midwives do not eschew pharmacological pain relief. However, the training of midwives differs from that of obstetricians. In the former, the emphasis is on the normal process of labor and birth, as well as the many variations that, while not common, do

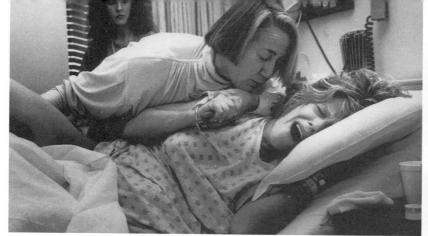

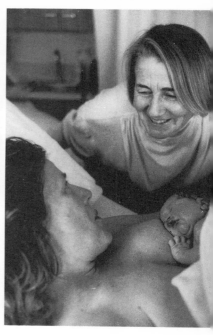

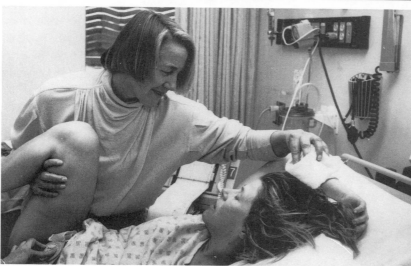

not require intervention. Doctors spend many more hours learning what to do for cases that need help. Doctors know more and have more skills than midwives, but more is not always better. Plato observed that a beautiful movement accomplishes its goal without anything that is not necessary. I think that holds true for a birth too. A cesarean section is beautiful if that is what is needed to deliver a healthy baby. But when all goes well and the mother wishes to do what she can herself, the beauty is in helping her stay in touch with the courage and perseverance this may take.

If you are willing to work hard and don't mind losing control over yourself a few times, a birth attendant who can give you compassion and guidance and who believes in holding back on offering technical assistance might be appropriate. This latter combination of a woman who is willing to work and, where necessary, endure some pain, guided by a doctor or midwife ready to support her but also able to offer her pain relief should this become appropriate, stands the best chance of avoiding an unnecessary cesarean section.

Interviewing a health-care provider, especially a doctor, can be a difficult task. We somehow feel deep inside that doctors are above the common human weaknesses such as lack of caring, taking advantage of others, or dominating them unnecessarily. This is probably because we want them to be so. Of course, some are, but there is nothing in medical school and very little in midwifery training that teaches practitioners how to be more aware of themselves and overcome their own personality weaknesses. Fortunately, a good health-care provider prefers to be consciously chosen and will therefore be willing to give you an interview or to hold a talk for a few prospective new patients. If possible, check out a few practitioners before making your choice.

If your insurance does not allow you to select who will attend you during labor, it should at least grant you some control over which staff member you see for your prenatal care. If you cannot interview the practitioners available to you and are not happy with the one who has given you routine gynecological checkups, ask the nurses or other women who use the same health plan whom they recommend. On the positive side, your health plan probably uses facilities where all the lifesaving equipment, staffed by experts, is available around the clock. Since such group insurance aims at keeping costs low, unnecessary use of this equipment is not likely. Not being able to select your birth attendant is not a matter of life and death, and I have heard many touching birth stories from women who had no say over who attended them during their labor. Health-care practitioners who work for a salary can be just as dedicated to their work as those who are paid by their clients. Women with prepaid insurance plans seem to have fewer cesarean sections, yet equally good outcomes.

If you do not yet have medical insurance and are considering a home birth, be aware that many insurance policies cover hospital and birth-center births only.

If you do have a choice, and you select a midwife, make sure that she was trained at an accredited school and is a member in good standing of the American College of Nurse Midwives. This ensures that she has up-to-date knowledge and skills and that she is tied into the rest of the maternity-health-care system, so that she can ask for consultations and/or a timely transfer to a reputable medical center. Some midwives attend both home and hospital births, and some do only one or the other. Ask the midwife who her backup doctor is and meet with him or her. Because of the unpredictability of labor, make sure that she agrees with you that more pain than you are willing to handle, anxiety, or a long and exhausting labor are valid reasons for a transfer to a hospital. Some women have found it helpful to ask for a few names of women who recently gave birth at home and to talk with them.

If your choice is an obstetrician, check where he/she trained and whether he/she passed the boards in obstetrics and gynecology. Most doctors display this kind of information in their office. More important than having a specific list of questions is finding a practitioner who will take what questions you have seriously. Think about such issues as group versus solo practice. In the case of group practice, do you like the partners? In the case of solo practice, how many patients who will give birth in the same month is the doctor committed to? Does this doctor use the many new diagnostic tests, such as chorionic-villi sampling, amniocentesis, and ultrasound, routinely or in accordance with individual needs and preference? If a test is needed, is it done in the office, or is the patient referred to a center that specializes in the procedure? (For complex procedures, including ultrasound, the latter is usually safer and gives more reliable information.) Does the way your practitioner talks about labor coincide with how you feel and what you know? (Medical procedures such as intravenous-fluid administration, continuous electronic fetal monitoring, pharmacological pain relief, and surgical widening of the vagina to prevent tearing are most beneficial when they are used according to individual need rather than as standard procedures.) If all is well, will you have a choice over the position in which you give birth, or does this doctor prefer the traditional, legs-up-in-stirrups position? What kind of birth facilities does he/she use? Does this place have a good reputation, and do you like the atmosphere there? What kind of pain relief will be available, and is this administered according to your needs, or does the doctor prefer to use it routinely or not to use it at all? Will this doctor be supportive if you decide to give birth with as little medical assistance as possible? Also, especially if a pregnancy is still in the planning stage, discuss how you can store your own blood. Blood can now be frozen and stored on a long-term basis. Should the need for a blood transfusion arise, having one's own blood available lessens the risks of transfusion reactions, suppression of the immune system, and the transmission of viruses.

You may wish to ask for the cesarean-section rate of both doctor and hospital. If you do, you should take into consideration whether the doctor being interviewed specializes in high-risk obstetrics or not. Some hospitals report a cesarean-section rate of 35 percent. It is generally believed that between 15 and 20 percent is more desirable, but all contributing factors to the higher rate are not understood. Doctors say that private patients have more cesareans than others, because many of them are looking for optimal health and development of their babies, as well as a good experience. At the slightest doubt about the effects of labor on the baby, or after a few painful contractions, they are ready for a surgical delivery. Also, doctors say a larger percentage of these women are over the age of thirty, and complications with pregnancy and birth go up, especially after the age of thirty-five. Moreover, health-conscious women are likely to eat extra well during pregnancy, and their well-nourished babies sometimes have more difficulty fitting through the natural birth passage. This group of patients and the doctors they choose are also probably more comfortable with technology and have a harder time trusting in nature's wisdom and timetable.

Once you are pregnant, you have a chance to get to know the person you selected a little better with each prenatal visit. These visits are not just health checkups—they provide you and the person who now shares the responsibility for your health a chance to exchange ideas and information.

If doubts arise about your birth attendant's competence, consider calling the labor and delivery department of the hospital where your doctor practices and asking the nurses for the names of their personal doctors. If your doctor's name is not mentioned, call again the next day and ask for the names of the respected doctors on the staff. If your doctor's name is not among them, bring up his or her name and listen carefully for the response. If you detect hesitation, make an appointment with one of the doctors the nurses do recommend. Sometimes we don't recognize quality until we see it. If this doctor seems more respectful of your wishes and/or makes you feel better cared for, consider changing doctors, or discuss your doubts with your present doctor. Do not push your anxieties into the background or hope that they will be proven wrong during labor. Doubts and fears interfere with your body's ability to handle labor effectively. When one goes sailing on the open sea, one needs a reliable compass. During labor, trust in one's birth attendant is just as important.

ABOUT AGENT X

At this point, especially if you read through this first section in one breath, you may need to reestablish a balance between taking control and living with a sense of trust. When knowledge and information, premeditation and planning lead to more, rather than less, tension and worry, it is time for reflection. Everyone needs this, but how each person does it best varies. I rearrange things in my house, put fresh flowers here and there, place clippings and notes in a "read later" file, put books that might have contributed to my overload back on the shelves, stare out a window, and avoid those who know the truth about too many things. Once I calm down from the relentless shower of facts that modern life bestows on us so freely, I wander into my study and look at my friends there, the authors, who are always available but who do not speak unless I take them off the shelves.

Once, while looking for something that could help me get some perspective on our modern notion of control over ourselves, our lives, and our reproduction, I opened Nabokov's *Lectures on Literature* and read:

> Three forces make and mold a human being: heredity, environment, and the unknown agent X. Of these the second, environment, is by far the least important, while the last, agent X, is by far the most influential.

Then, fearful that I might leave too much to a greater power, I reread an article in which Lawrence D. Longo, M.D., a well-known professor of obstetrics, urges his readers (it was published in the *American Journal of Obstetrics and Gynecology*) to stop thinking that the environmental problems of our era are outside our purview or too overwhelming for an individual to deal with. He ends his plea for responsible action with a quote from the Talmud:

> It is not for you to complete the task but neither have you the right to desist from it (Aboth 2:16).

With a sense of peace, I realized that the more I trusted that I would do my share, the more I could trust agent X. I believe it was a medieval saint who said, "Act as if everything depends on you and pray as if everything depends on God."

Health
and Fitness
in Pregnancy

GENERAL GUIDELINES

During pregnancy, fitness takes on new dimensions. "I want to do the best for myself and my baby," women say. "I also want to be strong for my labor, and I would like to recover quickly." Even women who never exercised before begin to work out regu-

larly, saying it makes them feel better. For years I've watched this desire on the part of women to actively help nature. It makes a pregnancy-exercise class a beautiful sight. If your health and schedule permit, join a class, taught by a good instructor. It can also be a great way to meet other pregnant women and develop a new network of friends.

The ultimate test of an exercise class is how it makes you feel. After a good class you should be invigorated yet more able to relax, and after a few good classes your awareness of posture should improve. It is a good sign if you find yourself correcting bad habits, such as sitting in one position with tense muscles while you barely breathe, that you had not even noticed before. In the process of leading the class, the teacher should help you see how you can better use your body and relieve tension—for instance, just by taking a few deep breaths.

Be wary of those who treat all pregnant women as if they are the same. The different trimesters impose restrictions, but the greater restricting factor is the mother's pre-pregnancy fitness level; a pregnant marathon runner need not worry about some of the things that apply to a woman who finds it hard to walk one block.

There are a few restrictions that every pregnant woman should observe. The complex hormonal changes that allow the remarkable expansion of the pregnant body and its equally phenomenal expulsive abilities have a blanket effect. They help the tissues surrounding the uterus to stretch, but they can stretch all other connective tissue too. The numerous joints of the feet have more mobility, as do the knees, hips, and vertebrae. A lot of vigorous bouncing might overstretch the ligaments of these joints, perhaps causing permanent joint instability. (Many new mothers notice a slight increase in the size of their feet after they have shed all their pregnancy weight. This, it seems to me, is due to the gentle but continuous stretch from the increased weight of pregnancy on the softened ligaments of the feet.) Run only if you have learned how and if you have the muscles to support the joints. In an exercise class, replace high- with low-impact aerobics, especially when working out on a concrete floor, and wear supportive and protective shoes.

The connective tissue inside the muscles becomes more elastic too. Curl-ups should be avoided once they visibly push the pregnant womb against the softened connective tissue that holds the left and right rectus abdominus together, causing too much separation in this muscle sheet. When you see your abdomen take on an A-frame-like shape as you lift your head (this usually begins to happen around the fifth month), replace curl-ups with exercises that work the abdominal muscles more gently, such as diaphragmatic breathing. Also, from now on, turn on your side and push yourself up rather than rising as in a sit-up. This seems better for the stretched muscle cells too. Some exercise physiologists suspect that working those too hard could cause microscopic tears.

When stretching, position the body carefully and do not stretch more than you can (it should not hurt), in order to avoid the risk of injury to ligaments. Do not stand on one leg unless you are able to do so without letting the body weight sag and pull on the hip ligaments of that leg.

Don't compete with others or with yourself. Even if you did all of a particular exercise with ease yesterday, if you feel exhausted two-thirds of the way through today, stop. Try again tomorrow. If an exercise hurts, check to see if you are doing it correctly. If you are, leave the exercise out for a few days and try again later, when the baby may have changed position slightly.

If the first trimester hits you with fatigue, wait until this changes without worrying that you will lose ground. Listening to your body is more important. If you have not exercised in years, allow your body to adjust to the pregnancy first, especially if you feel very tired. When you start, you can try to do all the exercises but work up only gradually to the suggested number of repetitions. Stop when you need to during the aerobics. It is better to let your body achieve fitness gradually. If you are fit and participating in a program you enjoy, there is no need to switch to a pregnancy class until some of the exercises of your regular class become uncomfortable or you want to be with other pregnant women.

Schedule your fitness program in such a way that it does not add stress to an already stressful life. If you work full-time, go to school at night, and entertain on the weekends, reevaluate your schedule and drop something before you add regular exercise to your must-do tasks. Who can shop, clean, or garden for you so that you can have a bit of time just for yourself? Pregnancy does take calories, and burning calories requires energy. It is all right to do less now. Doing absolutely nothing some of the time is quite nice too; it gives the mind and body a chance to regroup.

Eat well without fear of weight gain. You can try to maintain an active, fat-burning metabolism by engaging three to six times per week in an aerobic activity. Avoid nonnutritious snacks and eat foods low in fat, but don't become fanatical about a few extra pounds. Scales weigh water as well as fat, and anyway fat is not an enemy now.

On a hot day drink extra water; on a regular day take a few sips whenever you feel slightly thirsty. If more than two hours elapse between your last meal and your workout, have a complex-carbohydrate snack (a banana or some raisins, for example) before you start. Your baby cannot say, "Please, Mother, I am hungry," but it would like to if you exercise on an empty stomach. Also, your own metabolism will go through unnecessary upheaval if you ask muscles to work without giving them fuel. Your body will burn some of your fat deposits, but the by-products of that combustion, in the absence of carbohydrates, are potentially toxic for your baby.

Avoid working up a dripping sweat. Raising your internal heat might be harmful to the baby's nervous system, and sweating profusely can lead to dehydration, which causes uterine contractions. Moreover, your heart now has to pump a greater volume of

blood a longer way, and making it work extremely hard is not as good for it as making it work a little harder than normal.

Music probably does not sound the same to the little passenger in your womb as it does to you; sound is transmitted differently underwater. Don't let this scare you out of enjoying a workout to music with a good beat. Babies seem to like all kinds of music. But until the baby can say, "Turn it down, please," or signal by fussing that it would like less volume, protect it from prolonged exposure to loudly amplified music. We do not know what loud noise can do to the tiny sound-conducting bones in the middle ear. In adults repeated exposure to very loud music causes gradual hearing loss.

There is no need to give up a sport you enjoy if your body is used to it. If you continue to run, you might want to carry a water bottle and choose a route that offers a bathroom. During a weekend in the mountains you might walk rather than run, since it takes about a week for the body to increase its oxygen-carrying capacity and the baby probably counts on a steady stream. If you ski or water-ski, assess for yourself how good you are at these sports and how big the risk is that you might fall. If you love riding and you are good at it, there is no problem with continuing. Just don't take it up as a new sport. And be aware that sports such as scuba diving might interfere with the baby's ability to breathe. Changes in atmospheric pressure and oxygen saturation should be approached with caution and if possible avoided.

Yoga is great, especially with a good teacher. Women whose bodies were trained in this ancient discipline before they got pregnant often continue to do the inverted poses till the very last because it relieves so much pressure, particularly in the lower back. Those not so advanced in the postures may use the support of an orthopod or other device to place themselves upside down. If you feel tempted to try this, be aware that the inverted position can increase blood pressure, especially in untrained bodies. Check with your health-care provider to make sure it is safe for you, and do not stay upside down for too long at first.

JANE FONDA'S PREGNANCY WORKOUT

For approximately ten years now, our program has served dancers as well as women who hate to exercise, women who have just learned they are pregnant and women who are a few days past their due dates, health-food fanatics and women who have a hard time staying away from french fries and a chocolate milk shake, women of leisure and working women, and women of every variety between these extremes. Many of them have come back after their babies were born to show them off, share their birth stories, and get back in shape in the recovery exercise class. Here they often

continue to work out until the baby refuses to sit through the class because he or she has learned to crawl.

Thus, we have had the pleasure of meeting and getting to know thousands of mothers who exercised during their pregnancy, as well as their babies. The health, strength, and beauty of those babies has convinced me that exercise in pregnancy is good for the baby. I am in good company with this thought. The Spartans ascribed the strength of their young men to the strength of the women who bore them, and Plato thought that the motion of rocking strengthened an unborn child. When the Egyptians noticed that their Hebrew servants had much shorter labors than they, they concluded that it was because the Hebrew women were physically active. While we have not noticed an increase in short labors among our students, we do often hear them say that their birth attendants were astounded by their endurance and strength, as well as by their ability to bear down well with the expulsion contractions in positions such as squatting or kneeling. And we have helped numerous women look and feel better during both pregnancy and recovery, which no doubt contributed to the health of their babies.

For your exercise program to be as safe as those at our studio, make sure that your doctor or midwife is aware that you are working out, knows what kind of exercises you do and how often, and will be available to you should any questions come up (for example, if you experience twinges of pain, you will need to know whether they are contractions or are just pressure the baby is placing on a nerve). Always stop any physical activity if you notice more than five contractions per hour or feel cramping or low pelvic pressure reminiscent of a menstrual period, and report these symptoms to your health-care provider. These can be signs of preterm labor (the professional term for contractions that dilate the cervix before thirty-seven weeks of gestation), and your practitioner must examine you. If there are any changes in your cervix, you may need to stay off your feet.

Our exercise classes last one hour and fifteen minutes. The program outlined here is taken from these classes. At home you can do the whole class in one session or fit the different parts— aerobics, muscle strengthening, stretching, and relaxation—into your schedule however best suits you. To maintain or obtain a good level of fitness, do aerobics at least three times a week and muscle-strengthening work at least twice a week; stretch after either activity. At first do the relaxation only when you feel like it, but closer to your due date, practice it on a regular basis, as part of your preparation for labor.

To get started, read the information on each section and look at the pictures of the exercises, but avoid the detailed instructions. Then, pick the section you want to start with, read about one exercise at a time, and practice in front of a mirror, comparing yourself with the pictures.

About Warming Up, Aerobics, and Cooling Down

Warm muscles get more oxygen; more blood flows through them, and the blood releases oxygen more readily at higher temperatures. They also metabolize waste products better and can respond more quickly and effectively to specific demands. As the muscles warm up, the increased circulation makes the fluid inside the joints less viscous, and their ability to move improves. Therefore, warm up gradually before you embark on strenuous work. It will improve your performance and reduce the risk of injury.

According to the American College of Obstetricians and Gynecologists, pregnant women should keep their heart rate below 140 beats per minute and limit the aerobic part of their exercise regimen to fifteen minutes. For fit women who love the exhilarating feeling of exercising the circulatory system, these rather conserva-

tive restrictions are depressing. Exercise physiologists say that more than fifteen minutes of aerobic activity leads to quantum improvements in the cardiovascular system. From the runners' world comes constant evidence that women who continue to run at a level adjusted to their individual ability, rather than to general guidelines, give birth to healthy babies around their due dates and recover quickly. World-class athletes often improve on their own records shortly after a pregnancy, and some claim that the physiology of pregnancy and the training they did while pregnant improved their performance ability.

An obstetrician in Tokyo, Dr. Yasuhiro Tanaka, M.D., who teaches aerobic fitness in a studio equipped for telemetric heart-rate monitoring, divides his pregnant patients into three categories: beginners, advanced, and superadvanced. The beginners may work for half an hour, during which their heart rate may go up to 150 beats per minute for short periods of time; the advanced work for forty-five minutes with a maximum heart rate of 165, and the super-advanced can go up to 170 beats per minute for short periods and sustain a heart rate of around 135 beats per minute for approximately fifty minutes. When Dr. Tanaka visited us in Los Angeles, I was struck by his vigor (I had never met an obstetrician who looked like an aerobics instructor) and by the pride with which he spoke of the radiant health of his patients, their fast recovery, and the health of their babies.

Ten years of watching women find a class appropriate for their fitness level at the Jane Fonda Workout Studio has taught me that

fit women have a built-in sense of what they can do during pregnancy. Some continue the advanced aerobics until their due date. For them, I have stopped worrying about the risk of overheating while exercising vigorously in pregnancy. A trained body is more able to cool itself, because of better circulation of the blood to the skin and a greater ability to perspire. Moreover, fit women have a sense of when to stop. I see them slow down and then join in again, and they stop to drink water or go to the bathroom throughout the class. So if you are healthy and fit and your pregnancy is firmly established, don't be scared out of an aerobic workout that takes a bit longer than fifteen minutes (we do twenty minutes of low-impact aerobics in our pregnancy exercise class). Nature loves a bit of stress; it is how she renews, replenishes, and restores. I am sure this is true in pregnancy because for a healthy woman pregnancy is not an illness but a state of super health.

A woman who is unaccustomed to exercise may need a bit more help, not only to choose an appropriate training level but to stay with it for the first couple of weeks, the time it takes for the heart and circulatory muscles to get stronger. Working too hard during this time is not only unhealthy, it is defeating. The muscles that help us move get their energy from two fuels, fats and carbohydrates. Their combustion requires oxygen. When forced to work in the absence of enough oxygen, our skeletal muscles can burn carbohydrates anaerobically, but this process, while much more efficient than that by which an automobile's engine achieves combustion, is quite inefficient compared with the aerobic one, in which fat and carbohydrates are burned together. Anaerobic energy produces more wastes, and one of these, lactic acid, accumulates in the muscles, making them immediately sore. Moreover, the stored carbohydrates are used up quite rapidly, especially in nonfit people, and all-out fatigue—what athletes call "hitting the wall"—results. Carbohydrates are our cells' kindling wood; they get us started until the heart has a chance to send enough oxygen to the working muscle. Then, the stored fat molecules—the logs that keep the fire going—join in. They can burn only when there is enough oxygen. Extra breathing does not get the oxygen to the muscles; it requires a good pump (the heart) with powerful hoses (the arteries, veins, and capillaries). The only way to make the pump and hoses strong is by systematic stimulation. If you don't exercise hard enough, you do not stimulate the system. If you exercise too hard for your fitness level, you make the muscles work anaerobically. In an effort to give the muscles oxygen, you gasp for air and hyperventilate, and you are forced to give up after a few minutes. A few minutes is not enough to improve the heart. And when you give up because you feel bad, you'll end up telling yourself that exercising is not good for you.

To find the level that is safe and appropriate for you, learn to count your heartbeats, either at one of the carotid arteries (just below the chin at either side of the neck) or at your wrist (two fingers above where the thumb emerges). If you can't find your pulse, ask your instructor or health-care provider to show you how.

When you feel a beat, you feel the wave of the heart's contraction as it spreads through the arteries. In the pause between beats, the heart muscle itself gets nourished. The maximum heart rate is estimated at 220 beats per minute; past that rate there is not enough time in between beats for the heart muscle to be replenished. The maximum heart rate decreases with age, and one's individual maximum heart rate can be estimated by deducting one's age from 220. Most hearts can be trained safely and well at between 65 and 85 percent of this level. Therefore, if you are thirty-five, your training-sensitive zone is between (220 − 35) × 0.65 = 120 and (220 − 35) × 0.85 = 157.

For a beginner it is better to work at the low side of the training zone. In an unfit person the ability of the muscle cells to handle oxygen is not very good, and the cells cannot burn fat efficiently, because the level of fat-burning enzymes is low. An added benefit of not working too hard at first is that one can work for a longer period, and fat-burning ability improves with duration of stimulation. At age thirty-five you should look for an activity that will bring your heart rate up to 130 beats per minute (monitor your pulse for ten seconds and multiply by six rather than counting for a full minute). Exercise for five to seven minutes the first time and a little longer every time thereafter. All through your aerobic workout take the breath test—make yourself say a sentence of at least five words. If you cannot do this, you are working too hard and have switched to anaerobic fuel-burning.

Don't push yourself when you are overtired, but don't trust all your excuses either. It takes a bit of discipline to stay with it until the oxygen-delivery system improves. Once this happens, every system in the body begins to work better, and the brain gets the message that it feels good to work hard on a regular basis. Continuing on from there is much easier than getting started.

If the activity you choose is walking, you do not have to do a specific warm-up. Simply start out by walking slowly for at least five minutes and then gradually increase your tempo and the swinging of your arms and legs. The same holds for bicycling or rowing. A warm-up similar to the main activity is as effective as any other, if not more so. The important thing is to give the muscles a chance to get warm through improved circulation before you make them work hard.

Equally important as a good warm-up or the exact number of heartbeats per minute is the cool-down. Movement and breathing help the veins return blood to the heart. If movement is stopped abruptly, the venous return is impaired, while the heart continues to pump hard. Pregnancy adds two new problems: The muscles along the blood vessels relax in response to pregnancy hormones, and the enlarged uterus puts pressure on the veins. Especially difficult to empty, because of its location, is the large vein on the right of the vertebral column, the vena cava, which carries all blood back to the heart. Reclining or lying down on the back places the uterus on top of this important stream and impairs its flow. Therefore, always cool down in a position where the uterus rolls away from the vena cava. The veins in the legs also have a harder time getting the blood back out because the uterus tends to obstruct the veins in the groin. They do better when you move your legs, and they have a very hard time when you lock your knees at a standstill. The leg muscles should be stretched after any weight-bearing activity, especially if the work did not challenge their full range of motion. Therefore, first slow down gradually to give your blood the maximum chance to return to the heart, and then stretch, still keeping in mind the importance of venous return.

WARM-UP

Starting Position

Stand with your feet slightly more than shoulder distance apart, knees slightly bent and directly over the toes, tailbone dropped, chest lifted, shoulders relaxed, crown of the head reaching for the ceiling.

1. Torso Stretch

1. Inhale and lift your arms up from the sides. Reach overhead.
2. Exhale, drop the shoulders, bring the arms down. Repeat 4 times, breathing a little deeper each time.

2. Neck Stretches

1. Drop your head with the right ear toward the right shoulder and place your left arm behind your back, the back of the hand touching the spine between the shoulder blades, to keep the left shoulder down. Keep your chin tucked in, knees slightly bent. Breathe; try to hold this position for 15 seconds.
2. Lift the head up and reverse sides.

3. Upper-Body Stretches

1. Lace your fingers behind you and stretch your arms away from the torso, keeping the knees soft and the pelvis tucked under. Breathe, holding the stretch for 15 seconds. Release.

2. Bring your arms in front of your shoulders, cross them at the wrist, palms together, and lace the fingers. Stretch while you gently round the upper back. Hold this stretch, letting it ease the tightness between the shoulder blades. Release.

4. Shoulder Rolls with Knee Bends

1. Lift your left shoulder and bend your left knee. Drop the shoulder and straighten the leg as you . . .

2. Lift your right shoulder and bend the right knee. Drop the shoulder and straighten the leg as you shift to other side.

3. Alternate sides, 8 times.

5. Side Stretches

Keep the legs moving the same way as in last exercise. Now reach up with the right arm and then lower it as you reach up with the left arm. Reach 8 times, one arm up, one arm down.

6. Spine Stretch

1. Bend both knees and clasp the hands overhead. Drop the tailbone, lift the pubic bone, lift the chest, drop the chin to the chest, drop the shoulders, and reach with the arms. Breathe; feel your spine lengthen. Hold for 15 seconds.
2. Bring the arms down.

7. **Pelvic Tucks**

1. Place your hands on your hips, keeping the spine long and the knees soft and over the toes. Tuck the pelvis under and lift the baby inward.
2. Release the tuck without arching the back, then tuck under again, 8 times.
3. Turn the feet out, making sure your knees are over your toes, and do 8 more pelvic tucks to warm up the inner thighs.

8. **Pliés**

1. Place both hands on the shoulders and plié down with the knees over the toes. (If your knees are not directly over your toes, turn your feet out less.)
2. Straighten the legs and reach up and to the right with the left arm, dropping the right arm; don't rotate your torso.
3. Plié again, both hands to the shoulders.
4. Straighten the legs, reach to the left with the right arm, dropping the left one; don't rotate. Repeat 8 times.

9. *Upper-Calf Stretch, Left*

1. Pivot your left and then your right foot 90 degrees to the right; let your upper body follow the turn.
2. Bend your right knee and place your hands on the thigh just above the knee. Keep the left leg straight, heel down, and keep the head and spine in alignment with the left leg by looking slightly downward.
3. Hold the stretch in the left upper calf for 20 seconds. Straighten the right leg.

10. *Lower-Calf Stretch, Left*

1. Hands on hips, step forward with the left leg to bring it closer to, but still behind, the right one.
2. Bend both knees and keep your hips directly above the left foot.
3. Hold this stretch in the left lower calf for 20 seconds.

11. Hamstring Stretch, Right

1. Straighten the right leg and keep the left knee bent.
2. Place the hands on the lower back and bend forward from the hips, then lift the toes of the right leg. Keep the head in alignment with the spine, looking downward even though it is tempting to lift the head, as the model on the right demonstrates.

3. Hold the stretch in the right hamstring for 15 seconds.

4. Drop the toes, bend the right knee, and raise the upper body.

12. Hip Stretch, Left

1. Shift your weight onto the right leg, take a small step back with your left leg, keeping that heel lifted, and bring your body midway between your legs.
2. Bend the left knee to deepen the bend in the right one, drop the tailbone, and push the left hip forward.
3. Hold the stretch for 20 seconds.

13. Shin Stretch, Left

1. Shift your weight onto the right foot and place the top of the left foot on the floor.
2. Hold the stretch in the left shin for 20 seconds. NOTE: Omit this stretch if it causes cramping of the calf muscle.

Reverse exercises 9, 10, 11, 12, and 13 to stretch the right upper and lower calf, left hamstring, right hip, and right shin.

14. Thigh Stretch

1. Stand tall with the feet together, knees soft, and tailbone tucked under.
2. Bring the right foot toward your buttocks, grasp it behind with your right hand, and let the knee point straight down to the floor while you keep the hips forward. (Do not let the knee go out to the side). Keep the left knee slightly bent.
3. Stretch the front of the right thigh for 15 seconds.
4. Release the right foot and repeat the stretch with the left leg.

AEROBICS

Wear well-cushioned shoes and avoid thick carpet. Trust your ability to come up with fun steps to a record you like. Movements in which you use both arms and legs (especially if you lift the knees high and swing the arms overhead) will bring your heart rate up fast, and if you sing along it will go up even more. Don't start out with something that vigorous; warm up to it with some simple side steps or by marching in place. Pretend you are part of a band or are at a great party, and people are looking at you because you are such fun to watch. Don't get carried away and change directions too fast. Avoid twisting movements, and remember to take the breath test by talking or singing along regularly. And have a good time. Your baby will probably love it.

COOL-DOWN

1. Slow down gradually

until you are stepping in place, then stop with your feet slightly turned out and a little more than hip distance apart. Drop the tailbone, lift the chest, and clasp your hands together above your head; think of making your spine longer and of holding your baby in a muscular sling in front of your hips.

2. Side Stretches

1. Bend your arms, take your elbows in your hands, reach up, and inhale.
2. Let your torso stretch out of your hips and to the right as you exhale.
3. Breathe deeply and try to hold this stretch for 15 seconds. Then come back to the center, lengthen the spine, and stretch the left side the same way.

3. Back Stretch

1. Place your hands on your thighs just above your bent knees.
2. Inhale and round the back upward.
3. Exhale and flatten and lengthen the spine. Repeat steps 2 and 3 for a total of 8 times. When you inhale, think of rounding gently outward, especially the vertebrae at and below the waist. When you exhale, lengthen the spine from the base of the skull to the tailbone.

4. Leg Stretches.

Repeat exercises 9, 10, 11, 12, 13, and 14 from the warm-up.

NOTE: Warm muscles can stretch a little deeper, and the stretches can be held longer. You might want to keep more distance between your feet. If you have a problem with balance, hold on to a strong and stable doorknob or a sturdy chair. Inhale and think of all the muscle fibers lengthening; exhale, let go of tension, and picture the muscles lengthening just a little more. Keep breathing with this image of helping your muscles stretch. The stretching should not be painful. If it is, lessen the stretch by bringing the feet closer together.

STRENGTHENING AND STRETCHING THE MUSCLES

Balanced strength enhances posture and the grace with which we move. Skeletal muscles have two kinds of strength: One is capable of great force at a moment's notice and fades rapidly; the other lasts for hours. The strength we need for our daily tasks is the latter, the endurance kind. Training muscles for that kind of strength does not involve a lot of time or suffering, and the benefits appear rather quickly.

Muscles become stronger when the movement they are designed to make is resisted. If you make the resistance so strong that it wears the muscle out within six to eight repetitions, you train it for power; if you make it such that you can continue without exhaustion for fifteen to twenty repetitions, you train it for endurance. For quick improvement in muscle tone, work each major muscle with three sets of fifteen repetitions, taking a thirty- to sixty-second rest between each set. For slow but steady progress, start with two sets of eight to twelve repetitions of each exercise, and gradually increase the number of repetitions.

The initial gain in strength is believed to be primarily due to the recruitment of more messengers from brain to muscle, enabling more muscle fibers to work; overcoming psychological inhibitions also probably contributes. Next, the connective tissue gets stronger, and then the muscle fibers begin to change. They learn to handle oxygen more efficiently, which helps them burn fat; they store more glycogen, the muscles' kindling wood; and, in endurance training, the fibers within the muscles learn to take turns working so that they don't become exhausted and give out.

If you are not used to exercising, start by doing movements against the resistance of gravity—do not use any additional weight. Once you can do a particular exercise correctly and with ease for two sets of twelve repetitions, add some resistance: small weights that fit around the wrist or ankle, hand-held weights, or rubber bands. If you do not want to buy weights, fill two small bags with sand and hold those in your hands. For the leg exercises weights are less important, because the daily increase in the baby's weight will challenge the muscles in the legs.

On days when you find yourself wondering, Why am I doing this?, picture yourself with a baby who needs to be held. Strong wrists and hands will be very helpful. The chores that used to keep these muscles strong (washing and wringing clothes by hand, weeding a garden, stirring a big pot of food) are no longer with us, and the resulting weaknesses can give new mothers tendinitis. An orthopedist friend tells me that he can spot new parents among his patients by a particular pain in the wrists or shoulders. Then picture yourself with an eight-month-old little person who loves to go everywhere with you in a pack on your back. The closeness of his/her face near yours as you talk about the things around you can be delightful, but only if you have a strong upper body.

Yet another incentive for upper body strength

Warm up by stepping in place, riding a stationary bike for five minutes, or doing the warm-up exercises on pages 79–86. If you have just completed your aerobic workout, cool down to let your heart gradually return to normal, then move on without warming up again.

Do all standing exercises with slightly bent knees. This protects the lower back, and if you stand with locked knees, the ligaments do all the work of holding you up. When you soften the knees, the muscles are called into action. Always follow a series of strengthening exercises with a series of stretches for the same muscles.

Strength is only half of what makes a muscle function well; the other half is flexibility. When you bend your elbow, the muscle in the front of the upper arm, the biceps, shortens, while the muscle in the back of the arm, the triceps, lengthens. If the triceps is tight, bending the elbow all the way is more difficult, and eventually the

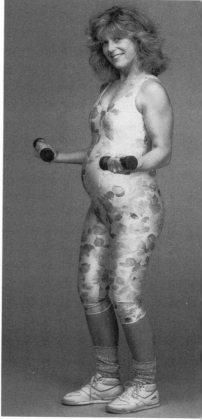

ligaments of the joints shorten and stiffen, causing the arm to lose some of its phenomenal range of motion. Such loss is more common and more troublesome in the hips and the shoulders, where the muscles are more complex. Lack of balance between strength and flexibility in the muscles that govern these two major joints is a common cause of aches and pains and injuries. Don't regard stretching as an afterthought or as something you can do quickly. Stretching takes time and thought, and it is essential to muscular fitness.

STRENGTHENING THE UPPER BODY

Starting Position (for the next four exercises)

Stand with the feet hip distance apart, knees slightly bent, tailbone tucked under, pubic bone and chest lifted, the baby held nicely in front of the hips by the complex sling of abdominal muscles, arms down at your sides. If you are using a rubber band, place it in a loop under one foot and hold the ends in each fist with the palms facing the outer thighs. If you are using weights, hold them in your hands, palms facing inward.

1. Upright Row

1. Bring your arms in front of you, turn your palms, fisted, toward the front of the thighs, thumbs close together, and inhale.
2. Exhale, bend your arms at the elbows, and bring the hands under the chin, elbows higher than the wrists.
3. Inhale and return the arms to where they started, fully extended. Control the return movement, especially if you are using weights or a rubber band. Repeat 8 to 12 times.

2. Front Raises

1. Inhale with your arms at your sides, palms facing inward.
2. Exhale and lift the arms straight out in front of you to shoulder height. Keep the elbows slightly bent.
3. Inhale and, with a controlled movement, return to the starting position. Repeat 8 to 12 times.

3. Biceps Curl

1. Inhale and place your arms, fully extended, in front of you with the back of the hands touching the front of the thighs.
2. Exhale, bend at the elbow, and bring the lower arm as close to the upper arm as you can. Keep the wrists neutral; don't flex them.
3. Inhale and control the return movement. Repeat 8 to 12 times.

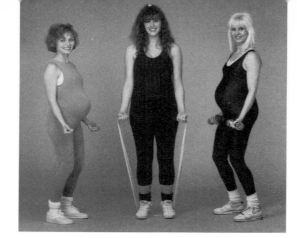

4. Lateral Raises

1. Inhale and place your arms at your sides, palms facing inward.
2. Exhale and lift your arms outward and up until they are on a line with the shoulders.
3. Inhale and control the return movement. Repeat 8 to 12 times.

Give yourself a moment of rest. Move your legs, do some shoulder shrugs, and release your grip on the rubber band if you are using one. Then replace it under your feet and repeat the series once or twice.

If you are using a band, look for something sturdy to wrap it around for the next series, such as a towel rack or a doorknob. At the Workout we use the barre. Face away from where you fastened the band, holding the ends of the band in your hands.

5a. Chest Press with rubber band

1. Stand with knees slightly bent, arms level with shoulders, elbows bent so that the hands point forward, palms facing down. Inhale.
2. Exhale and straighten your arms in front of you.
3. Inhale and, with a controlled movement, return your arms to the bent position. Repeat 8 to 12 times.

5b. Chest Press with or without weights (Wall Push-Ups)

1. Stand a good step away from a wall, feet hip distance apart, palms against the wall at shoulder height and width, elbows bent. Inhale.
2. Exhale and straighten your elbows, pushing your torso away from the wall.
3. Inhale. Go back toward the wall by bending your elbows. Do not let your buttocks stick out; stay in a straight line from the crown of the head to the heels.
4. Exhale and push yourself away from the wall. Repeat 8 to 12 times.

6a. Reverse Press with or without weights

1. Kneel with one knee on the floor and the other leg bent in front of you. Drop your arms along the bent leg, back of hands toward the floor. Inhale.
2. Exhale and bring your arms out to the side. Inhale and return them toward the floor. You should feel this between your shoulder blades. Repeat 8 to 12 times.

6b. Reverse Press with rubber band

1. Turn and face the object on which your band is fastened. Extend your arms in front of you, and raise to shoulder height. Inhale.
2. Exhale and bring your elbows out to the side while keeping them at shoulder height. Inhale and control the return movement. Repeat 8 to 12 times.

7a. Long Row with rubber band

1. Extend your arms in front of you, palms facing each other, and inhale.
2. Exhale, bend your arms while keeping your elbows close to your body, and bring your fists next to your torso.
3. Inhale and control the return movement. Repeat 8 to 12 times.

7b. Long Row with or without weights

1. Stay on one knee as in the Reverse Press. Rest one arm on your knee and drop the other hand to the floor.
2. Exhale, bend your elbow while keeping it close to your body, and bring your hand toward your torso.
3. Inhale and drop your arm toward the floor. Repeat 8 to 12 times. Repeat with the other arm.

8a. Triceps with or without weights

1. Standing with the feet hip distance apart, the knees slightly bent, and the torso leaning forward, inhale and bend the elbows to bring your fists, thumbs up, close to your shoulders, as woman on the left is doing.
2. Exhale and bring the torso slightly further forward while you straighten your arms all the way, until the hands are slightly behind the hips.
3. Inhale and control the return to starting position. Repeat 8 to 12 times.

8b. Triceps with rubber bands

1. Still standing with the feet hip distance apart and the knees slightly bent, inhale and bend the elbows to bring the hands close to the shoulders.
2. Exhale and straighten the arms down and back until the hands are slightly behind the hips. Keep your elbows close to your body.
3. Inhale and control the return movement. Repeat 8 to 12 times.

Rest a few moments, then repeat all the upper-body exercises.

UPPER-BODY STRETCHES

1. Triceps

1. Inhale, bring your arms overhead, and reach.
2. Exhale and bend the right arm at the elbow, keeping the lower arm behind your head.
3. Take the right elbow in the left hand and gently press backward, stretching the muscle in the back of the arm. Hold for 20 seconds.

2. Deltoid

1. Place the left arm across the chest.
2. Place the right hand on top of the left upper arm.
3. Gently stretch the left upper arm and the top of the shoulder for 20 seconds by pressing them toward the right.

Repeat exercises 1 and 2 for the other side.

3. Middle- and Lower-Trapezius and Rhomboid Stretch

1. Inhale, bring the arms overhead, clasp the hands, and reach for the ceiling.

2. Exhale, keeping the body tall and the chest lifted. Drop the shoulders, bend the elbows, place the fingertips on the shoulders, and bring the elbows, level with the shoulders and parallel to the floor, together in front of the chest. Hold for 20 seconds.

3. Keeping your fingertips on shoulders, drop your elbows to your sides, press the shoulders down, stand tall, breathe, and hold for 20 seconds.

4. *Pectoralis Stretch (familiar from the aerobics warm-up)*

1. Inhale, clasp your hands together behind you, lift your chest, and drop the tailbone.
2. Keeping your arms straight, move the clasped hands away from your torso. Hold for 20 seconds.

STRENGTHENING THE LOWER BODY

For this series you will need something sturdy to hold on to, such as the back of a chair or a tabletop, and something to kneel on, such as a mat or a folded blanket and some pillows.

The legs get a lot of extra work because they carry the daily increase in the baby's weight. The following three leg exercises make full use of this weight.

1. Lunges (buttocks and thighs)

1. Stand beside a sturdy chair or tabletop, the inside hand holding on to this support for balance, and place one foot in front of the other. (The distance between your feet should be determined by how strong and flexible you are; keep it small if you are just beginning.)

2. Inhale and bend the front knee over the toes to bring your torso forward and down, letting the back heel lift off the floor. Do not bend the front leg more than 90 degrees at the knee.

3. Exhale and push your torso back and up to the starting position. Repeat 8 to 12 times, then turn around to work the other leg.

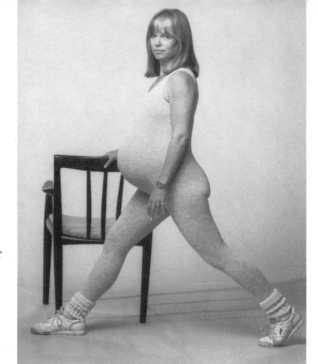

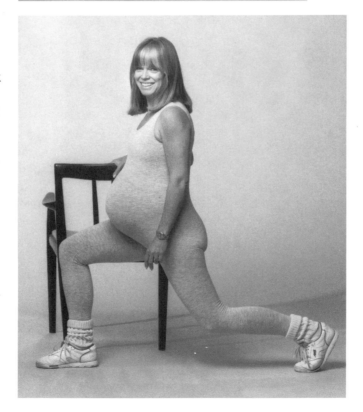

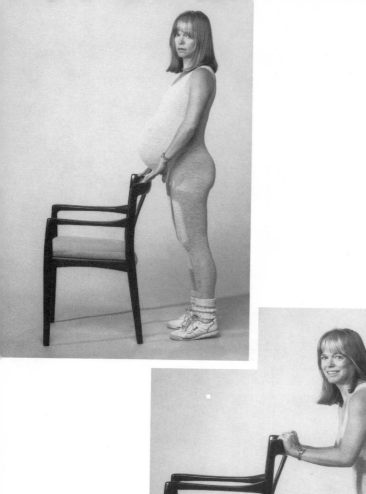

2. Squats (buttocks and thighs)

1. Place both hands on the back of the chair or tabletop, and with feet parallel, or turned out slightly if you need more balance, place feet a bit more than hip distance apart.
2. Inhale and bend the knees over the toes. Let your buttocks move back so they stick out a bit. Do not bend the knees beyond a 90-degree angle.
3. Exhale and push yourself back up to the starting position. Repeat 8 to 12 times.

NOTE: This exercise, if done regularly and with attention to balance, is good for learning to squat to lift heavy objects. It is okay to descend into a full squat at the end of this series to rest a moment, but coming down all the way again and again is too hard on the knees.

3. Calf Raises

1. With both hands still on the back of the chair or table, feet parallel or slightly turned out and about hip distance apart, exhale and come up on the toes. Don't arch the back.
2. Inhale and lower the heels. Repeat 8 to 12 times.
3. Stay up on your toes, raise your hands overhead, drop your shoulders, hold, and breathe. Lower your arms, lower your heels, and shake out your legs.

Repeat 1, 2, and 3 if you feel up to it and like the extra work.

LEG STRETCHES

These stretches will be familiar from the aerobics warm-up and cool-down. Continue to use your support; it will help you hold the stretch longer.

1. Calf Stretch, Left

1. Lift the baby inward with your abdominal muscles, take a good step back with the left leg, and bend the right knee over the toes. Hold this stretch in the left calf for 20 seconds.

2. Bring the left leg in, about twelve inches from the right heel, keep the left heel down, and bend both knees. Hold this stretch in the lower calf for 20 seconds.

2. Hamstring Stretch, Right

Bend your torso toward the chair. Keep the left knee bent, straighten the right knee, lift the right toes, look down to the floor and align your head with your spine, straighten your arms, hold, and pull on your support. (If your partner is nearby, ask him to weigh the chair down for you so that you can get a better stretch.) Think of lengthening the spine and the muscles upward from the back of the right knee. Hold for 20 seconds. Lower the right toes, bend the right knee, tuck the buttocks under, and round up through the back to a standing position.

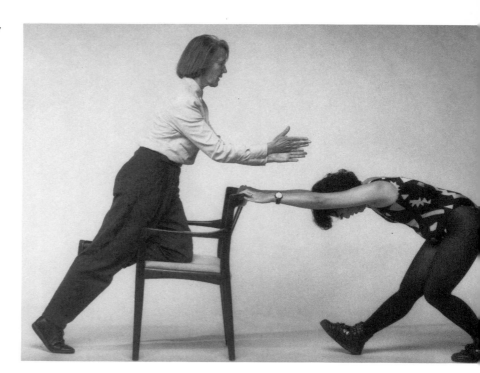

3. Hip Flexor Stretch, Left

Place the left leg a small step behind you, resting on the ball of the foot. Bend the knees, keep the chest lifted, tuck the buttocks under, and press forward gently with the left buttock to stretch the left hip flexor. Hold for 20 seconds.

4. Quadriceps, Left

Reach behind you to take your left foot or ankle in your left hand. Slightly bend the right knee. Stand tall, baby lifted inward, tailbone dropped, and stretch the top of the left thigh for 20 seconds. Keep the knee pointed to the floor, not turned to either side. If you do not feel the stretch, you can bring the knee slightly farther back. See if you can keep your balance when you let go of the chair and raise your arm up over your head.

Reverse and repeat all leg stretches for the other side.

1. Abdominals

1. Stand with the feet hip distance apart, knees slightly bent, tailbone dropped, baby lifted inward, chest lifted, crown of the head reaching up. Exhale and reach with the torso to the right.
2. Inhale and come back up to center.
3. Exhale and reach with the torso to the left.
4. Inhale and return to center.

You may hold weights in your hands if you like. Repeat 8 to 12 sets.

2. Abdominals (continued)

1. With the feet hip distance apart, bend your knees and place your hands above them on your thighs. Inhale.
2. Exhale and lift the baby inward. NOTE: The lower back and the pelvis do not move; the work is done strictly by your abdominal muscles. The movement is small, but it strengthens the

muscles that go across your belly.

3. Inhale and let the abdomen move out.

4. Exhale and lift the baby inward again. Repeat 8 to 12 times. Rest and try to do another series.

3. Abdominals (continued)

1. Get down on your hands and knees, the knees directly under the hips, the hands directly under the shoulders. Keep the back flat rather than letting it be pulled downward into a swayback position. Inhale.

2. Exhale, tuck the buttocks under, and round the back up.

3. Inhale and lengthen the spine from the base of the skull to the tailbone.

4. Exhale and tuck the buttocks under. Lift the baby inward and round the back. Repeat 10 more times.

While you are in this position, if you have time and feel up to it, you can do some extra leg work as follows (make sure you are on a folded blanket or a mat):

1. Buttocks Toner

1. Bend your elbows and let your arms and hands support you (you can use a thin pillow if you like). Shift the remainder of your weight to your left knee and lower leg.

2. Exhale and lift the right leg with a bent knee until the thigh makes a straight line with your torso, and no further.

3. Inhale and control the return movement. Repeat 8 to 12 times.

4. Straighten the right leg, toes touching the floor. Inhale.

5. Exhale and lift this leg until it forms a straight line with your torso, but no higher.

6. Inhale and control the return movement. Repeat 8 to 12 times.

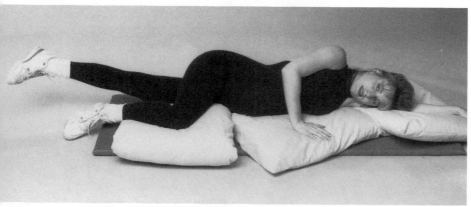

7. Turn on your left side. Toward the end of your pregnancy, support your belly and upper body with pillows. Bend your bottom leg in front of you so that your thigh is at a right angle, to let that leg support some of your weight. Inhale.

8. Exhale and lift the top leg up; don't rotate at the hip. Keep the top hip pointed toward the ceiling.

9. Inhale and control the return movement. Repeat 8 to 12 times.

10. Straighten the bottom leg, bend the top leg, and rest it on a pillow. Keep the top hip right above the lower hip and don't let the pelvis tilt backward or roll forward. Inhale.

11. Exhale and lift the bottom leg with your inner thigh muscles.

12. Inhale and control the return movement. Repeat 8 to 12 times.

Return to your hands and knees and reverse and repeat Buttocks Toner to work your other leg. Then get back on all fours for the final stretches.

COOL-DOWN STRETCHES

1. Buttocks Stretch and Pelvic Floor Toner

Begin on all fours, with your weight evenly distributed and your back flat. Open your knees wider to make room for the baby, sit back on your heels, place your arms in front of you, and rest your chin on your hands. (Use pillows under your arms if your upper body gets uncomfortable.) Rest for a moment in this position. If your partner is nearby, you might ask him to place his hands at the middle of your back, then move one hand up and the other down along your spine with slight pressure, until one hand presses on your lower back and the other holds the base of your skull. Ask him to press down gently on your lower back with the image of moving his hands away from each other. Breathe, let the pressure from the baby release, let your spine lengthen, then focus on the complex and important muscle sling between your legs. Lift those muscles gently and slowly inward—the movement you would make if you were trying to stop your bladder from emptying. Release, lift inward again, release. Work up to 15 repetitions.

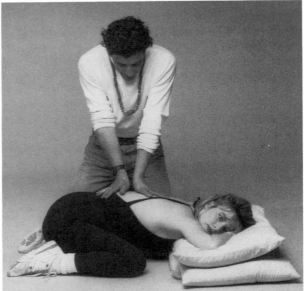

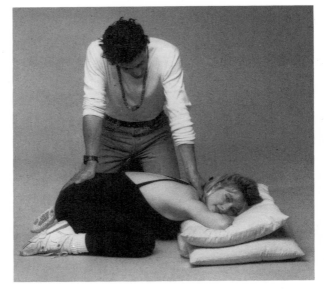

Push your upper body up, curl your toes under, and rock back into a squatting position.

2. Squatting Stretch

Squat with your feet flat on the floor if you can; otherwise stay up on your toes. Make sure your knees are directly over your toes—don't let your feet turn out too much, forcing your knees to drag inward. Turn your feet out less or, with your arms on the inside of your legs, gently press your thighs farther apart. Then ask your partner to grasp your hands and gently pull on them, while you think of reaching toward the floor with your tailbone and of letting your spine lengthen and your lower back release some of the pressure from carrying the baby. Then place your hands behind you on the floor and bring down your buttocks.

3. Abdominals

1. Keep your knees bent and your legs open from the hips. Sit squarely on the "seat bones" of the buttocks (if necessary, lift back the fleshy part of each buttock) and rock back and forth with your pelvis a few times. Place your hands on your lower legs for support. Inhale.
2. Exhale and round the spine outward by bringing your chin toward your chest and pulling away from your hands while you lift the baby inward.
3. Inhale, sit up straight, and lengthen the spine. Repeat 12 times.

4. Hip Stretch

Place the soles of your feet together, let your knees fall open, and reach with your forehead toward your toes. Breathe and stretch for 20 seconds. Round up through the spine to a sitting position.

This position, as well as lying on the side with the top leg lifted, kneeling, and squatting, is often used during the expulsion stage of labor. Doing this series regularly can make it easier for you to move from one of these positions into another.

5. Low Back and Hamstring Stretch

1. Open both legs as far as is comfortable. Lift back the fleshy part of each buttock, bring your hands in front of you, and sit up tall on the seat bones. Inhale.

2. Exhale and walk your hands forward to lower your torso. Keep your spine straight. Think of releasing the muscles in the hips.

Do not come down farther than your hips allow.

6. Side Stretches

1. Keep the right leg extended and bend the left leg in front of you, bringing it in closer. Lift back the fleshy part of each buttock and sit up tall on the seat bones. Inhale, bring your arms up, and reach.

2. Exhale and stretch your arms and torso to the right. Place your right arm inside your right leg for support, bring the left arm alongside the left ear, and elongate the torso at a diagonal to the right. If you are used to this stretch, you may come down over the right leg to grasp your right toes with your left hand. Don't roll forward— keep the left ear facing the ceiling. Breathe with this stretch. Inhale and let your body expand; exhale and let tension flow out. Hold for 20 seconds.

3. Come up with your torso facing front, and change legs to stretch the other side.

7. Buttocks Stretches

1. Fold your legs in front of you with the right leg farthest away from your torso. Place your hands on the floor in front of your legs. Gently walk your hands out until you feel a stretch in the right buttock. Breathe and stretch for 20 seconds.
2. Reverse legs and stretch the left buttock the same way.

RELAXATION

In the ancient discipline of hatha-yoga, the relaxation at the end of an exercise session is as important as the workout itself. To understand why, interlock the fingers of both hands in hook-and-eye fashion in front of you. Now pull, as if to pull your hands apart, and slowly let your fingers straighten and unlock. Inside each muscle there are millions of locks like this. When you strengthen muscles, you create more and stronger locks; when you stretch muscles, you increase the ability of these locks to release. Thus, stretching improves relaxation. Aerobic work and strengthening exercises improve stretching, because they make the muscles warm and activate messengers from muscle to brain. So when you want to relax, warm the muscles and stretch them before relaxing, and your relaxation will be deeper and more rejuvenating.

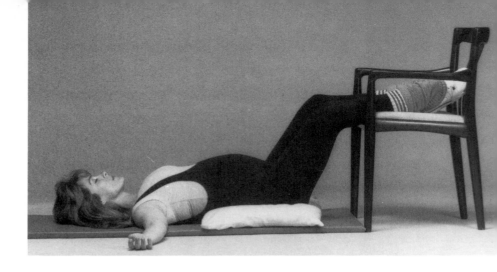

Lie on your back with your legs bent at the knees, the lower legs propped up on a couch or a chair to relax the pelvic region, and your arms extended out from your shoulders to relax the upper chest and facilitate breathing. If you are past the seventh month, place a folded sheet under your right hip to help the uterus fall away from the vena cava. Let your body get very heavy on the floor, and let your legs lean on the couch or chair. Let the stale air gush out, then let your body expand as you inhale deeply. When you feel full, allow for a slight pause, then let the air flow out. When you feel empty, allow for a slightly longer pause, then take air in again. When the air goes in, imagine a feeling of expansion, of opening up. When the air goes out, imagine breathing out your tension and fear; let go of everything you do not need to hold on to. Each breath finds you a little more relaxed.

As you relax, your breathing will slow down and become more superficial—your body will need less oxygen and produce less carbon dioxide. Let your body move with each breath. Notice how it takes in and gives back in an even flow, how holding on is self-defeating. Relax your mind, and picture for a moment one cool hand pressing inward and upward on the bony ridge behind your eyebrows, another on the ridge at the base of the skull. Maybe your partner can do this for you. Notice how this relaxes the muscles over your skull. Now visualize your brain expanding slightly when you inhale. When you exhale, let go of stale air, and thoughts you don't need, and anger and resentment. Thinking is not just tossing old thoughts around; it is also emptying and opening the mind so that new thought can be born. Close your eyes and cast them downward. Relax your temples; relax your tongue in the floor of your mouth; relax your lips and your jaws; relax down your neck

to your shoulders, down your spine to your pelvis. Turn your mind inward and picture the uterus, cradled by those big bones, rocking gently with your breath. Picture your baby inside, temporarily rooted into you with the placenta. Picture the intimate exchange between the two of you. If you notice no obstruction in your circulation—you can breathe easily and feel great—stay as you are. However, if you have any difficulty breathing or experience dizziness or slight nausea (signs of excessive pressure on the vena cava), or if you are more comfortable on your side, turn on your left side, supporting the belly, the top leg, and your head with pillows, and allow yourself a few minutes of deep relaxation. During the latter part of your pregnancy, picture yourself relaxing similarly between your labor contractions. Try at times to relax deeply while sitting up with your back supported or kneeling with your upper body resting on a couch or on your partner's lap.

Awaken your body by making circles with your hands from your wrists and with your feet from your ankles. Then stretch your arms overhead and stretch your legs long. Come to a sitting position and, when your circulation has adjusted, stand up.

HINTS ON POSTURE FOR WORK AND REST

By the time we reach adulthood our genetic endowment for posture, together with our cultural and social climate, have produced very particular habits of movement. Thus, general rules for posture need to be adjusted to each individual to make them usable, especially during pregnancy, when localized weight gain adds a new challenge.

In general, the human body prefers moving to being stationary. A sitting job or a job where one is forced to stand in one position for long periods of time is harder on its structure than one that involves movement. The effects of a sitting job are compounded when one sits for the ride home and sits again for relaxation and entertainment. If you have become a truly sedentary person, give some attention to how you sit. Try not to slump, which squashes your stomach, liver, and spleen and impairs your ability to breathe. Instead, lift your body up from the midriff. Also, try not to cross your legs all the time. It impairs your circulation at the knee and in the groin. Place your feet a bit apart instead, and open your legs from the hips to make space for the growing uterus. Consider periodically placing one and then the other leg on a footstool to relieve the lower back.

At work, get up and move your arms and legs or stretch regularly. Fidget and move in your chair instead of staying put in the same position. Check your chair. The seat tends to be easier on the lower back when it is inclined forward slightly and of a height that bends your knees at a 90-degree angle or slightly more; the cushioning should consist of about an inch and a half to two inches of foam padding, and the seat should be contoured so that the pressure of sitting is evenly distributed. The backrest should be adjustable to your spine's curvature. Use a footstool, supply your own foam padding, and/or get an adjustable lower-back support if you find your chair inadequate.

At home, sit on a pillow on the floor with your legs folded in front of you some of the time. If you can, push yourself up into a squat every once in a while to relieve the lower back from the tremendous pressure that sitting imposes on it. When you sit down again, try sitting for a few minutes with your legs straight in front of you; this posture is hard to maintain but it does strengthen the muscles with which we maintain proper sitting posture. Lie on your side or on your back with your legs folded up on a chair to watch TV or read. Change positions often and always have lots of pillows around. Don't be embarrassed to be always shifting, rocking, leaning forward, looking for comfort. When your back is tired, try sitting on a kitchen or dining-room chair with your arms on the back of the chair to support your upper body. And let someone massage the tension out of your lower back.

While driving, wear a seat belt over your hipbones and try to adjust the seat so that it is parallel to the floor and the backrest so that your upper body is supported. Play with the distance between your seat and the foot pedals; your knee should not be completely straight when you step on a pedal, because this tends to put strain on the lower back.

If your job is a standing one, try to stand some of the time with your knees soft rather than locked, to help the blood return out of your legs. Also try stepping in place and alternately placing each leg on a low footstool for a while to relieve the lower back. Wear supportive shoes as much as possible and, if your legs ache, see if wearing support stockings helps.

When lifting, carrying, or moving heavy objects, be aware that the levers of the human body are designed more for agility, speed, and precision of movement than for strength, and that, in spite of all equality, the male body is better designed for lifting heavy weights than that of the female. If you must move something heavy, pushing is better than pulling and far better than lifting and carrying. If something must be carried, hold it close to the body. To pick up something heavy from the floor, get down into a semi-squat, feet flat on the floor and hip distance apart; keep the spine straight or slightly rounded, never arched; and lift by straightening the legs rather than by pulling with the arms and back.

Even though the body likes to move, it does not like to do the exact same movement over and over. If you have a job that requires such machinelike repetition, try to take regular short breaks. The human body cannot work continuously without losing efficiency. Also, giving the body recovery time greatly decreases the risk of chronic pain and injury.

ACHES AND PAINS, WORRIES AND FEARS

Pregnancy is a bit like a new marriage: Friends and relatives expect the couple to be happy, and few if any acknowledge the hard work and problems inherent in creating something new. Yet pregnancy, especially with a first baby, is also an adventure. It is harder on modern women because they are no longer surrounded by other women who have experienced it numerous times and who can teach by their example.

Time-tested and normal as it may be, pregnancy is a process of growth and change. And when the baby is planned, the feeling of responsibility can be almost too much. The Ingalik Eskimo tribe believed that somewhere in the sky was a room where babies watched and waited until they saw the right parents, at which point they let themselves be conceived. Maybe in some way babies do choose their parents. Knowing a lot about human reproduction does not mean we know everything, and even if we did know everything, we still would not be able to control it all. Try to let go of the idea that you *made* your baby. You conceived it.

Don't expect a book to tell you whether or not you need a particular medical test and which one is best. The information in a book is of necessity quite general, and when something concerning your own or your baby's health comes up, you need specifics. In any case, discoveries are made all the time. Good health-care providers keep up with these advances.

Prenatal care is without a doubt one of the greatest medical innovations of this century. The idea of prenatal care originated around the turn of the century with a Mrs. Putnam of the Instructive Nursing Association in Boston. The infant-mortality rate was still high, probably between 100 and 150 per 1,000 births. (Precise figures are not known, because the law requiring registration of infant births and deaths was not passed until later.) When local physicians responding to her concern about high infant mortality insisted that this was nature's way, Mrs. Putnam approached J. Whitridge Williams, M.D., professor of obstetrics at Johns Hopkins University. In 1912, in his presidential address to the newly formed American Association for the Study and Prevention of Infant Mortality, Dr. Williams presented a landmark paper, "The Limits and Possibilities of Prenatal Care." Infant mortality among women who receive good prenatal care and take good care of themselves is now less than 10 per 1,000.

Prenatal care works best when the health professional provides information and support as well as health checks. Not all healthcare providers do. If your doctor does not answer questions very well, dismisses your concerns, or expects you to submit to tests and procedures without an explanation, ask if there is a nurse on the staff who can explain things to you. If not, make it clear to your doctor or midwife that he/she is your guide but not your dictator. If you have always been healthy and are not used to seeing a doctor regularly, learning to use prenatal care will be excellent preparation for interacting with your child's doctor later.

If your doctor proposes a test or procedure that goes against your beliefs, talk it over with him/her, and if you still feel unsure, consider a consultation with another pregnancy expert. Medical procedures are better tolerated and have better results when they are understood and accepted by the person who undergoes them. If important topics such as whether you should have amniocentesis, or whether chorionic-villi sampling is better, are up for discussion, bring along your partner and/or a trusted friend. Important decisions take time and thought, and once out of the doctor's office it is hard to remember all the information. Two people hear and remember more than one, and your decision-making process will be better that way.

Make sure there is a sound medical reason for any procedure, even for the now almost routine one of looking at your baby with ultrasound. Tests, including ultrasound, should be used only when the benefits outweigh the drawbacks. One of the benefits of ultrasound, especially for fathers, is the thrill of watching their baby in the womb; one of the drawbacks may be expense. Ultrasound is currently considered safe, yet informed sources, including the National Institutes of Health, caution against unnecessary use of or overreliance on this one tool.

The increasingly wide application of ultrasound, combined with the growing custom in medicine of telling a patient every concern, has many women unnecessarily worried. Ask questions when your doctor makes the kind of statement that will set you worrying

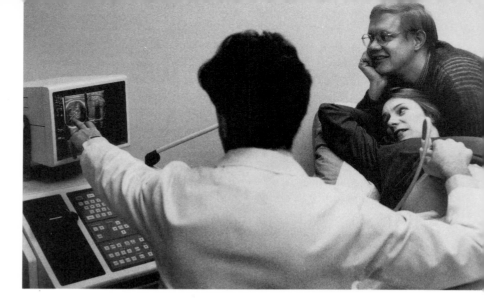

when you get home, and if the answers are not satisfying, ask for a consultation. Many women become anxious when the ultrasound reveals that their baby is small for its stage of development. If the consultant also concludes that your baby is small, it might be necessary for you to cut down on activities or to go on bed rest to help your baby catch up. While bed rest can be beneficial in cases of slow growth, when all is well it is better to remain active. Try not to judge the size of your baby by the size of your belly, and ignore comments like "My, your baby is large" or "Aren't you small for this far along?" Women carry babies very differently. Some hardly show at five months, while others are already uncomfortably large.

It is fun to learn to feel the pregnant belly for your baby's position. Fathers especially enjoy this because it makes watching the baby move more fun. Past the sixth month, you might ask your care provider to show you how. You will be amazed to discover how large the baby's head is in proportion to its body. Once you know the baby's position it might be relatively easy to hear the heartbeat. It is best heard closest to the baby's left upper back, so if the baby is head down and facing its mother's left hip, its heart will be heard in the lower right quadrant of the mother's belly. Try listening with the cardboard tube from an empty roll of toilet paper or some other instrument that will focus the sound waves and bring them to your ear.

Past the sixth month, if your care provider has not volunteered the information, ask him/her to teach you how to watch your

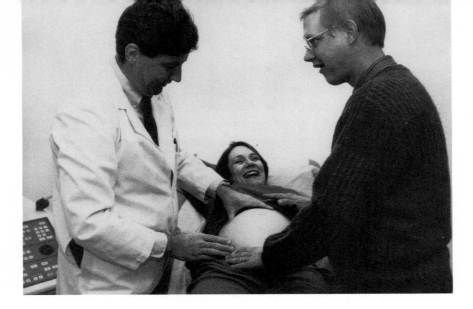

baby's movement patterns and to identify which changes might warrant medical attention. Also learn the signs and symptoms of preterm labor. Mothers who know what to be on the alert for can often recognize premature labor early enough so that any further opening of the cervix can be stopped with bed rest and medication.

Don't be overly concerned about gaining too much weight. Doctors don't care that much about a few extra pounds if you don't. Normally, you should gain between 16 and 35 percent of your pre-pregnancy weight. Thus, if you weighed 120 pounds before you conceived, allow yourself to gain between 19 and 42 pounds. If you were underweight for your height at 120 pounds, you may gain a little more, perhaps as much as 50 pounds. If you were overweight, your gain may fall at the lower end of the scale, but being overweight before conception does not cut down on the need of the baby to get sustenance from things you eat during its gestation.

Trust your body more than exact numbers. If you are gaining too much, make the portions smaller instead of cutting down on variety of foods. You are eating for two, but not for two adults. According to nutritionists, growing a healthy baby takes about 300 extra calories per day. Of those, about 30 grams, or 120 calories, can be proteins. The rest should be mainly complex carbohydrates and a little fat. The danger of measuring calories is that they might not have much to do with nutrients. A can of soda, a candy bar, and some french fries may surpass the required extra calories, but they don't provide the essential nutrients. To develop to its potential, a baby needs proper nutrients—especially micronutrients, such as zinc, copper, magnesium, and selenium—more than a specified number of calories. The safest and surest way to meet your baby's needs is by eating a variety of unrefined foods. Refining grains removes zinc, vitamin B6, magnesium, and vitamin E. These usually are not added when refined grains are fortified, and even if they are, the proportions might be off. Fortunately, better preservation and transportation of food brings a great variety of fresh fruits and vegetables and all kinds of grains and animal products to places where previously people had to rely on a few items for balanced nutrition. Yet now, when more good food is available, many people are turning to vitamin supplements. Oversupplementation can be toxic and may interfere with absorption of other nutrients. For example, too much folic acid, especially the kind that is in some prenatal vitamins, interferes with zinc absorption; too much zinc interferes with copper absorption; and calcium supplements containing bonemeal or oyster shell are high in lead. If you take a supplement at the recommendation of your care provider, ask if he/she checked that particular one out with a good nutritionist or biochemist, or do the checking yourself. The only

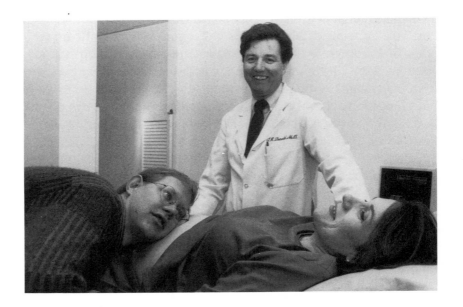

supplement that virtually all experts agree is healthful for almost every pregnant woman is iron. Also often suggested are supplements of calcium and vitamin C.

Don't get frantic about sudden weight gain. If you gain five pounds in one week, your doctor may seem concerned because sudden weight gain can be one of the first symptoms of the still unresolved complication of pregnancy called preeclampsia. In most cases, however, the extra pounds will be the result of temporary water retention. Go swimming, reduce other activities, and try to relax for a few days. Add watermelon, including some of the rind if it is an organically grown one, or some cantaloupe, figs, and prunes to your diet, and avoid very salty foods, and the problem will probably correct itself.

Be careful with drugs but don't be fanatical about not taking any. If you come down with strep throat, taking antibiotics is better than avoiding them. Trust your health-care provider on this issue. The medical profession has become very careful with prescription drugs. Do not take over-the-counter drugs without checking with your care provider. And do stay away from all recreational drugs. It might be hard but it is necessary. Babies addicted to PCP, downers, or cocaine in the womb are a sorry sight at birth.

If you took cocaine just once or twice, your baby will not be addicted and probably will not be affected. The important thing is to stop before it might be. Cocaine use in pregnancy is associated with sudden detachment of the placenta, so don't take it again.

If, before you knew you were pregnant, you took something else, including a prescription drug that is usually not recommended for pregnant women, talk it over with your health-care provider. Realize that what is done is done and that worrying about it all the time will only add stress. I know quite a few women to whom this happened, and their babies were fine. Nature does have a certain resiliency. Many of us would not be here if it did not.

See aches and worries as signals from your body or mind that you have something to investigate. Learning to worry is a step toward learning to assume adult human responsibility. And the desire to do the very best for the baby is the root of parental love —human beings find profound delight in the belief that through their best effort a new and beautiful person with better opportunities and fewer flaws will come into being. When aches and worries occur, you might jot down what they are and what brings them on, and discuss those that recur at your next health-care visit. The more you know about a symptom, the easier it is for your health-care provider to ascertain what the problem is.

When a new ache or pain worries you, yet you are afraid to call your doctor because you have already called so often, try changing positions or lying down and relaxing for a while. After a few hours, if there is no improvement, you should call.

Pain or a burning sensation while emptying the bladder should be reported at once, because bladder infections often bring on premature labor. Any flare-up of the now prevalent herpes virus should be discussed with one's health-care provider too. If the virus is active in the vagina around the time of the due date—and herpes can act up at the last minute—it is safer to schedule a cesarean section than to risk exposing the baby, because it can make an infant very ill. Expectant parents with an active infection should also learn precautions against passing on the infection after the baby is born. If the virus was discovered in your blood during a routine medical test, try not to feel too bad about it. It is a very contagious disease and can be transmitted by forms of contact other than sexual intercourse. Since pregnancy alters a woman's immune response, it is not uncommon for women exposed to the virus earlier to have a first outbreak of herpes during pregnancy.

Always make sure a complaint is not the kind that warrants medical attention before you consult someone such as an osteopath, a chiropractor, a physical therapist, or a masseuse. The first two have been trained to know which nerves govern which muscle or organ and where they enter the spine. Sudden movement, lifting, or carrying a heavy burden can pull one of the vertebrae slightly out of alignment, causing nerve pressure with resulting symptoms in the corresponding muscles and/or organs. Osteopaths and chiropractors can adjust these so-called subluxations. One treatment usually relieves the symptoms considerably, but if the muscles have gone into a spasm, full correction might not be possible the first time, or things might not stay in place. Usually a few visits are necessary. Gentle adjustments are better than forceful ones, especially in pregnancy, when the ligaments are flexible and corrections are easy to make.

Physical therapists relieve spasms with deep-tissue massage. They usually also teach corrective exercises. Masseuses do alleviate muscle spasms, but they usually do not teach corrective exercises. They might combine Western massage with some of the Eastern techniques such as shiatsu and acupressure.

Which of these approaches is better probably depends more on the skill of the individual practitioner than on the field in which he/she was trained. This is not as strange as it sounds. Illnesses too can be cured by different approaches. The body is complex, and it wants to be well. When given a hand or a hint, it tries to do the rest.

Once you have clearance from your doctor, seeing a practitioner of one of these healing arts can be very helpful. I have seen crippling lower-back aches disappear after a few treatments. If your doctor seems skeptical, remind him or her that these healing arts are based, not on faith healing or any new-age notions, but on the sound physical principles of alleviating muscle spasms or nerve pressures and restoring good circulation.

After a ritual bath with water that has been blessed and scented with herbs, midwife and relatives slide an egg inside the expectant mother's dress: "May the birth happen as easily." This ceremony, the Tingkĕban, is held in the seventh month of a first pregnancy when "the unborn fruit is considered viable." (West Java, Alit Veldhuisen-Djajasoebrata 1981)

Getting Ready for Your Baby's Arrival

PREPARING FOR THE BIRTH PROCESS

Thinking about birth and hoping that it will go well is perhaps as old as the human race. Before the advent of modern obstetrics, it was all people could do. At one time women practiced sympathetic magic to help them overcome their fears, such as letting a smooth stone fall to the ground inside one's dress and wishing that the baby would leave just as easily, or untying knots in clothing and hair at the onset of labor and hoping that the birth passage would be similarly unobstructed.

While science and reason are very important, they are not everything. Make room in your mind for some symbolic ideas. Cultivate thoughts that help you feel that your mind and body are uniting behind the process for which every cell in your body is preparing.

Don't dismiss your need to learn about what lies ahead. Women have always helped each other prepare for birth. Until recently, such learning came not by way of professional instruction but by example and through storytelling. My mother went to live with a pregnant sister a few weeks before her sister's baby was due,

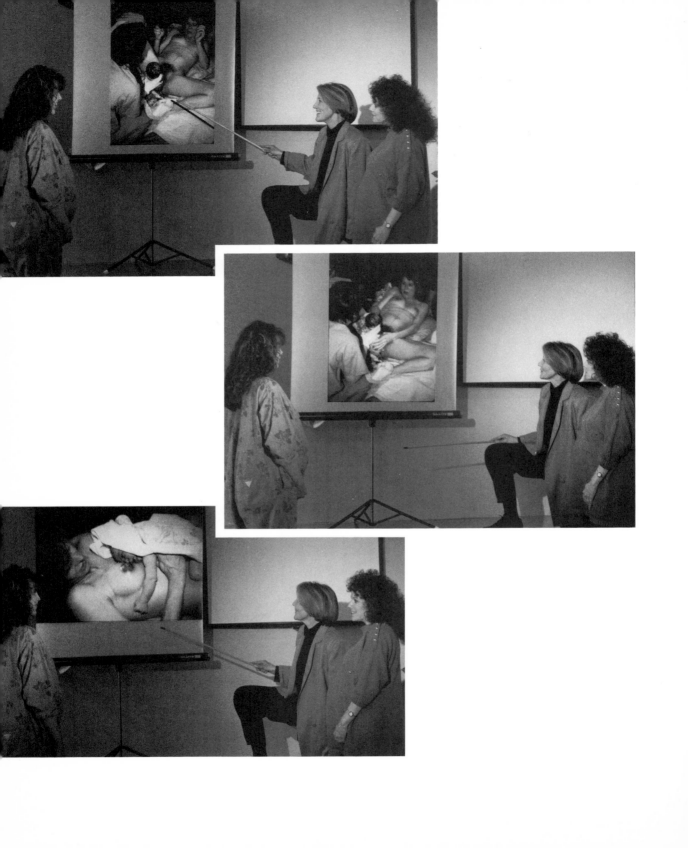

stayed with her throughout her labor, and helped her take care of the baby for the first ten days. Her sister had learned by helping a cousin, who had learned by helping an aunt, etc. This way of learning has largely disappeared from our lives because of the move of birth from home to hospital, the emphasis on school and career for females, and the decline in birth rates. At the same time, as a modern woman you are more aware that knowledge and skills improve anything you undertake, and this holds for birth and new parenthood too.

While education is helpful, indoctrination usually is not. The term "natural birth" has become associated with methods by which women are indoctrinated to believe that they, mostly through the power of their mind, can and must cope with the pain of their travail. When labor and birth are accompanied by an amount of pain that is manageable, watching a woman's power of concentration and devotion and strength is very inspiring. But when the pain changes to suffering, whatever relieves it without harming mother or baby is like nectar from the gods. Making use of it is perfectly natural.

The idea that concentrating on relaxation and breathing techniques, coupled with an understanding of the physiology of labor, can help women with their labor pains originated sometime before the Second World War in the minds of two very different men, Dr. Grantly Dick-Read, of England, who called his method "Natural Childbirth," and Professors A. P. Nikolayev and I. Z. Velvovsky, of the Soviet Union, who called theirs "Psychoprophylaxis in Obstetrics." Natural Childbirth became popular in the United States through the books of Dr. Dick-Read (the anthropologist Margaret Mead was one of his pupils) and through the work of Dr. Robert A. Bradley, an obstetrician in private practice in Denver, Colorado. Dr. Bradley taught all his patients how to cope with contractions using Dr. Read's methods, and he worked with them during their labor. After many grateful hugs and kisses from the women he helped, he decided to teach husbands how to do the coaching. His book, *Husband-Coached Childbirth,* published in 1965, introduced the idea of husbands participating in labor not only to expectant parents but to birth educators and eventually to doctors and nurses. And what was once called the Read Method of Natural Childbirth now became known as the Bradley method.

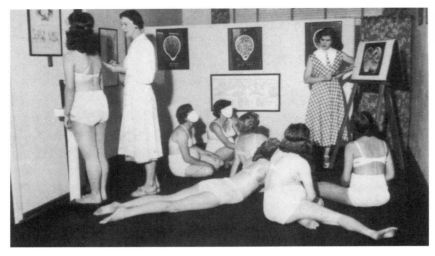

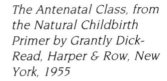

The Antenatal Class, from the Natural Childbirth Primer by Grantly Dick-Read, Harper & Row, New York, 1955

Psychoprophylaxis became popular in the United States thanks to a book called *Thank You, Dr. Lamaze*, published in 1959, in which the author, Marjorie Karmel, tells American women of her wonderful birth experience under the guidance of French obstetrician Fernand Lamaze in Paris. In 1951 Dr. Lamaze had gone to the Soviet Union to learn Velvovsky's method, about which he had heard at an obstetrical congress.

Both methods were probably inspired by publications from the Pavlovian school, particularly by the doctoral thesis of a Mrs. N. Erofeeva, published in 1912, in which she proved (on paper) that pain is perceived by the conscious part of the mind, that it has a conditioned nature, and that pain perception can be suppressed by the intervention of a new conditioning. In *Painless Childbirth: The Lamaze Method*, Dr. Lamaze takes this philosophy to its logical extreme. "The strength of the inhibition of pain," he writes, "depends on the strength of the focus and the strength of that focus depends on the strength of the effort contributed by you; hence the success of your labor is entirely in your hands. The success of labor is a direct variant of a woman's contribution."

I wish it were true. Many of us would like to believe that our mind has the power to bring the process of birth, or at least its pain, under control. And in some women this is possible. A number of years ago, when I worked as an obstetrical nurse in the labor and delivery department of a large hospital in Los Angeles, I was assigned to work with a woman whose labor was to be induced. While we waited for her doctor to start administering the Pitocin, which would bring on her contractions, I explained what would be happening in her body once labor started (this was before birth-preparation classes or books had become popular) and taught her the simple relaxation and breathing techniques of the Lamaze method. We worked closely together once her contractions began, and when her doctor, after a few hours, offered her pain relief, she said, "I don't need it yet." She pushed her baby out with complete control and no drugs. She was ecstatic. It was her third child, and for the first two she had used all the drugs offered to her. What kept her going once the contractions became painful this time, she said, was a sense of power over herself and the belief that what she was feeling was normal and not to be feared or fought. Her labor was over in couple of hours.

The duration of labor and the amount of pain women experience are variable, as is the ability of a person to be conditioned or hypnotized or helped with any other nonmedical remedy. These differences are genetically based and reinforced by our upbringing and our present lifestyle. Pain in labor is hard, and the longer labor lasts, the more difficult it becomes. If a woman has been led to believe that there would be no pain if she handled the contractions properly, it can become unbearable.

Equally misleading are remarks that diminish a woman's hope that she may be able to handle birth without drugs or surgery. Doctors often do this to avoid disappointment. Yet negative predictions can throw a woman into turmoil and sap the strength she gets from believing in herself. Each baby's birth and the labor that will lead to it are new events. We don't know beforehand exactly how it will go. Learn the skills that have helped other women and learn from each birth story, but keep an open mind. If a friend tells of a difficult labor, realize that long labors are not contagious but fear is.

Don't be afraid of your fears. A little fear is a good thing. It can make you nurture your strong points and help you be both cautious and courageous. However, there is no need to be overwhelmed by fear, thanks to modern medicine. Take your big fears to your doctor or midwife and learn to trust their skills. Don't expect them to guarantee you a great experience, a painless labor, or a perfect baby. If your health-care provider did, that would be a reason to doubt his/her insight or sincerity. One of the challenges

of our era is learning to accept the uncertainty that has remained in spite of science, technology, and statistics. Such uncertainty has its good sides. Women who, according to modern medicine, could not conceive sometimes get pregnant; women who were told they would not be able to carry a baby to term sometimes deliver past their due dates; women who were told that their babies were small have delivered babies of normal weight; and women who were told they could never deliver vaginally sometimes have a relatively easy spontaneous birth. If everything could be predicted, something in us would die.

Think about your innermost wishes for this birth. If it makes you feel surer of yourself, write them down in order of importance. Allow them to change as your pregnancy progresses. Notice how your priorities change when you imagine that your wishes have an impact. The Sioux Indians believed that their wishes would be heard and fulfilled if they climbed a particular peak in the Black Hills and stayed there overnight. They did not go very often, for fear that they would wish for the wrong thing. What is it that you want most? And next? and next? Don't confuse such a list of wishes with a plan. Wishing is more like praying than like planning; it helps you focus on what you want, but it keeps you humble and ready to change in the face of complications. See how your doctor or midwife responds. Are your wishes respected, and is your health-care provider able to help you bridge any gap between what you see as important and what he/she as a professional has learned about birth? Does every visit reinforce and increase your sense that your doctor or midwife has you and your baby's well-being at heart and that he/she is a skillful and insightful person?

Talk, too, about what you are learning in your pregnancy-exercise and/or birth-preparation classes, from your reading and from the stories of friends and acquaintances. If your teacher says things that go against what your doctor has told you, talk it over with your doctor. If what you learn in your classes opens your eyes to the fact that you do not like your doctor's or midwife's attitude or birth practices, select another health-care provider. If you prefer your care provider's approach to your teacher's, change teachers. Do not go into labor with opposing instructions or a lack of faith in your birth attendant. Such inner division will take away from your strength and from your ability to let go and trust.

Birth-preparation classes can be helpful and fun. There is very little difference between the Read, Bradley, and Lamaze methods in terms of techniques. The better teachers usually incorporate what is good from each method, often adding ancient self-help techniques such as acupressure, visualization, and self-hypnosis. Classes should prepare you for hospital equipment and for medical procedures in case of complications, and teach you about recovery, breast-feeding, and infant care rather than emphasizing the birth process to the exclusion of other relevant information. How much you like the teacher and the way she interacts with people, how knowledgeable she is, and how comprehensive her course is seem to be more important than which organization accredited her or the size of the classes. There are no university-based, state-approved courses of accreditation for birth educators.

The breathing techniques are not difficult to learn If you don't like the idea of going to classes, or are on bed rest or live too far from a good teacher, you will be able to learn what you need to know for handling labor from the next two chapters.

Also, talk with your partner, as honestly as you can, about what you expect from him. Do not associate his willingness (or lack thereof) to help you during labor with his ability to be a good father. Men from cultures where women and men live separate lives often cannot bear the thought of participating in something so distinctly female. Also, do not confuse his inability or unwillingness to coach you with lack of love. At one of the most romantic births I ever attended, the father could not touch his wife during labor because of his religious beliefs. He could only stand in the doorway of the labor room and sit next to the door of the delivery room with his back toward her. When she cried out in pain, his reading from the prayer book got louder and faster. And when suddenly her cries merged with those of a baby and her voice said, "A girl! Oh, a beautiful girl!" he bowed his head in grateful silence.

If you are one of the many modern women who do not have a supportive relationship with their child's father, do not feel shy about needing help from someone. It is very rewarding to help a new mother and her baby. Women and their newborns have stayed at my house to recover, and I probably got more out of being allowed to help at such a special time than they got from my assistance. People's natural desire to help is revealed by their tendency to shower advice freely on expectant and new parents; it becomes more useful when it is channeled into some concrete form of assistance. Allow one or a few people to help you out; without anyone to encourage you and give you a hand here and there, the transition is harder and lonelier. Don't be afraid that you will not have the strength and the resources to raise your child alone. Being alone is easier than being in a troubled relationship, because one is less divided. Some of the women I have admired most as mothers were single.

If all is well, continue to exercise. Aerobic fitness, strength, flexibility, discipline, greater awareness of muscles, and the ability to move smoothly from one position to another—from kneeling to squatting, to sitting with the legs folded in front, and back to squatting, for example—will all make you better prepared to handle labor. Pay special attention to stretching and to the way you breathe when you hold your body in the position that makes a particular stretching exercise work. Women have often told me that it was this practice of unifying the mind, the breathing, and the body's activity that most helped them cope with their contractions.

Keep your body well hydrated—drink about six to eight glasses of water per day—and well nourished on complex-carbohydrate snacks—whole-wheat crackers or toast, fresh or dried fruit, and the like—so that your muscle cells will have a good store of carbohydrates with which to supply you energy during labor.

HANDLING BED REST

While fitness is helpful, if you are on bed rest for medical reasons, the resulting lack of fitness will not place you at a great disadvantage. It is more important to overcome the condition that warranted your bed rest. Make the experience nice for yourself. If you can't take your work to bed with you, read all the books you have always wanted to read. Don't read about birth and babies all the time. The conflicting opinions and sometimes doctrinaire tone of those books will drive you crazy or make your blood pressure go up. Read some poetry or a good novel and maybe some children's books. I remember loving Winnie-the-Pooh when I was pregnant (and I did get a willful little girl with the imagination of a Christopher Robin).

More than 10 percent of expectant women have to stay off their feet temporarily during pregnancy, for a variety of reasons. Try to enjoy the unexpected rest. Don't worry too much about losing all your muscle tone. Ask your doctor if you can do some simple exercises and stretches that do not cause added pressure on the cervix. It is much easier to relax after you have moved and stretched a bit. Maybe you can continue some of the exercises and stretches from the pregnancy workout. Ask your doctor which ones seem safe for your condition.

It is common for doctors to tell you to lie on your left side for better circulation, but one position, even a good one, becomes uncomfortable very quickly. It's all right to rest on your right side intermittently, and, unless there is a specific problem, it is okay to lie on your back for brief periods too, especially if you place a small pillow under the right hip. It's also perfectly safe to turn on your hands and knees for a while, and in that position the circulation is even better. On all fours you can do some stretches, rock the pelvis, and maybe crawl around a bit. Crawling can be an excellent exercise, especially if the knees are protected with padding. It strengthens the body, arms and wrists included, without placing any pressure on the cervix or compromising circulation. Women on bed rest for preterm labor have told me that crawling to get something they absolutely had to have brought on fewer contractions than walking. And, as anyone who has been on bed rest for more than three days knows, one can suddenly need something so badly that waiting is not an option.

Twins rarely surprise us anymore. Today a so-called multiple pregnancy is usually detected with an ultrasound exam, and the mother is almost always placed on restricted activity or bed rest —very uncomfortable and worrisome, especially since one cannot help but wonder how it will be with two babies. Try to get help for the first few months, even if you have to borrow the money. And read up on twins. They can be great fun!

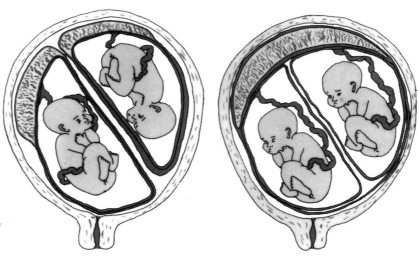

Nonidentical and identical twins

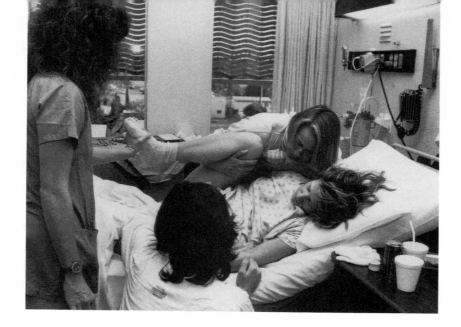

ABOUT THE IDEA OF A COACH

In any culture, women rarely face labor alone, and even more seldom are they expected to labor among people they do not know. This did become a practice in the developed world for a brief period, when women were separated in labor from all family and friends, to be attended by nurses they had never met, while the doctor, the one professional who was familiar, often did not arrive until the delivery was imminent. In this climate, husbands became spokespersons for their wife's rights, as well as caring labor coaches and sharing partners.

Like male doctors 300 years earlier, expectant fathers had to fight for their right to enter the birth chamber. Doctors discouraged men from participating, warning that after the sight of childbirth they might never again be able to make love, and hospitals banned all nonprofessionals from the labor and delivery department. One man chained himself to his wife's wrist during her labor, and after the birth he won in court the inalienable right for fathers to participate in the birth of their children if they and their wives so wished.

Since then it has become customary to call fathers coaches. But fathers are much more, and the word "coach" perhaps implies that helping a woman with her labor consists of telling her what to do, when, and how. While precise and detailed instructions can be helpful, they are only part of coaching. The other part is sensing when such instructions are relevant and how to give them so that the person who needs them can hear them. This requires a clear understanding of the birth process and sensitivity to the woman's personality and needs.

Some fathers have it in them, some don't. Some women have a friend, sister, or mother who would love to coach and who is devoted to learning how. Some women develop a trusting relationship with their midwife or doctor, who promises to be with them throughout labor. Labor nurses can be very good at coaching too, but usually one does not get a chance to choose one in advance, and on a busy night nurses may have to take care of two or three women at the same time. Take a good look at the birth facility you selected, evaluate your relationship with your birth attendant, and decide whether or not you need a coach and, if you do, who it should be. If around-the-clock obstetrical anesthesia will not be

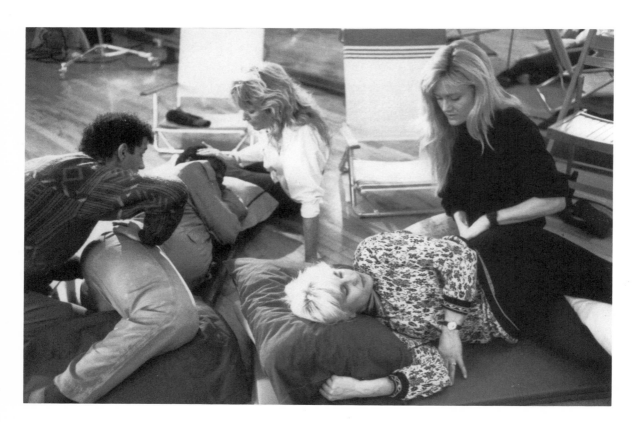

available to you, or if one-on-one nursing care is not guaranteed, I recommend that you bring an extra coach unless your birth attendant assures you that he/she will work with you through every contraction. Women often say that looking up into the face of a trusted woman friend who had gone through labor herself once or twice was very helpful. An extra coach does not diminish your partner's importance; nor does his not coaching you at all. If you do not feel comfortable with the thought that your treasured lover will see you in the pangs of labor, respect that feeling. Throughout the history of birth practices it has been more common for women to help each other than for men to help women. While we have learned that man and woman, as well as the relationship between them, may benefit from the father's participation, this need not be true for everyone.

ESPECIALLY FOR FATHERS

You have a number of advantages over all other possible coaches: your intimate knowledge of your partner, including her body and what pleases or relaxes her; the fact that you care as much as she does about the outcome; and the fact that you do not need to schedule practice sessions and labor rehearsals. You can practice making her more comfortable and being caring and supportive on a daily basis.

Becoming a good coach does not take a lot of studying and rehearsing, but it might involve some inner work. Learning the physiology of the birth process is relatively easy. Picking up the touches, words, and positions that have helped other women is not too hard either. But applying them to an individual woman without the need to prove something or be right is harder. And even more difficult sometimes is to trust one's intuition and observations and respond accordingly rather than simply do what was learned beforehand. Yet the more authentic and vulnerable and real you become, the better the chances that your suggestions will be useful to her. Coaching is a bit like courting—you do what works, and when it works you can feel it.

Don't worry that you cannot know what labor feels like. First, it feels different from woman to woman, and second, if you too felt

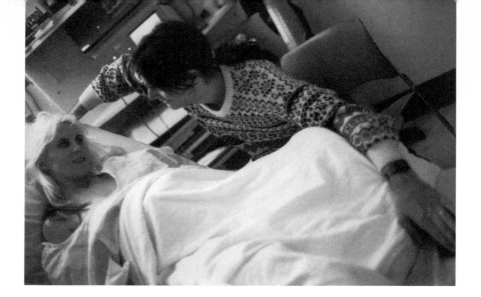

the pain, you could not possibly help her. A good coach does not need to play the game himself; he needs to understand the game and the players. If it goes against your nature to see her in pain and help her cope with labor, be honest about it. She might have a trusted friend who is willing to take on the function of coach, and you could still be there as much as is comfortable for both of you.

If coaching her during labor does not seem right for you, you might still want to learn some of the comfort measures that are part of the coaching techniques. Many women can use a little help those last weeks of pregnancy. Also, after the baby is born, it will still be quite dependent on an adult body for comfort and sustenance, and by then that will not always have to be the mother's. Consider learning about infants and how to help them. Participating in the care of your baby is at least as important as helping your partner with labor.

If this is your first child, you are, like her, making a transition. On the surface it seems harder for her—she has to do the job of carrying, giving birth to, and nursing the baby, while your life can go on almost unchanged. But it really can't; becoming a father affects you to the core of your being. It's just that you have choices as to how you will let it affect you and how much of the burden you will help your partner carry. When actions are based on choice, doing what is right is harder. It is also more rewarding.

Pregnancy and new motherhood make women more vulnerable and dependent. So much of their energy goes into nurturing some-

thing totally dependent that they in turn look for someone to take care of them. Before it became customary to move away from home and trusted friends to start a family elsewhere, women usually received support and advice from a number of relatives and friends. Today, with our emphasis on small nuclear families, there is a heavier burden on the expectant father.

Over the years, many fathers have thanked me for my program at the Jane Fonda Workout. It gave their wives a place to go, they said, and a support system, which took some of the burden away from them. And it gave them as a couple a perspective on what was going on and how to navigate the changes. Thus, if at times you feel unsure or overextended, don't become threatened or conclude that you are inadequate. Such feelings are a by-product of impending fatherhood for many highly competent and successful men.

PREPARING FOR PARENTHOOD

Pregnancy and new parenthood often activate long-forgotten rules about family life. Partners who, until they became parents, saw eye to eye may find they differ on issues surrounding parenthood. It reminds one that the attraction between lovers has nothing to do with similarities in upbringing or agreement on child-rearing practices—as a Chinese proverb says, no girl ever got married by studying how to suckle an infant. It also makes one realize that the mind of a young child has the ability to deduce general rules from what it hears and sees. This faculty may well be similar to that by which one learns language. By age three, children usually master the complex grammatical rules of the language(s) spoken around them. They cannot spell out the rules by which they speak, but they use them correctly. The same seems true for rules of behavior.

If a boy grew up with a nurturing father, he probably learned how to be a caring man. If his father was the kind of man who always appeared unemotional, he may find it hard to trust his strength while admitting insecurities and fears. We learn things from our parents that they never intended to teach us. A child whose mother gives a lot of warmth and attention when the child is sick and little when it is well may conclude: To get my mother's full warmth and attention I must be sick. The mother did not intend to teach that.

Most of us have incorporated a few rules like that. When we formed them we were dependent for our survival and happiness on the people from whose behavior we deduced them. Even if they did help us get what we needed at that time, they may not be valid in our present situation. Look into your heart and at some of your actions to see if you too are not partly living by rules that go against your innermost feelings and that you no longer need.

Try to let go of notions that are better forgotten: A more pointed belly is not a sign that the baby is a boy; reaching up to get something from a shelf does not cause the cord to wrap itself around the baby's neck; jumping up and down on those very last days does not bring on labor; breathing according to precise instructions does not take labor's pain away; and bonding is a lifelong process, not something that needs to take place within an hour after the baby is born. Similarly, reexamine the rules that you deduced from the way you grew up. If one of you has a rule that says, "I must never go into my parents' bedroom at night," and the other has one that says, "I can always get into my parents' bed," see which one of you can change the rule a bit. Many men believe it is a rule that taking care of a baby is woman's work. Many women have been quite disappointed that their partner, while helpful if asked, never seemed to feel that caring for their child really was his task as much as hers. To help the father assume more of the nurturing aspect of parenting, the mother may have to change some of her rules too. Deep down, women often carry fears such as "He won't like the baby if it cries while I'm gone," and by not trusting their partner, they make it harder for him to trust himself.

Earlier and greater participation of the father in child-rearing may well be of advantage to the developing child. Children whose parents are equally involved often do not show the exclusive preference for the mother in times of fatigue or hurt that children who are nurtured mostly by their mother display.

If you experienced any form of abuse from people who were important to you while you were growing up, changing some of the rules you wrote in your mind a long time ago is essential. Don't be afraid of it. In ensuring that the hurt done to you will not be repeated on your child, you heal yourself. The Bible's troubling assertion that the sins of the fathers are visited on the children need not be true. But you have to make a sincere effort to keep the hurt from being passed on to another generation.

ABOUT CARING FOR BABIES

Once the size of your belly and the movement inside become a constant reminder, it is natural for you to want to learn more about babies and how to care for one. In choosing classes, avoid the kind where the father is made to bathe a baby doll. There is no resemblance between that and bathing your own baby, and such specific skills are more fun to learn in the hospital the day after your baby is born or from the visiting nurse who comes to your house. "There are," says Heywood Broun in *Seeing Things at Night,* "one hundred and fifty-two distinctly different ways of holding a baby, and all are right." It is the same with bathing. And, judging from the variety of child-rearing practices that have led to healthy, well-functioning adults, the same applies to raising a child too.

Yet advice to parents, like books for pregnant women, frequently suffers from a doctrinaire tone. It limps between artificially created opposites such as environment versus genes and maternal versus other care, and it tends to perpetuate the idea of a "critical period," a specific time during which an aspect of character must be formed. And new parenthood seems to make otherwise open-minded people into dogmatists on the subject of child-rearing. Mothers who stay home with their babies tend to make women who return to work feel as if they are lesser mothers, while mothers who work try to make women at home feel that they are unproductive. An emergency-room physician once told me that she found a day on the job easier than one home alone with her two small children. It is, in part, because it can be so difficult to take good care of a small child that parents often do better when the task is shared.

Don't feel guilty about wanting or having to work. Babies need good and preferably individual care, but across the world and throughout history, among rich and poor, many more babies have been, and are, cared for part of the time by someone other than the mother than by their mothers exclusively. Babies can form attachments to two or three people at the same time from birth on, and they seem to enjoy a change, especially since their needs are so great and so specific that they tend to wear out even the most loving and patient caretaker.

Good mothers can stay home or go to work. Good mothers do whatever it is that helps them and their baby live and grow. In preparing for your baby's arrival, assess the circumstances of your life and decide. Some parents take different shifts and thus share in the care. Some can work part-time for a while or take their work home. Some have child care available on the job. If an employer can grant only a limited amount of time away from the job, women whose health and energy level permit often work until their due date in order to have as much time as possible to recover and be with the baby.

If you plan to go back to work soon after delivery, you might want to check out now what kind of child care is available in your area. Usually the options are hiring someone to come to your house (a relative, au pair, nanny, or someone who likes babies, such as a woman whose own children are grown), taking your child to someone else's house (family home day care), or bringing your child to a child-care center. Some couples who find individual care too expensive jointly hire a nanny. Studies suggest that until the age of eighteen to twenty-four months, most children fare better with individual attention, but after that, group care can become beneficial, especially for intellectual growth and the development of social skills. However, even for an infant, good group care is better than poor individual care. Group care, especially when the ages of the children vary a bit, resembles the extended family of old. Some children thrive in such a setting; others prefer a more quiet one.

Children in group care do have more illnesses. Not only is this more hazardous for the child involved, but every illness puts stress on working parents. Also, some of the illnesses the child catches from other children are passed on to the parents. Check that the area where babies are diapered is completely separate from food-preparation and eating areas, and make sure that there is a sink and clean towels close to the changing table and that hands are washed every time a baby is changed. In terms of location, where possible avoid places on or near busy intersections or near gas stations. The air pollution, and consequently the amount of lead in the soil of the outdoor play area, will be worse there. Yet, a good center near your workplace may be preferable to one with cleaner air if choosing the former means that you can stop in during your coffee or lunch break. Be wary of any child-care center that discourages unexpected visiting. Unannounced visits are a good way to ensure that no neglect or abuse is taking place.

As for the issue of environment versus genes, babies grow and change very fast according to an inner plan that interacts with an environment even before conception. One of the first groups of cells the embryo forms are those that will enable it to reproduce later. These cells, two generations away from the possibility of becoming a person, are affected by the womb in which the future parent is developing. Thus, even before we are conceived, we are a complex intertwining of genetics and environment. Identical upbringings will not produce equally happy people. Each baby will need and in its own way solicit different care. Mothers of more than one child often say, "My children were different from each other even in the womb." That is why a manual for child-rearing is not a good idea. Love, patience, and wisdom are more important for good parenting than detailed knowledge of child development. While some factual information enhances perceptions, too much of it tends to lessen the power of observation and takes away some of the rapture of discovery. Learn from books, but don't raise your baby by the book.

The "critical period" of growth that you may have heard about is a theory that probably has a grain of truth in it. During the first four months of life, a baby learns, from looking around, how to integrate what each eye sees into binocular vision. After the age of four months, eye doctors say, such integration becomes harder, and eventually it is no longer possible. Yet, in general, if physical growth is temporarily slowed down, due to a deficiency of nutrients or an illness, a child can, without permanent ill effects, catch up when circumstances improve. It is most likely the same with emotional and intellectual development. Consistent absence of love, of any kind of stimulation, or of acknowledgment and respect does serious damage, but a small shortage every once in a while will be forgiven. Thus, as parents you receive many chances to do well; you can build and improve on what you have already done instead of fearing that the first three months or three years form an unalterable foundation, and that any imperfections on your part will keep your child from reaching its full potential. Some mothers handle infants very well but have a hard time with toddlers. Some don't much like either stage but absolutely love child-rearing from there on. Recognizing one's limitations and one's own needs is a very important aspect of motherhood. Try to be authentic, and be prepared to change as you go along. I have seen prominent career women who never thought they would be able to stay home during their maternity leave ask for an extension or a part-time job because they found the interaction with their infant so thrilling. Avoid taking on too many financial obligations; that way, if one of you wants to spend more time with the baby, you will have that option. Children—who, according to an American adage, are God's message to us that the world should continue—can help us rediscover the immense joy of being alive.

If you are looking forward to staying home and caring for your baby yourself, be aware that tending to a baby by yourself, without other adults around and without contact with other mothers and babies, is difficult for most people. Primates do not care well for their offspring in isolation either. They groom and look after their babies much better when a few females and their babies live in close proximity to each other. I see the same in human mothers. The need for peers more than the desire to exercise attracts women to our recovery classes. If you are not part of a circle of friends with small children, try to meet some people in your pregnancy-exercise or birth-preparation classes with whom you can stay in touch. Another good way to meet new mothers is through the La Leche League, an organization dedicated to helping mothers with breast-feeding.

Count on needing some help the first week to ten days after your baby is born. Someone who does the shopping, laundry, cooking, and cleaning might be more helpful than a baby nurse, because a lot of contact between mother and baby helps to get breast-feeding established. And once established, mother's milk keeps flowing whether mothers work, go out a lot, or are with their babies day and night.

SELECTING A DOCTOR FOR YOUR BABY

Selecting a good doctor for your baby may be as essential to its health as taking good care of yourself and receiving quality medical care during pregnancy. If possible, choose one during the seventh month. Getting around is still easy for you at that point, and if, later, a health problem that puts you on limited activity or bed rest should arise, or if your baby is born early, you will have its most important health need covered.

Two types of physicians, family practitioners and pediatricians, are trained to help parents with the health care of children. Family practitioners have completed a three-year residency in family medicine. Unlike the general practitioner of old, family doctors do not usually make house calls. This is not due to unwillingness on their part. Cars have made the transportation of a sick child to the doctor safe and easy, and doctors have more resources for proper diagnosis and treatment in their offices or in the hospital emergency room.

A pediatrician's expertise is children and their illnesses. Some also study developmental psychology, family dynamics, or pediatric nutrition, but these subjects are not mandatory. Many pediatricians, especially those who see breast-feeding as important to the baby's health, employ a pediatric nurse practitioner with special training in this area or a lactation consultant, who may make house calls. This is a great plus, particularly with a first baby and more especially for those women who live at great physical and/or emotional distance from their mothers. First-time motherhood is a very special state. A woman needs an experienced and respected person to assure her that what she is doing for her baby is the very best, and such trained baby experts usually have a lot of simple tips on how to handle the practical aspects of infant care. If you know people whose approach to child-rearing you like, ask who their child's doctor is and why. Ask your health-care provider, or your birth educator or pregnancy-exercise teacher, for names of good baby doctors in your vicinity. The nursery nurses at the hospital of your choice can be helpful too: they know each doctor's routine, including his/her attitude toward breast-feeding. If you are planning to return to work, you might want to check if there are pediatricians with evening or Saturday office hours.

Don't feel embarrassed about asking for time for an interview. Doctors often cherish the opportunity to talk with the parents of their prospective patients, and a good doctor likes to be carefully chosen rather than picked from the yellow pages. If you feel that you do not know enough about well-baby care to make an educated choice, read Part Seven, "More About Babies," before you make your first appointment with a baby doctor.

A doctor's credentials are usually displayed in the office. If not, inquire about them. Ask at which hospital the doctor practices, and if this is not the hospital where you will have your baby, ask if he has staff privileges there too. If there is any problem with your baby, you will want it tended to by the doctor you selected, not by a substitute whom you do not know and who is not going to help you later with the care of your child. Find out if you will be able to stay with your child should it need to be admitted. Breast-feeding, the nursing mother's nutrition, whether or not you should have a

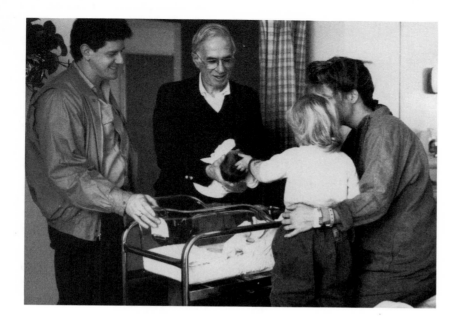

baby boy circumcised, how this doctor prefers to treat the baby's eyes at birth (with silver nitrate or an antibiotic), how vitamin K is given (by injection or orally), and how neonatal jaundice is treated if it occurs are important subjects to discuss, especially if you are trying to decide between two physicians. Injury prevention, including car safety, and the pros and cons of immunization are also good topics for a first interview. On a more practical level, it is useful to know about fees, frequency and duration of regular visits, and who covers if your doctor is unavailable during an emergency. How accessible will this doctor be in those first weeks, when you may have lots of questions? Will you feel free to call? Does he/she have a time set aside for calls from new parents? Finally, you and your baby's doctor should have similar child-rearing philosophies. If you wish to let your baby gradually establish its own schedule, for example, do not choose a pediatrician who tells you that you should nurse every four hours and/or let the baby cry at night.

If allergies run in your family, ask what you can do in the last two months of pregnancy to avoid oversensitizing your baby. The tendency to be allergic is genetic (if there are allergies on both sides of the family, there is a greater-than-50-percent chance that your child will be allergy-prone), but specific allergies are not inherited. By trying to avoid dust and molds and cutting down on milk, wheat, and other common allergens in the last weeks of pregnancy, mothers can protect babies from developing allergic reactions early in life. If the doctor you are interviewing does not know how to advise you on this subject, consider asking for a reference to a pediatric allergist.

New parents frequently complain about the inability of their baby's doctor to provide the nursing mother with concrete information and guidance. The ins and outs of breast-feeding are not part of the curriculum of any medical school. Since the information is of a basic, subtle nature, many doctors consider the topic beneath them. Many prefer formula because they can "see what the baby is getting." Of course, it is also important to note that formula companies sponsor conferences on infant health and development and provide research grants. Breast-feeding has no powerful sponsors, because no one but a baby gains directly from it. Some doctors have overcome all these cultural biases and studied the subject on their own. When you find a doctor you like, feel free to ask how he/she learned about breast-feeding. If the doctor employs a lactation consultant, meet with her and make sure the two of you communicate well.

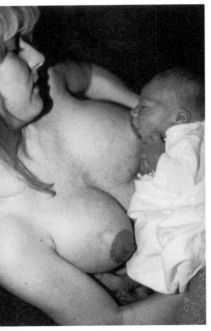

PREPARING FOR BREAST-FEEDING

Nursing is a natural step in the ancient mother-baby dance. For most it comes easily, but for others it presents physical or emotional hurdles. Where possible, it is healthier, for both mother and baby, not to interfere with the body's normal process of producing and secreting milk. Artificially stopping milk from flowing, with hormones or other drugs or devices, may not be the healthiest thing to do. There appears to be less breast cancer in women who nurse. Don't let the fear of losing the youthful firmness of your breasts keep you from trying. The continued beauty of the breasts is determined by heredity, age, and pregnancy as much as by breast-feeding. Exercise and good nutrition are a better way to preserve your breasts' shape.

A woman's milk is called white blood among many peoples, and like blood, it is a species-specific fluid with living cells that fight infections. The milk that comes closest to ours is that of baboons, but ours is higher in a milk sugar called lactose and lower in fat. Human milk helps the development of the nervous system and brain without placing unnecessary strain on the kidneys and other vital organs, and it gives the immune system a chance to develop to its full potential. The newborns of other species breathe more irregularly, with longer pauses between breaths, when fed milk from a different species. Formula-fed babies have a much higher rate of infections and allergies, and there is a higher incidence of crib death among them. A number of medical experts have angrily called the $15-billion-a-year formula business the world's greatest experiment without controls. If your mother did not nurse you and you believe that formula is fine because you are fine, please reconsider, in the light of modern knowledge, how best to feed your baby. For those who cannot or do not wish to nurse, formula is a good alternative, but an even better one would be the old custom of hiring a wet nurse. These days, when women borrow or rent each other's wombs, it would seem a natural step to let one woman help another with her breasts.

In thinking about nursing, accept the fact that it will tie you to your baby. It is that unique tie that makes it so special. Before we could control when and how often we got pregnant, there was probably a reason to fear the extent of involvement with our babies. But for women who can choose whether or not the baby inside will be their only experience with motherhood, there is much less reason for such fear and a greater reason to explore the process to the fullest. The greatest intensity of physical contact is during the "fourth trimester." And even during that period, it is possible to lose weight and/or return to work.

The hormones of pregnancy, including some secreted by the placenta, signal to the breasts that they will soon be needed as food-producing glands. It is thought that in cows the calf hormonally signals how much milk will be needed. A similar process may take place in human mothers. Thus, a woman whose nursing failed with one baby may well be successful the next time.

About eight weeks before term, ask your health-care provider to examine your breasts to see if you need any special preparation. If your doctor or midwife says your breasts are normal and fine, trust that your body is willing and able. If your obstetrician is not sure whether your breasts need preparation or does not seem knowledgeable about the subject, check with the pediatrician who will tend to your baby or with a lactation consultant.

The profession of lactation consultant is a new one. It arose in response to the medical profession's lack of knowledge about breast-feeding. As with birth education, there are no university-based, state-controlled licensing programs. Quite a few birth educators have added this training to their curriculum vitae; otherwise, a nurse with a background in neonatal nursing and a certificate from a lactation-consultant training program should be able to help you. If no such person is available to you, and neither one of your doctors seems well informed about breast-feeding, try to find a local chapter of the La Leche League and see what you can learn at one of their meetings. Many nursing mothers need not only expert guidance but also support, especially during those first five or so crucial days with a first baby.

If it is your instinct that a woman shouldn't need expert guidance for this natural function, keep in mind that the knowledge that was once quite naturally passed on from generation to generation is largely lost. Many mothers of women now expecting babies did not nurse. There is an advantage to this gap in the handing down of traditional information—we've learned more since our grandmothers' day. For instance, a number of studies have shown that toughening the nipples by scrubbing or rubbing them does not prevent soreness those first days, when they suddenly get a lot of friction, and such scrubbing, especially with soap, removes the oil secreted in the tiny glands on the nipple and the areola. Some soreness can be prevented if the mother understands the mechanics of how a baby suckles and learns to help her baby take the nipple properly from the start. Almost as important as helping the baby "latch on" properly is giving the baby free access to the breast from the start and allowing it to suckle for a few minutes whenever it desires. Another preventive measure for nipple soreness is learning how to deal with engorgement, the common swelling in the breasts in response to the onset of milk production. These techniques are very simple, but to put them into practice when everything is new may require an experienced eye.

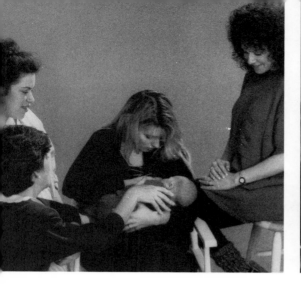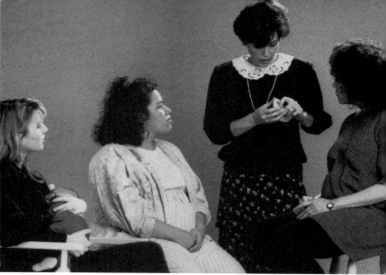

If your breasts are firm and somewhat inelastic (that is, you cannot easily take a sizable fold of skin between your thumb and forefinger), regular massaging may lessen their swelling when the milk comes in. It is probably easiest to do this while bathing. Don't make it into a science; just stroke the breasts in a circular fashion. Don't be afraid to slide your hands over your nipples and gently pull on them or roll them. Touching improves the circulation to your skin, while nipple pulling and rolling begins to stretch the tissue, and prepares you for the sensations of nursing. If your nipples are not visible and do not come out during caressing (this is called inverted nipples), it will help to wear a breast shield, which is designed to correct this particular problem, inside your bra some of the time during the last few weeks of pregnancy. Some experts say that you can also begin to bring the nipples out with a breast pump; however, since such stimulation of the breasts can bring on contractions, it should be done only in consultation with your health-care provider. Electric breast pumps provide the safest and most effective suction.* You may also want to arrange for an electric breast pump to be at your bedside after delivery so that you can pump for a minute or two and, when the nipple has come out, quickly give the baby a chance to grasp it. Another item that is helpful in case of inverted nipples is a Lact-Aid nursing trainer, which you can use to give the baby the colostrum or milk you pump until it learns to suckle hard enough to bring your nipple out.

The shields designed to bring out flat nipples can also catch a sudden release of milk. If this milk has been in there for a while, it should not be used, because milk may spoil rather quickly at body temperature.

* See pages 329 and 330 for organizations that can be helpful.

More common than inverted nipples are flat ones (nipples that seem almost part of the areola instead of extending distinctly). Here, too, the best remedy is probably to wear a breast shield inside the bra some of the time. Flat nipples present a problem only for babies who do not suckle strongly at first. Again, having an electric breast pump on hand right after delivery will be helpful. Some babies open their mouth so wide and suckle so strongly that even an inverted nipple is no challenge; others have a hard time with any nipple. Nature does not always give a mother with a flat nipple a baby with a strong sucking reflex, or a mother with an inverted nipple a baby with a mouth large enough to get a hold of her breast.

Don't judge your ability to nurse by the size of your breasts. Small breasts often produce in abundance. If you have large breasts, nursing bras that close in the front will be better than bras with flaps that come down, because the frame of the latter often cuts into the breasts and prevents proper emptying. Something to catch the milk that occasionally escapes between feedings will come in handy. You have a choice of disposable paper pads, washable cotton ones, or small cups that fit inside the bra to catch rather than absorb the milk. Cotton pads are kindest to the skin.

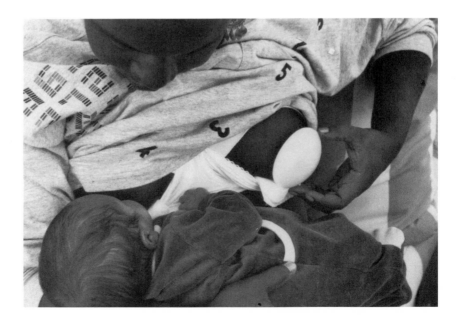

The cups are great when you have an abundance of milk and you have to dress up, but if you use them all the time, their milking action on the breasts will increase milk supply and prolong the problem of leaking between feedings.

A breast-fed baby is usually better off without bottles the first few weeks, because the technique of sucking on a bottle is very different from that of getting milk from the breast, and some babies prefer the bottle over the breast if they are given a bottle too soon. Although it is a good idea to give a baby a relief bottle regularly once nursing is going well, the chances for it to get to that point are greater without bottles around.

ABOUT BABY EQUIPMENT

When you make your first visit to a baby store, bear in mind that it is human nature to want the best and the most beautiful for our babies, and it is the nature of a consumer society to exploit that desire to the fullest. You do not need it all, and since you do not yet know your baby's likes and dislikes—nor your own as a parent—postpone buying anything that is not immediately necessary.

Avoid baby furniture made from plywood, because it contains formaldehyde. Also, if there are allergies in your family, avoid things like ruffles and drapes and other pretty items that collect dust. If you have a taste for antiques or have inherited items such as a crib, check whether or not they are up to current safety standards. Follow your natural inclination to watch parents with babies, and ask them why they chose a particular stroller, car seat, baby carrier, or other item that strikes your fancy.

When purchasing a car seat, shop at a store that offers a good variety and allows you to try out the seats you like; take each one in and out of your car a few times to see which handles best. If you have friends with a small child, ask if they will go with you and try some seats with the child in them. If you are offered a hand-me-down, check to make sure it conforms to Federal Standard 213. If you are short of funds, you can purchase a big seat right away and make it suitable for an infant by placing a rolled-up blanket on each side. Quite a few local chapters of the Child Passenger Safety Association offer loaner seats.

Small children used to get injured due to the lack of a car seat; now that federal law requires a special seat for children, they get hurt because the seat is not used correctly. The safest place for a car seat, everyone will tell you, is in the middle of the backseat. This is true, yet if, as a new parent, you find yourself constantly glancing over your shoulder, it might be safer to put the baby next to you. Some parents fasten another mirror onto the rearview mirror in order to watch their baby in the backseat. If you live in a sunny climate, also consider a movable window shade to keep the sun off your baby. In a cold climate, wrap a blanket around baby and seat instead of trying to place a bundled-up baby in a car seat. Take all loose objects out of your car. In a collision, a Kleenex box, flying through the car, can cause serious injury if one corner hits a baby at its temple. Station wagons are safe for transporting strollers and cribs only if such items are fastened down or if a strong net separates the luggage area from the baby's seat.

Before you settle for paper diapers, like so many other parents around you, reexamine the pros and cons of buying and laundering your own, hiring a diaper service, and using throwaways. Don't be misled by the term "disposable." Paper diapers with a plastic covering are not biodegradable, and they add tremendous bulk and disease-causing bacteria to the garbage dumps. Even biodegradable disposable diapers (available in some health-food stores

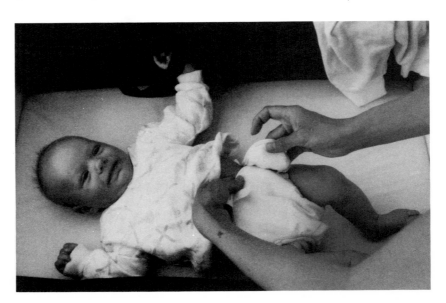

Cloth diapers come prefolded and don't need pins.

and by mail order) take five years to disintegrate. Using cloth diapers does not mean pins and plastic pants, and if you live in an urban area, a diaper service can take care of the laundry. There are wonderfully soft flannel and cotton diapers, preshaped so that they can be held in place with a tightly woven, water-resistant wool or cotton outer covering that fastens with Velcro. These materials allow the baby's skin to breathe; plastic and paper do not. Be especially cautious with ultradry diapers. The baby's waste should not stay in contact with its skin for long periods, but because of their absorbency (and, perhaps, their expense), disposable diapers can trick parents into changing their baby less frequently. A properly cared-for infant will need between ten and fifteen diaper changes per day. Thus, if you choose throwaway diapers, you will need around 350 for the first month. A diaper service usually provides 80 to 100 per week. If you decide to launder your own, the amount you need will depend on how often you wash them. Since cloth diapers can also be used in other ways, you should get another dozen or so for burping and other purposes. In terms of expense, laundering your own costs the least, using a diaper service costs somewhat more, and relying solely on throwaways is the most expensive. In terms of the ecosystem that sustains us, a diaper service is the least costly choice; when every family washes their own diapers, more water, soap, and electricity are used.

Thirteen babies with one day's supply of nonbiodegradable disposable diapers. Multiply by 365 to see the mountain of potentially toxic waste just thirteen babies would produce in a year. These diapers take a few hundred years to disintegrate. In contrast, diapers with biodegradable plastic will disintegrate in about five years. However, millions of small shards of undegradable plastic will remain. No one knows the implications of a world filled with plastic sand. Experts say plastics should be used with restraint, handled with care and recycled as much as possible.

Cotton is the fabric that is most soothing and neutral to the skin, but it cannot be made flame-retardant. Many states legally require children's sleepwear to contain a flame-retardant, even though one popular flame-retardant (Tris) had to be taken off the market because it was found to cause leukemia. The best way to prevent children from burning is not by treating clothes and bed sheets with a chemical, but by better protecting the house from fire and by observing basic safety rules. Be careful with open flames, install smoke alarms, buy a fire extinguisher, and turn the water heater down to 105 degrees so that your tap water is not scalding hot. If you decide that you prefer all-cotton fabrics, look at playwear to find something appropriate for sleeping. In terms of design, V-necks are best because babies have virtually no neck, and the rubbing of the chin against fabric can cause irritation.

All new clothing should be run through a full wash cycle, without soap, to remove sizing. To launder your baby's clothes, use soap flakes rather than a detergent and avoid bleach. If you purchased some flame-retardant items that cannot be washed with soap, use only a small amount of detergent and include an extra rinse cycle, because even traces of detergent can irritate a baby's skin.

You don't need a lot of bathing equipment right away. Your baby's doctor will most likely advise against giving your baby a tub bath until its umbilical cord has fallen off and the belly button is dry, which usually happens between the sixth and the tenth day. By then you may be comfortable enough with your baby to take it

in the tub with you (ask your partner to hand the baby to you once you are in the tub). Another easy way to bathe a newborn is in a plastic dishpan next to the sink in the bathroom or the kitchen. By the time the baby outgrows this simple setup, you will know your and your baby's likes and dislikes, and you can buy what you will both enjoy.

Even though a lot of babies do not sleep as much as their parents had expected, babies do sleep more than we do. Where they sleep best depends on their temperament and that of their parents. Strong-willed babies often have strong-willed parents; alert, unrelaxed babies often have parents who do not spend a lot of time sitting around; and restless sleepers often have a parent who has difficulty sleeping too. So when you think about where your baby should sleep, take into consideration what kind of a sleeper you are. If you love to cuddle all through the night, you might like having your baby in bed with you some of the time. If you wake up easily and have a hard time getting back to sleep, chances are you and your baby will sleep better if you each have your own place from the start.

Most babies go to sleep when they need to and wake up when they are ready, no matter where they are, as long as they are not hungry or suffering from some other physical discomfort. They love waking up near one of the parents or caretakers. Many mothers find it convenient to have the baby sleep near them, but not in bed with them, so that they can reach over and pick the baby up when it wakes up hungry in the night. Parents and babies usually

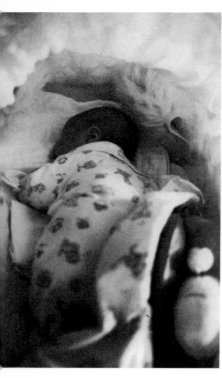

outgrow this temporary setup within two to four months, so if you don't have a lot of money to spend, don't waste it on an expensive bassinet. A basket, a box, or even a drawer removed from a desk will do. Babies are so beautiful, they look great in the simplest of settings.

If you do not already own a hot-water bottle, consider getting one. Babies like their beds, clothes, and bath towels preheated, and a hot-water bottle is safer than a heating pad, especially if left in bed with a sleeping baby. One other item many babies seem to like is a piece of lambskin. They're handy because they make an instant soft surface for a nap anywhere and they are washable.

Many mothers find it easier to change the baby right on their bed, using a pad, rather than to get up and go to a changing table, especially in those first days. If the baby is soiled, they use cotton balls and warm water from a thermos to clean it, or they move baby and pad closer to running water. And many mothers don't use a crib much those first weeks either. Thus, if you are short of time or money, cribs and changing tables can wait, and for some they prove altogether unnecessary. You may prepare a basket with diapers, diaper covers, undershirts, suits or gowns, and receiving blankets, which you can move near where you decide to change your baby or fold the laundry. A basket, a foldable mat on which to change the baby, and a cradle could get you through the first months while you decide how to set up your house as a parent. A washing machine and an extra pair of hands to help with shopping, cleaning, and laundry do more to make those first weeks less hectic than a lot of equipment.

SECOND AND SUBSEQUENT BABIES

Second and subsequent pregnancies often surprise parents. "All it seemed to take," some say, "was a fond look at each other with the thought of having another one." Others manage to plan carefully again and decide on the time for another conception. In general, the mother's body benefits from two years between pregnancies, and children adjust better to a new baby when they are three or older. Yet, here, too, nature is flexible, and for healthy women who have taken good care of themselves, two pregnancies in close succession seem to be fine. Three or more pregnancies without a rest in between is a different story, but this is becoming increasingly rare in the developed world. Women caring for two small children at home while pregnant with a third are at greater risk for miscarriage than those employed outside the home in physically demanding jobs. Avoid lifting and carrying your toddler constantly when you are pregnant. Squat or kneel down to your child's level some of the time, and use a stroller rather than your arms whenever possible.

A second pregnancy never duplicates the first one: We cannot step into the same river twice. The chemistry between the mother and the new baby is different, as are the mother's body and her mind-set. Most women notice the baby's movements earlier, and they find themselves bigger sooner. They also carry the baby lower, and uterine contractions come earlier and are more frequent. This combination of being bigger, carrying lower, and feeling more contractions makes many think that their due date is off and that the baby will come earlier. This usually is not the case.

A baby carried by muscles and ligaments that stretched once before sits at a different angle to the birth passage. This often prevents it from entering the bony exit until a strong labor contraction lifts it inward and pushes it down. Thus, even though they seem lower, second babies often do not drop.

In general, labor with a second baby is shorter than with a first. Experts say the longer the time in between babies, the smaller the decrease. However, length of labor is determined not only by the mother's body, which is experienced now, but also by the chemical exchange between mother and baby and by the size of the baby. Second babies are often slightly larger, and sometimes second labors are longer than first ones.

Women who, with their first child, took twelve hours or more to dilate to three or four centimeters often progress past that point within two hours with their second. From there, dilatation usually occurs in two-thirds or less of the time it took with the first baby, and expulsion, especially if the baby is in a good position, is faster too. Faster does not mean less painful, but coping with the pain may be easier, especially if fears, disappointments, and pain over the first labor were effectively dealt with and left behind. Many women experience a great labor the second time even though their

first was long and hard, and many women are able to give birth vaginally after a cesarean delivery of their first child. The secret is to see the second birth not as a repeat performance but as a new and unique event. If the memories of the first birth are frightening, this may take some inner work or counseling. If the first birth went well, taking one review class or rereading the book that gave useful information before should be all that is needed.

If a cesarean was necessary because of a narrow pelvis, it might not be reasonable to try for a vaginal birth, because the pelvis does not get larger, and second babies are often bigger than first ones. At least this time the surgery can be performed at the onset or after a few hours of labor instead of after many hours of work, and that will facilitate recovery. Unless a medical condition such as high blood pressure or diabetes requires otherwise, it is better to let the mother go into labor and then schedule the surgery. There is less bleeding, and the uterus heals better when the lower segment has had a chance to thin from the contractions. Also, the baby gets a warning sign and can prepare for the impending change.

The contractions that take place after baby and placenta have been delivered are usually stronger and more painful with each baby. The colostrum comes in faster and is more abundant if the mother nursed her first child, and the change from colostrum to milk often occurs with less engorgement. The joy of infant care is greatly enhanced by the parents' sense of confidence, but it can be troubled at the same time by insecurities and pain over the responses of the child that has to adjust to a sibling.

Be aware of false analogies when you try to prepare yourself for the feelings your first child may be experiencing. For your other child or children, the arrival of a new baby is not, for example, the equivalent of your husband saying to you, "Honey, I still love you, but you'll have to share me with this younger woman." There is no comparison between the relationship of husband and wife and that of parents and children. Lovers who form a partnership are a dyad. Parents and child form a triad. If husband and wife decide to have another child, the first triad does not become a foursome.

Instead, a new and different triad is created. The more secure the first triad is allowed to remain, the less pain there will be between the three members that form it. And the better the parents recognize that between them and the new child a new and different triad will form, one that is affected by all the natural forces of their life, including the fact that there is already another child, the better the chances that each child will be able to flourish and that the children will be able to love each other.

Don't overprepare a child in hopes of avoiding turmoil after the baby's arrival. Adults have a hard time letting knowledge and understanding help them with feelings, and for children this is even tougher. Don't be threatened when the child you found so perfect suddenly shows feelings of jealousy and aggression. Those emotions are difficult to control for an adult, and the fact that your child has them does not mean that you did not do a good job raising him/her. Don't insist that number one love number two either. Allow your child to discover its love instead. It will come, especially if the first one does not have to give up too much. This is easier to accomplish when there are a few years between children, but it can be done when they are close together. It will just be harder work for the parents.

Do not reject nursing to make it easier for your first. There is no evidence that giving up something so vital for the well-being of

the baby will help the adjustment of a toddler or child. Instead, set up a corner somewhere in your house with toys and books and a comfortable chair for yourself. Then, as you nurse the baby, you can read to or talk with your other child, and nursing will become a special time for both.

Do not feel guilty that you are not giving your second baby the same kind of attention that you gave the first. Your second child benefits from having experienced parents and a sibling to watch and imitate. Your first child also benefits, because finally there is someone in the house who is less competent and who is likely to be, from very early on, an admiring imitator.

Be subtle when telling your child about the new baby. After the initial introduction of the subject, wait a while for questions and feedback that show that the child has processed what you explained and is ready for more. If your child seems to have forgotten altogether, realize that at this point the subject is more important to you than to him/her. If it feels right to you and your child shows an interest, discuss with your birth attendant whether or not your child can visit you during labor and/or attend the birth or visit you shortly afterward. Even if your child shows a great interest in being there, be ready to change your mind once labor starts and the child shows signs of wanting to leave. It is best to have a trusted adult present as a companion to play with and watch the child, who can leave with it should that become preferable. With that kind of flexibility and sensitivity to their needs, children do not seem to be traumatized by watching the birth of a sibling. Quite a few families feel that it created a special bond from the start.

Insights and Skills for Labor and Birth

PART

4

THE PHYSIOLOGY OF LABOR

The main actor in the drama of birth is the smooth muscle tissue of the uterus. Smooth muscle cannot be voluntarily controlled— it does not become stronger from exercising, as the striated skeletal muscles do; one cannot will it to contract or stop contracting; and it gets energy only from aerobic combustion. The hormonal

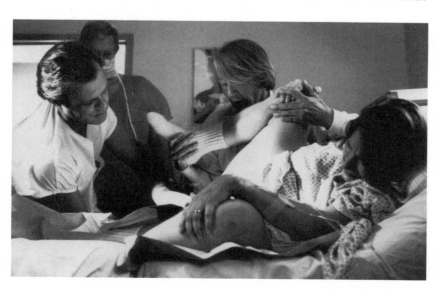

changes of the last weeks of pregnancy, brought on by the interplay between mother, baby, and the baby's supportive structures (mostly the membranes and the placenta), make the uterine muscle cells more sensitive to oxytocin and other contraction-stimulating substances. The body secretes these in steadily increasing amounts, and they prepare the connective tissue between the muscle fibers of the lower uterus, cervix, and vagina for the stretching that will occur. Thus, when called upon to open up and expel the baby, the uterus, stretched to many times its nonpregnant size, is able to contract with more strength than ever before, and the cervix, the area that needs to be pulled over the baby's head, is more able to stretch.

Of almost equal importance is the pelvis. External appearance tells us little or nothing about the internal dimensions of this structure; small-hipped women may have a spacious birth passage and vice versa. In all women the passage is easier to navigate at the end of a pregnancy than at other times, because the ligaments that tie together these strongest bones in the body (the triangularly shaped backbone, the flaring hipbones, and the pubic bone) become slightly elastic with the hormonal changes that prepare the body for birth. This makes the passage a little wider and more mobile.

While the uterus first and foremost accommodates the baby, the pelvis is there for the mother, and the baby has to adjust to it. Thus, the drama of birth is a behind-the-scenes interplay between these two structures. Of the two key players—the mother and the baby—the baby is the more difficult to reach. We can see the mother, ask her how she is feeling, and take her temperature and blood pressure. A trained hand can slide two gloved fingers to the back of the vagina and assess how wide the cervix has opened and how far down into the birth passage the baby has progressed. If the cervix has begun to open, the examining fingers can feel the bulging, water-filled sac, and when the membranes have ruptured, they can touch the baby. Professionals can tell how the baby is positioned, but they cannot tell how it is feeling. The closest we can get to knowing that is by listening to its heart.

The discovery that one could hear a baby's heart through its mother's belly was made by a pupil of the man who invented the stethoscope. He held the new tool to a pregnant woman's abdomen, expecting to hear splashing sounds, and instead he heard a

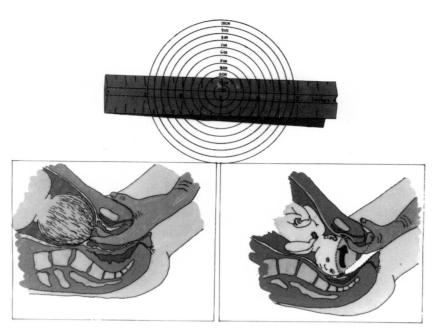

The arrow indicates the occiput posterior position.

heartbeat about twice as fast as that of an adult. Two hundred years later, the baby's heart rate is still one of the main indicators of fetal well-being. It should be listened to during every prenatal checkup and, depending on mother's and baby's health and the birth attendant's preference, checked intermittently or continuously through labor and birth.

While listening to the baby's heart is essential, it should not impair the mother's ability to change positions or get up and walk. Labor and the ability to cope with it usually improve when the mother feels free to move around. Moving also tends to make it easier for the baby to come down the birth passage.

From the baby's point of view, this passage curves slightly toward the mother's back, then forward to her vagina. At the pelvic entrance the diameter is widest from hip to hip but at the exit it is widest from front (the pubic bone) to back. The snug fit means the baby must make a ninety-degree head turn as it travels down its mother's pelvis, because its head is largest from front to back. Thus, it commonly enters the birth passage facing one or the other of its mother's hips and exits facing her back. The baby follows nature's path of least resistance when it turns its head to fit the structure into which it is being propelled. But at least 20 percent of babies make a wrong turn and end up looking up instead of down—occiput posterior, or "sunny-side up," as it is called.

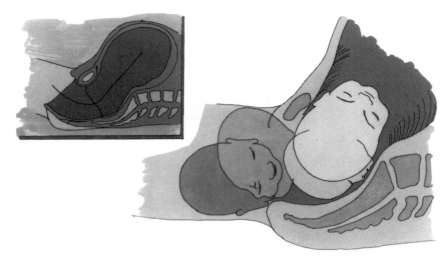

The birth passage curves toward the back, then forward. The baby's head enters sideways, turns toward the back, pivots up from behind the pubic bone, then returns to the sideways position during the delivery of the shoulders.

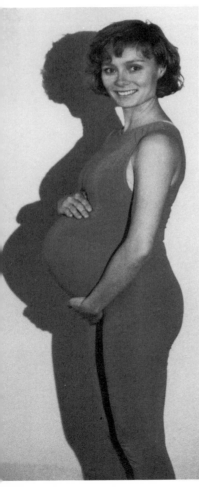

The baby usually turns on its head in the seventh month of pregnancy. Hippocrates and many medical writers since him thought that this move so exhausted the baby that it needed a month of rest, after which it picked at the cervix and membranes until they gave way, and then made its way out with swimming movements. It is now understood that the baby's active participation in the onset of labor is more subtle. When the baby's lungs have matured to the point where they can handle oxygen, they secrete an enzyme into the amniotic fluid. It seems the baby's brain, especially the pituitary gland, also sends signals in the form of secretions into the amniotic fluid. In response, the mother's cervix gets ready to be shortened and opened by contractions. The baby's size seems to influence the frequency and strength of contractions, which may explain why women with multiple pregnancies are at risk for an early onset of labor. When size, maturity, and age of the placenta combine, more and stronger prelabor contractions result, and the ligaments that hold the pelvic bones together, already softened from the pregnancy hormones, begin to yield a little. At this point the baby, grateful perhaps to have a little more space, slides its head behind the pubic bone. Women can often tell when their baby has dropped. The buttocks swing further outward, providing the mother with a place to rest her hands. Also, women say they can breathe deeper and their stomach can hold a little more, while the bladder holds virtually nothing. When you use the bathroom every time you see one, your baby has probably dropped. Don't worry; its head, now cradled in your pelvic bones, is cushioned by the water sac.

Prelabor contractions often initiate changes in the cervix too. They pull it up (this process is called effacement), and when that is nearly done, they begin to stretch it open (this is called dilatation). Some women dilate three or four centimeters (two inches) with these irregular and usually painless prelabor contractions. (Complete dilatation equals the diameter of the baby's head, about ten centimeters.) Other women do not efface or dilate until labor starts. This does not mean they'll have a long labor; I have seen women who started with a long and closed cervix give birth after six hours.

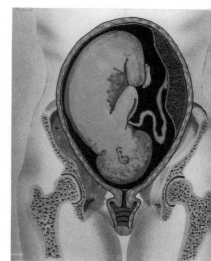

Labor begins when the contractions induce further opening of the cervix. In most cases, the contractions must occur at least every five minutes and last around a minute each to open the cervix past three centimeters; this is called active labor, and from there on dilatation usually proceeds at a steady rate. With a first baby, it commonly takes six to twelve hours of labor to progress from three centimeters to complete dilatation. But getting to three centimeters sometimes takes up to twenty-four hours. Fortunately, this is not as bad as it sounds. Early contractions are often not very painful, and, when all is well, they can be handled at home. Note that the distinction between pre- and early labor is often made in hindsight: When contractions stop after a few hours they are called prelabor (some still use the old misnomer of "false labor"), but when, instead, they begin to accelerate into contractions that last longer, occur closer together, and feel stronger, they are called early labor. Most women reach the point where they say, "That's why it's called labor" when they have dilated to between two and four centimeters. From there on, the birth process dominates over all other functions of the body—digestion usually slows down, and so does any thought process not directly related to what is going on inside.

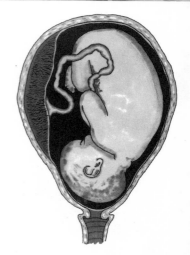

When the uterus shortens with a contraction, the baby is pushed onto the cervix, and, much like the collar of a turtleneck sweater, the cervix stretches up and opens over the baby's head. Since the uterus is anchored in the lower body with very strong ligaments, uterine contractions force the baby down through the steadily

During labor, as the uterus contracts the cervix retracts.

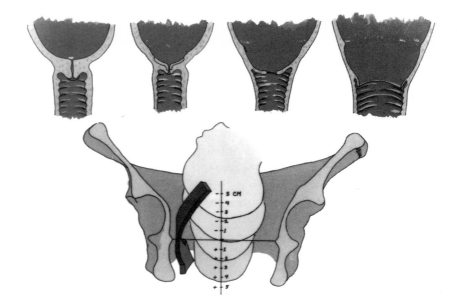

Dilatation and descent, portrayed here separately for clarity, usually happen simultaneously so that when the cervix is fully open, as seen in the upper right, the baby may have descended to the +1 or sometimes even +2 station.

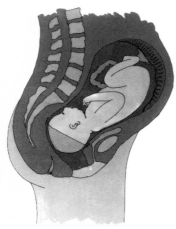

Note the alignment of mother and baby: The baby's face will slide over the muscles of the mother's perineum while the back of the head pivots around the pubic bone.

widening opening of the cervix into the vagina. Birth attendants measure progress in this downward journey by dividing the passage into ten stations, from minus five to minus one above zero, and from plus one to plus five below.

When the baby reaches "plus one," a good contraction will push it directly toward the mother's rectum, triggering a sensation similar to, but much stronger than, that of a bowel movement. The mother wants to bear down, but the cervix may not be open all the way. Now the contractions can become quite tumultuous. The mother, confused by conflicting messages—her body is saying, "Push it out," while the birth attendant is saying, "Wait, because the cervix is not quite ready, and extra pressure on it may swell it and slow its opening"—needs strong support and guidance. Fortunately, this transition from the dilatation to the expulsion stage, which women describe as the hardest part of their labor, does not usually last very long. When dilatation is complete, the fully open uterus contracts more strongly than before, because the muscle tissue from the cervix has moved up to reinforce the dome, propelling the baby through the open gate.

The baby's two-inch journey out of the uterus, through the vagina, and into a life of its own can require anything from two easy pushes to two hours of hard work. The muscles used for expulsion are well rehearsed, and bearing down with uterine contractions comes quite naturally from the practice of emptying the bowels. The first sign that the baby is coming is a bulging of the area between the vagina and rectum and some opening of the rectum when the mother pushes. The baby's passage will continue a little farther in the direction of the back before it curves toward the vagina. The resulting rectal pressure can feel as if the baby is going to leave through the wrong opening, but a contraction later the baby changes direction, the sensations change, and the vagina opens. The initial stretching of this sensitive opening often causes a burning sensation, called the "ring of fire." This usually disappears once another contraction pushes the baby's head down to a point where it blocks conduction of some or all of the pain.

While the emerging head can cause pain, there will be relief too, and some women also experience an emotion akin to ecstasy. The shoulders are generally easier to deliver, and once they come out, the mother feels the baby slide out. It instantly and forever outgrows the womb.

The work does not end with the baby's delivery. Contractions now shorten the uterine wall to detach and then expel the placenta. These contractions become stronger when the baby nuzzles the mother's nipples. Usually this complex organ, which in some cultures is reverently called the baby's little sister, slides out within forty-five minutes.

The detachment of the placenta stops the secretion of preg-

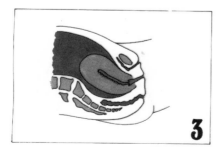
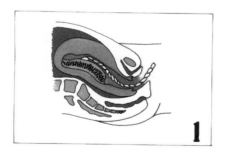

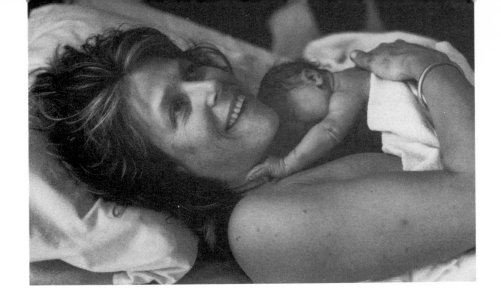

nancy-supporting hormones into the mother's blood. Upon registering the change, her brain signals that milk-producing hormones can be released. The combination of hours of exertion and this sudden biochemical change gives many women the shakes. Legs tremble; teeth chatter: All that is normal and usually lasts no more than twenty minutes. At about that time or slightly before, the baby's stomach begins to secrete acids that create hunger pangs, and it gets ready to nurse. The baby's active suckling releases more of the hormone that causes the uterus to contract, which now helps close the blood vessels that once went to the placenta, cutting down on the mother's blood loss. The colostrum from the mother's breasts coats the lining of the baby's stomach and bowels to protect them from bacteria, while the baby's suckling reinforces the message in the mother's brain that milk needs to be produced. And so their interdependent relationship continues.

SELF-HELP TECHNIQUES

Giving birth, said a composer a few weeks after her baby was born, is God's way of allowing us to take part in creation. Millions of women before us did it without specific instructions or detailed knowledge of what went on inside. The most important ingredients you bring to the birth process are trust that your body can do it and the ability not to fight your body as it goes about its work. Since pain tends to attack both trust and the ability to let go, some women find it helps to visualize the process in detail; others do better with just a little knowledge. If you sense that you fit into the first category, reread the preceding section until you know and understand the process. If you believe that you might do better with less detailed information, just picture your uterus, cradled by your pelvic bones and holding the membranes, the placenta, the cord, and the baby, its chin tucked to its chest, its knees up against its belly, its ankles perhaps crossed, and think about labor and what you and the baby need to do. In either case, as long as your contractions are relatively painless, you need no special techniques, just profound concentration.

Trust that you will find positions that help your body handle labor. Some women say getting in the bathtub, either in early or active labor, was great for a short while. If you try that, make sure both you and the tub are clean so that no bacteria will get in. Others recommend sitting backward on a chair under the shower, with a strong stream of warm water hitting the lower back. Some like walking about and pausing—with the knees soft, the hands on the partner's shoulders, against a wall, or on a tabletop for support—during a wave of smooth-muscle action. Some like kneeling, on all fours or with their arms resting in their partner's lap, on a couch, or on a chair, or on the backrest of the labor bed. Some lie on their side, supported with pillows, especially one or two between the legs, and some say that lowering themselves into a squat while holding on to their partner's hands or a doorknob for support relieved much of the back pain during the contractions.

Another remedy for back pain is counterpressure. This is usually best achieved by placing the palm of the hand against the area that hurts, often the very lower back. Hot or alternating hot and cold compresses can help too. Some American Indians used to place a heated rock against the back of a kneeling woman; this provided pressure and heat at the same time, while the kneeling position allowed uterus and baby to fall forward, causing less pressure on the aching ligaments of the back. In early labor it is best to move about a bit after a contraction: Stretch, rock the pelvis a few times, roll the shoulders, rotate the head, change

positions or walk a bit, and then rest to get ready for the next one. Muscles let go of lactic acid, one of the waste products from contracting, much better when they work a little than when they are completely passive.

If you are not hungry, don't eat; if you are hungry, eat something your body can digest quickly. In general fat is digested the slowest, protein is next, and complex carbohydrates leave the stomach quickest. Digestion seems to slow down as labor progresses, and you could become nauseated when the body is going through this drastic change. Athletes eat a lot of complex carbohydrates a few days before an important event, but they don't eat just before or during their performance; research shows that it would slow them down. The same may be true for labor. If you are not nauseated, you could have some tea or juice. Cold water is absorbed the quickest, and when taken in regular sips it will keep the body well hydrated without aggravating the secretion of stomach acids. Sugar impairs the ability of the stomach to absorb water.

Breathe with the contractions. Use the imagery familiar to you from practicing relaxation. As you inhale, let every cell in your body breathe. When you exhale, let the stale air and the tension flow out. Inhale and think of your body opening up to the air. Exhale and think of letting go. Inhale and envision the baby's head on the cervix, as the cervix stretches open. Exhale and picture the baby's head sliding a little farther down. Relax the buttocks, the thighs, and the muscles in between the legs and the lower abdomen. Let the body move with each breath. Allow your body to dictate the rate of breathing while you try to breathe in and out rhythmically (pain tends to make people hold their breath or exhale more than they inhale, and the latter can lead to hyperventilation). When a contraction is over, give a sigh of relief—one less to go. Women often say that simple thoughts—such as "One at a time," "Maybe the next one will be easier," or "Each contraction has a beginning, a middle, and an end"—helped them.

Special breathing techniques can come in handy when the contractions start to hurt. Pain, like anything that costs us great effort, causes us to hold our breath. But strong contractions need oxygen. They can also make regular breathing, the kind where the belly moves out when you inhale and relaxes when you exhale, more difficult, because during that kind of pain one wants to keep the belly warm and still. At this point, as you inhale, flare the ribs out and think of the shoulders lifting up slightly, then let them collapse as you exhale. Picture your diaphragm, the muscle that separates your chest from your abdomen and moves up and down as you breathe. The deeper you breathe, the farther it moves down and the farther your belly moves out. Take more shallow and faster breaths as the contraction gets stronger, then take slower and deeper breaths when it lets up. Give a sigh of relief when a strong and painful contraction is over.

If the contractions grow so strong they seem to take your breath away, switch to an even more shallow breathing. Open your mouth slightly, and relax your tongue, with the tip tucked behind the lower front teeth, in the floor of the mouth. Push the air out and let it rush back in, in a light, rhythmic, fast, and shallow way. Each exhalation should be barely audible and each inhalation silent but of equal duration. Try to let the incoming air travel over your moist tongue so that your throat will not get dry. Switch to this panting only when necessary, during a strong contraction, and resume slower and deeper breathing as soon as the contraction subsides (rapid superficial breathing expends more energy).

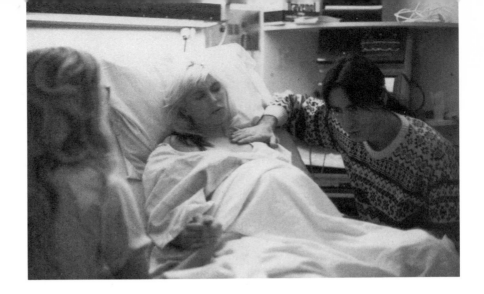

Once these strong contractions have begun, the first urge to push can occur at any time, especially if the baby has moved quite far down. To avoid giving in to this desire and bearing down, try blowing puffs of air out through relaxed lips. As you blow, imagine letting the baby stretch open the birth passage. Inhale as much as you exhale, and try to keep from holding your breath and bearing down forcefully. Some women combine panting and blowing by switching rhythmically from one to the other during these difficult contractions.

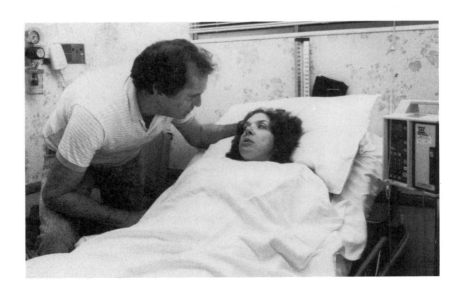

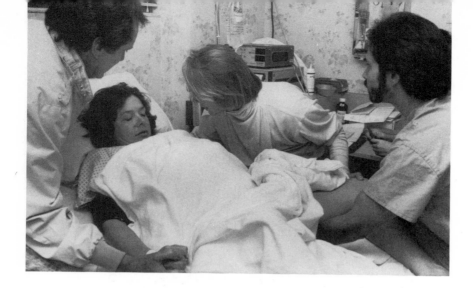

Trust that when your birth attendant says, "Go ahead and push," you will know how, but be aware that it may take a few contractions before you feel like doing it fully. The baby's head may feel really big when it comes down between your legs, but don't be afraid. Let your body stretch as you push the baby downward; the pregnancy hormones prepared your vagina for this. As you push, the muscles between the legs relax; that is why bearing down with an expulsion contraction often feels better than holding back. Once you discover that, you may want to push a little harder. Hold your breath and bring your chin toward your chest so that the abdominal muscles can contract better. Exchange the air as you need to; that way you won't hold your breath longer than ten seconds at a stretch, and you and your baby will continue to get enough oxygen. Push only when you have a contraction and rest in between.

There is no one best position for expulsion. A lot of women like sitting up with their back supported, knees pulled toward the chest, and legs open at the hips. From that position it is relatively easy to push yourself into a squat for a few pushes, then roll forward onto the knees. Kneeling can help the baby move down, and it relieves the pressure on the back. Squatting opens the pelvis more than most other positions, but staying in a squat for a long time tends to make the labia swell up. Sitting up with the back supported takes the least amount of energy, and that way the body can rest better between contractions. Each of these positions has an advantage of its own, and moving from one to the other is

184

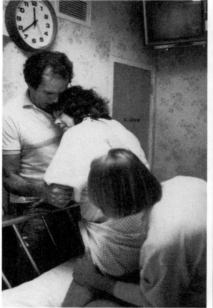
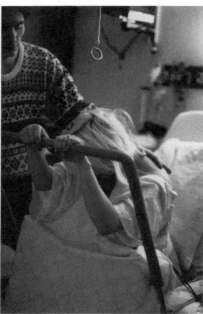

probably better than staying in the same one for long periods. This is perhaps why in old houses in Central European countries there is usually a hook in the ceiling above the middle of the marital bed. Women could fasten a rope to it and pull themselves up to get into these different positions. Modern labor beds often have squat bars you can use to pull and hold yourself up. If not, your partner and extra coach or the nurse can support you on each side.

If the baby has difficulty coming down, try to get out of bed and make a stepping motion, as if going up and down stairs. This is an old midwifery trick. The alternate lifting of the legs causes slight changes in the structure of the pelvis. If there is no progress after pushing in different upright positions, try pushing while flat on your back with your legs open at the hips, your knees as close to the chest as possible, your feet against the hands of the coach or birth attendant. Bring your chin to your chest, pull on your legs with your arms, and push against the hands that hold your feet. This position sometimes helps the baby negotiate the pubic bone.

Once the baby becomes visible, turning on the right side, upper body supported by pillows or in the lap of the coach, legs open at the hips, knees close to the chest, lessens the risk of too much sudden pressure and tearing. The idea of tearing such a sensitive part of the body easily arouses fear. But muscles tear all the time. Stretching them too much or making them work hard without first warming them causes many little tears, which repair themselves within days. And while the area in between the legs is very delicate, it is most sensitive from the vagina forward; tears usually occur closer to the rectum. In addition, improved surgical skills can re-pair any tear that cannot be completely left to nature.

Since a supple, well-nourished muscle stretches better than one not in optimal condition, a useful preparation would be to do pelvic floor contractions daily during pregnancy. Twenty-four to thirty-six repetitions should be ideal; too many might make the

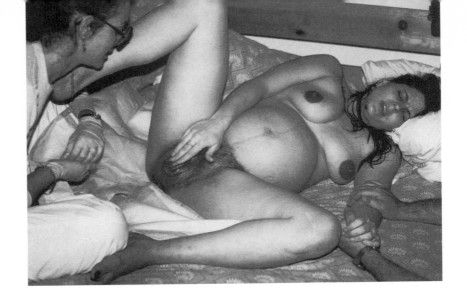

muscle overly tight. Also, a regular massage of the muscle and skin between the vagina and the rectum, the so-called perineum, might, by stimulating the circulation, improve the suppleness of the tissue. To massage yourself, place your thumb just inside the vagina and your index and middle fingers opposite your thumb on the skin outside. Massage in a semicircle and imagine stretching the fold of muscles and skin you are stroking. Avoid the area near the bladder opening. Some doctors advise their patients to place warm wet compresses on the perineum for about 10 minutes every night, starting about two weeks before the due date. Before you do this or the massage, wash your hands and the area in between the legs, especially around the rectum. Midwives say that a small tear heals better than an incision but midwives and doctors agree that when it becomes clear that the vagina cannot stretch enough, it is best to widen it with a small cut, called an episiotomy.

Birth attendants can usually tell when the contraction that will deliver the baby comes. They will ask the mother to listen for instructions. If you feel like it, bring your hand down to feel the baby's head while you wait for this last contraction. Push, release, and blow with relaxed lips when you hear the trusted voice of your birth attendant say, "Stop pushing—just blow. Let the head slide out; there it is. Hold it. Blow. Now give a little push for the shoulders." The next sound you hear may be your baby.

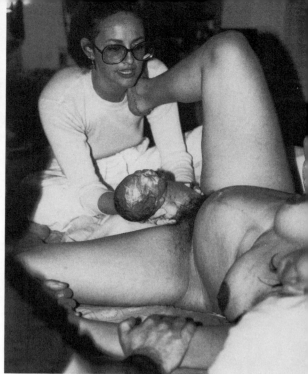

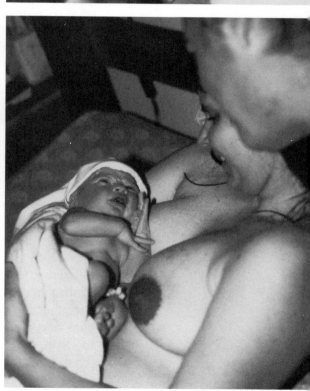

COACHING AND BEING COACHED

During active labor a woman may have two or three minutes to rest between contractions; then there will be a minute of pain, which will steadily increase before ebbing away. If she can relax in between, she will have more strength for the contractions, so first work on helping her get comfortable between contractions. Practice by taking care of her some evening when she is tired and her body aches. Use your voice in a suggestive, relaxing manner; stroke her in a way that you know makes her feel good; put pillows here and there; and encourage her to tell you what else she would like you to do or say.

If her back hurts, relaxing will be almost impossible. See if you can help her get rid of some of the pain. Have her lie on her back, legs supported by pillows. Kneel beside her and lift the leg closest to you, placing one hand under her bent knee and the other around her ankle. Make small circles with her leg, rotating it from the hip and supporting it carefully. Encourage her to relax the leg in your hands, to make it heavy, very heavy. When the rotations meet with no resistance, tell her to stay relaxed while you pull on the leg. Support it well, straighten the knee, and pull as you imagine lengthening the leg from the hips. Hold the pull for a few moments, release it, make a few more rotations, and position this leg so that the knee is bent and it is propped up by pillows. Move to her other side and repeat the procedure with the other leg. If her upper body feels tense too, you can rotate the arms in a similar fashion. Place the upper arm away from her body and, before you put the arm down, make one firm stroke from the top of her shoulder over her shoulder blade. This helps open up the chest. Next, have her turn on her side and support the top leg with pillows. Kneel behind her back and place the palm of one hand against her lower back, with the other hand on her hip to stabilize her; shift some of your weight into the hand that is against her back and rotate while you press inward. Don't let the hand leave the skin; just make small circles and try to relieve pressure and tension. Watch her closely and learn to see the difference between a somewhat tense and uncomfortable body and one that can relax and rest.

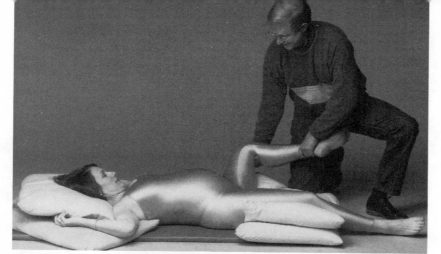

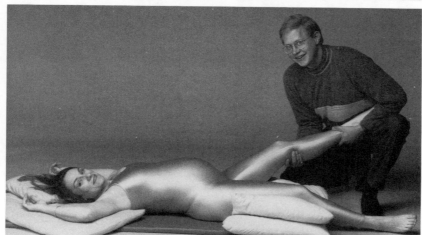

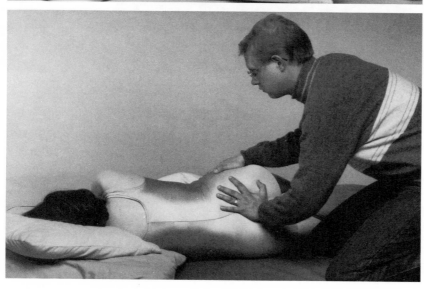

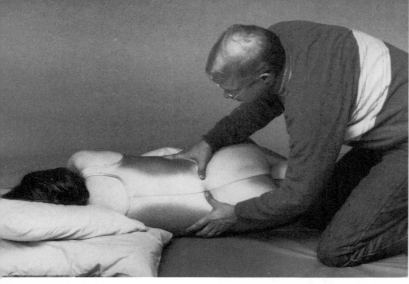

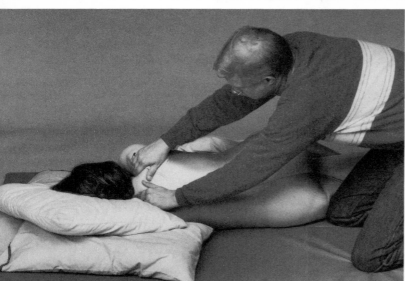

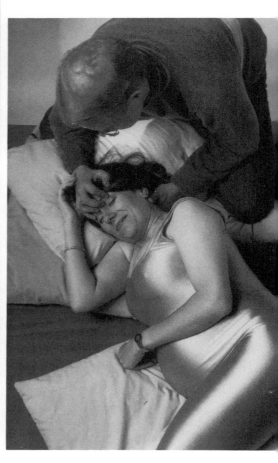

After a while, move both hands up and stroke the large muscles over her hips; rub the muscles along the spine, the top of the shoulders, and the neck; then place one hand on the bony ridge behind the eyebrows and the other at the bony ridge at the base of the skull. Gently press on both as if to bring the hands together. Maintain this pressure and say, "Turn your mind inward and watch your body move with each breath. Relax down your spine; relax the muscles around the bones that cradle the baby; relax your buttocks, your thighs, your knees, your calves, your ankles, your feet. Let yourself get very heavy."

Her trust in you as a coach will grow when your suggestions and your hands can make her feel so much better. Also, rubbing and kneading is, after active movement, the next most effective way to help clear out the lactic acid produced whenever muscles are used. During labor, when a woman has reached the point where she does not feel like moving about anymore, massaging her can help relieve the tension that comes with the accumulation of such metabolic waste. Some practice beforehand will help her accept your touching when pain has made her less willing to experiment.

When you touch her to help her relax, position yourself so you can work with the least amount of strain. Tension in you goes immediately into her. During labor, avoiding unnecessary strain is important for another reason: labor can be long, and you need to preserve your energy.

Touch can also be used to apply counterpressure at the lower back or to redirect the energy flow at specific points. The latter technique, called shiatsu in Japan and acupressure in China, is usually most effective when it is smoothly incorporated into one's overall style of coaching. Several pressure points are said to help women with labor. Three commonly mentioned ones are: at the lower back along the triangular bone called the sacrum (quite a few languages use a word meaning "holy" or "sacred" to name this bone), the area located four fingers above the inner ankle-bone, and the ball of the hands. Counterpressure applied with the

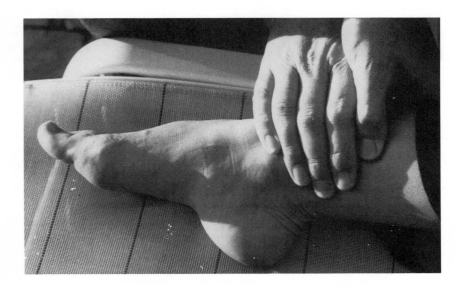

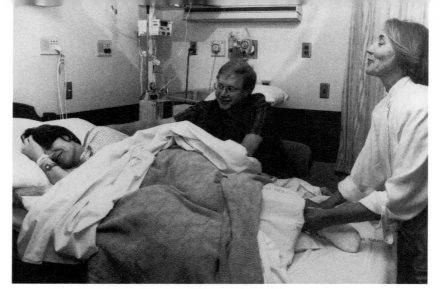

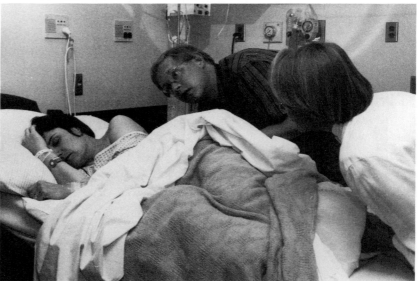

palm of the hand against the lower back will touch the points there. For those at the ankle, start by massaging the feet; then, when a contraction is felt, place your thumbs on the points above the ankles with steadily increasing pressure and suggest she relax the feet, the ankles, the calves, the knees, the thighs, all the way into the hips. The points in the ball of the hand are activated when the mother clutches someone or something. In Korea and Japan combs are made to fit the hand, and these are squeezed during labor.

Also take a look with her at the breathing techniques described in this book. Realize that when pain comes in waves, people tend to hold their breath or breathe irregularly. This makes it harder for the body to work properly. Slow deep breathing would be ideal during labor, but this seems impossible for many women at the peak of a strong contraction. Prolonged rapid breathing only speeds exhaustion. Thus, it is important that she learn to slow her breathing down once a contraction subsides. It may be easier to help her with her breathing by example than with words. When I help someone with a hard contraction, I often place my face close to hers, make eye contact, tune in to her tempo, and by my example try to lead her out of her turmoil. To be able to do this confidently you might want to practice breathing with her beforehand a few times. The breathing techniques work in much the same way as the gears on a bike as it mounts and descends a steep hill. As a contraction comes to its peak, the woman changes to more rapid breathing; when it recedes she slows her breathing down. Time a sixty-second period and watch your partner change pace—first faster, then slower—until she finishes with a deep breath. Next try breathing with her a few times to get a sense of her rhythm and to practice helping her slow down by your example during labor.

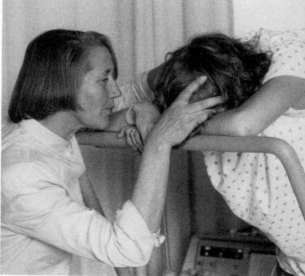

Be aware, too, of a tendency to exhale too much (hyperventilate) in response to pain. Signs of hyperventilation are a prickly feeling around the lips and then a tingling of the fingers; if improper breathing continues, the little finger and the thumb stiffen, and slowly all five fingers become spastic. Hyperventilation is especially likely when a woman is blowing in order to avoid pushing. If, in spite of your best efforts to help your partner regulate her breathing, she continues to exhale more, ask a nurse to help you. In pain or panic, one sometimes follows a voice of authority over a familiar one. If she mentions any of the hyperventilation symptoms, hold an open hand close to, but not quite over, her mouth to help her retain a proper level of carbon dioxide.

Don't expect any magic from the breathing techniques. If they help, it is because the two of you make them work. Don't fall into the trap of saying "Use your breathing" should she cry out and lose control. Instead, acknowledge her pain—compassion is essential when you want a person in pain to listen to you—and then try to help her continue to breathe, either by example or through tactful suggestion. Breath is the string that ties us to life, and a woman in labor is breathing for two.

It is normal for dilatation to hurt. Any sensation, including pressure and stretching, changes into pain when it reaches a certain intensity. Labor has been painful for women across the world and throughout time. Women can cope with it relatively well if their labor is not too long; if they feel loved, respected, and safe; and if those who care for them give acknowledgment and perspective. Try to reassure your partner by telling her, "I know you are hurting, but you are doing very well. Don't let the pain scare you. You will probably have the baby soon. This contraction is about half over. Relax your buttocks; relax your thighs; keep breathing. This one is almost over." To a woman in the throes of labor, soothing words spoken with sincerity and compassion are like an analgesic. They don't take the pain away, but they make it more bearable, because pain makes us lose perspective. No matter how well prepared and how willing to work with the pain one is, it is common to think that it hurts more than it should and to wonder if it is never going to end. Also, no matter how good one is at relaxing, in the middle of a strong contraction it is almost impossible. Yet, the ability of the cervix to dilate improves with relaxation of the surrounding

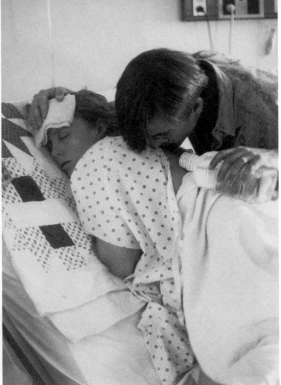

muscles. Hearing how much longer a contraction is likely to last, and being reminded to relax particular muscles, increases the chance that one can control some of the flight reaction with which we defend ourselves against pain. Try helping your partner visualize that the baby's head is pressing against the circular opening in the cervix. Think of what you can say to help her bear the pain. Encourage her to tell you after a contraction which of your suggestions are most helpful. Don't worry about repeating yourself. You don't need to be original; you need to be relevant, to the point, and sincere.

Ideally, with your voice and suggestions you help your partner accept rather than fight the pain. This is comparable to an altered state or hypnosis. Some people naturally have a hypnotic effect on others, and some have a talent for being hypnotized. During labor, tactful but simple instructions and eye contact tend to work best. Do realize, when you practice, that it is easier to help your partner relax and reach a special state when she is not in labor than when you are both tired from hours of contractions. Be willing to change tactics if it becomes clear that what seemed so helpful beforehand does not work during labor.

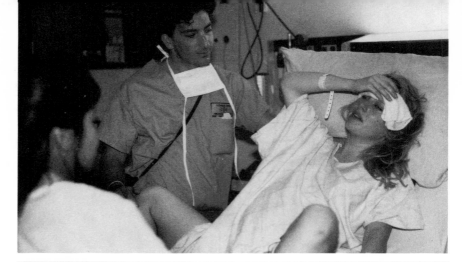

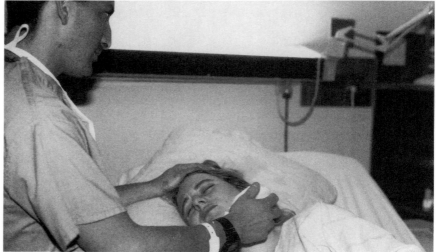

Between contractions offer her ice chips, a wet washcloth, lip balm—not by asking if she would like them but by giving them to her. If she does not want something, she will push your hand away or say no. This takes less energy than having to consider a choice. Try to make her so comfortable that she can actually doze off during these brief rest periods.

Toward the end of the dilatation stage, when the cervix is about seven centimeters open and the urge to bear down makes itself felt, it helps to say something such as: "This is the hardest part; you're almost there. Try not to push, but don't worry if your body makes you push. Just don't hold your breath and don't push forcefully." Breathing with her to make sure she inhales as much as she blows out can help too.

Not every woman gets the urge to push before the cervix is fully dilated. If the baby stays relatively high, there will be no rectal pressure until the baby is brought down by the mother's expulsive efforts.

Don't let her start specific pushing techniques until the birth attendant has given the go-ahead. At that point some women need four or five contractions before they can bear down well with each contraction. There is no rush, unless for reasons of health it is important to get the baby out fast. Some babies never need the mother's all-out expulsive efforts; the force of the uterine contractions alone pushes them through the passage. Some need her to push just a little. But when the fit in the pelvis is snug, the mother's ability to bear down can enable her to avoid a cesarean section. Thorough understanding of how to push can also condition a woman to do it even though a pain reliever may have taken away her ability to feel the bearing-down reflex.

You can best help your partner if you yourself know how to push. Pretend for a few minutes that you have to do the pushing. Recline against her legs or a couch. Open your legs at the hips, place your hands on your knees, and bring your knees as close to your chest as you can. Inhale, hold the air in, bring your chin toward your chest, bend your elbows up, and move your shoulders forward and down. Push as if your life depends on how well you do it. You

know how from emptying your bowels. Relax while you think about the following: The baby will come down when there is pressure on it, and when the pressure ceases it will slide back up a little. Thus, steady continuous pressure will help a baby advance farther in one contraction than intermittent intense pushes. Holding one's breath with the chin close to the chest places the abdominal muscles at the position of greatest strength and makes for the strongest push. But mother and baby need a fairly regular air exchange. Thus, she needs to inhale, hold her breath and push, exhale without letting the abdominal muscles relax, inhale, and hold the breath while continuing to push. An expulsion contraction usually lasts about sixty seconds, so during one contraction she will exchange air three or four times. Since pushing is less strong during such an exchange, it is best to exhale quickly, then take air in through the mouth rather than the nose. Try all this yourself before you practice it with her. Notice that you can push even harder when you pull on something with your arms. Now help her try.

Have her lie on her back (if this makes her dizzy, place a pillow under her right hip), pull your chair close so that she can put her legs on your knees and her hands on your ankles, and place one open hand on her lower abdomen, right above the pubic bone. Ask her to push downward. Notice that this makes her belly rise

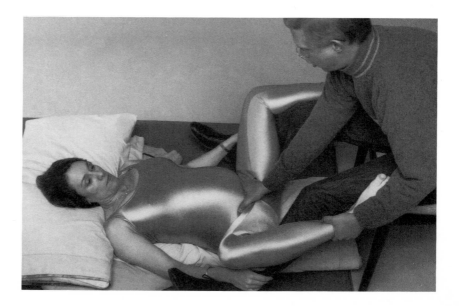

up and move down a bit and causes the muscles under your hand to harden. Let her rest a moment. Ask her to take a breath, hold it in, push downward, keep the abdominal muscles tight, exhale, inhale, and bear down again. Practice until she can hold the muscles under your hand tight while she exchanges the air. She should not push hard, just enough so that you can feel and see it.

Now pretend that she is experiencing an expulsion contraction. Let her inhale and exhale once—the so-called cleansing breath, which allows the contraction to pick up momentum. Next, have her inhale while she brings her chin toward her chest, pushes downward, and pulls on your legs with her hands. Count to ten while she holds her breath, then have her exhale and inhale quickly, count to ten, exhale and inhale quickly, release, take a deep breath, and rest.

During labor the nurse and your doctor will help. They will probably hold your partner's legs so that you can support her head and, when a contraction is over, wipe her forehead, give her ice chips, rub her shoulders, etc.

If the two of you are not sure whether she knows how to push, don't have her push hard or try over and over. Instead, suggest that at her next check-up she ask her health-care provider to examine her pushing and reassure or correct her. The pushing techniques are the same no matter what position they are used in. I

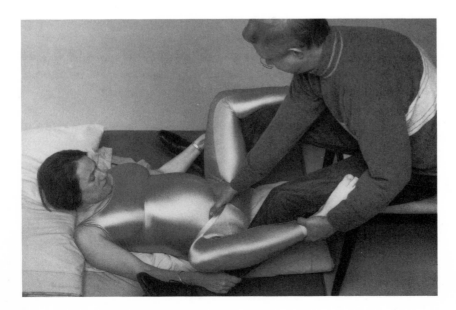

have seen babies slide out while the mother squatted, kneeled, lay on her back, rested on her side, or sat up straight.

While it helps to practice and think things through before labor, there is no evidence that a *lot* of practice is necessary. Training is most successful when the conditions are close to the reality, but no one can bring on a few real contractions just to practice.

MORE ABOUT PAIN
AND WAYS TO RELIEVE IT

Socrates, imprisoned for his teachings, rubbed his aching ankles after the chains were removed and mused that pleasure and pain, though opposites and never present at the same instant, seem to be related: "Their bodies are two but they are joined by a single head. And I cannot help thinking that if Aesop had remembered them, he would have made a fable about God trying to reconcile their strife, and how, when he could not, he fastened their heads together; and this is the reason why when one comes the other follows: as I know by my own experience now, when after the pain in my leg which was caused by the chain pleasure appears to succeed."

Similarly, many people believe that the pain of labor adds to a mother's delight in holding her new infant. Our human need to make that which we cannot change more bearable or acceptable may well account for this and many other ideas about labor's pain: According to the Old Testament, it is God's punishment to Eve; nineteenth-century obstetricians who opposed the use of ether in childbirth considered the pain a desirable and conservative manifestation of the life force. The Gros Ventres Indians of Montana believed that crying out in pain might drive the child back into the womb and that twisting and turning might entangle it in its cord. And Dr. Grantley Dick-Read, the originator of Natural Childbirth, wrote that over 95 percent of women in normal labor neither demanded nor desired to use "the gas" or trilene apparatus.

Yet efforts to relieve the pain are as old as ideas to make it acceptable. Theophrastus, a pupil of Aristotle, noted that dittany "is a plant especially useful for labor in women. People say it makes labor easy or stops pain altogether." Before the discovery of ether in 1844 and its successful application to childbirth by Professor James Young Simpson in Edinburgh (during the prolonged and painful labor of a young woman whose first baby had been stillborn), people used alcohol, opium, coca leaves, and marijuana as well as nondrug remedies such as acupuncture, acupressure, and hypnosis. Opium was finally recognized as dangerous, and the others were only partially or occasionally effective. Ether and other techniques of inhalation anesthesia had their drawbacks too. Epidural anesthesia is the first remedy that is almost always safe and effective. It has no effect on the mother's consciousness, and it can remove the pain once labor is well established. Without pain many women are ecstatic when they can touch their baby and admire its perfection. Instead of losing out, they get pleasure twice: first when the pain is gone and then when their baby is born. As to its effect on the baby, pediatricians say that they cannot tell by checking a baby's reflexes at birth whether the mother did or did not have an epidural. Traces of the local anesthetic are found in the baby's blood, because the immature liver has a hard time breaking it down. Some studies show that there might be more neonatal jaundice in babies whose mothers used an epidural, and some breast-feeding experts claim that it might affect babies' readiness to suckle at first, but even if those claims are true, these are not serious problems, they do not occur frequently, and they can be remedied.

Some physicians, proud of this relatively new invention (epidurals have been given to women in labor for a little over twenty years), wonder why every woman would not want to use the epidural. Women state a variety of reasons: "I want to try to do it myself; women have always done it, and I see no reason why I should not." "I want to experience as much of it as I can." "I have been so careful all through my pregnancy with what I ate, and I took no drugs, not even aspirin. I would prefer not to take any medications just when my baby has to make so many adjustments and might be under some stress." "I'm more afraid of the epidural than I am of labor. After all, labor is a natural process."

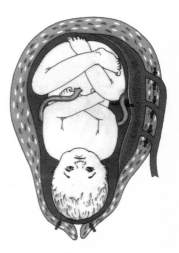

For a baby each active labor contraction may well feel like a full body squeeze, during which breathing stops or slows down. The resulting stress alerts the baby's system to the big change of birth.

The stress can be harmful if the birth passage is narrow, causing strong and prolonged pressure on the head; if the placenta does not open up to good blood flow between contractions; if the umbilical cord gets compressed because it is wrapped around the baby or is coiled between the baby and the cervix; if labor is prolonged and exhausting, thus altering the mother's energy metabolism; or if baby or mother approaches labor with a health problem. Thus, every baby and mother needs to be watched to make sure both can handle the natural process of parturition. In a healthy mother and baby, if the pain is such that the mother can handle it without a lot of anxiety and tension, it is best if she does. If the pain becomes too great, and the mother feels worn out and her body is tense, the by-products of her pain can become more stressful for the baby than the drugs that would give her relief.

Physicians must learn to understand and respect a woman's desire to do what she can for herself. I see three reasons why so few doctors do. The science of obstetrics emerged at the same time as its more admired sister, physics. When Newton described the forces that regulated planetary motion, doctors tried to put those that govern birth in similarly abstract and seemingly scientific terms. Thus obstetrical textbooks talked, and still talk, about a passage, a passenger, and a force. In this scheme, the mother as a complex individual whose state of mind will affect the force remains somewhat overlooked. Second, labor can be devastatingly hard. When it is, self-help techniques, or folk medicine, do not accomplish very much. What do work are the measures of scientific medicine. Doctors have devoted years of their life to studying what they can do for people when they cannot help themselves. Respect for self-help techniques is a strange thing to ask of a science that flourishes because these techniques so often are not sufficient. And, finally, the problem of using powerful drugs and equipment before they are needed permeates our culture, and medicine is no exception. In agriculture this tendency has created pesticide-resistant insects, ruined soils, and contaminated groundwater; in obstetrics it contributes to the increase in cesarean sections and to disrespect for the feelings of many expectant parents, especially the mother.

Pregnancy hormones may well activate an otherwise latent desire to experience birth. Even women who clearly understand that they must have a cesarean section can have a hard time with the decision. The labor and delivery nurses at one large and sophisticated hospital still talk about a time when the anesthesiologists were on strike and women in labor could not have epidurals. After their babies were born, quite a few new mothers said they were grateful that they had been forced to cope with their labors. There was something very fulfilling about the experience.

If you and your coach believe that our technology is generally smarter than nature and wish to remove as many hardships as possible from labor and birth, make sure that your birth attendant shares that view, and discuss with him/her what kind of pain relief will be available and at what point you can count on it. If you feel, as increasingly many do, that the time-tested processes of nature should be helped along only when necessary and would like to try labor without pain relief, talk with your birth attendant about your desire to have his support before he/she offers you drugs.

Coaching a woman is hard, especially when she is giving birth to your child. Fathers often feel they can do so little—if only they could take the pain of a few contractions for their wives! For a woman in labor, it is great to have a compassionate, strong, and admiring mate at her side. For an expectant father, it is very touching to see his wife do her best to give birth. Don't be afraid of pushing each other too far. If you approach the experience with the understanding that you have a hard and unpredictable task to accomplish, you will both recognize the point where you have done enough. Help from your doctor, be it drugs for pain or something else, will then add to rather than take away from your experience.

Which drug and manner of administration are best depends on the circumstances of one's labor, including what kind of expertise is available. Only an anesthesiologist can administer an epidural; that is why a birth center or a small hospital often does not offer this form of pain relief. For labor one does not choose one's anesthesiologist but uses whoever is on call. Large hospitals usually have a department of obstetrical anesthesia, and such experts are best at administering the epidural so that it relieves the pain without completely numbing the legs or causing headaches afterward. If you have had a back problem or suffer from a lot of allergies, it might be wise to call the department of anesthesia to see if an examination before labor is recommended.

What kind of pain relief to use and when is usually decided on

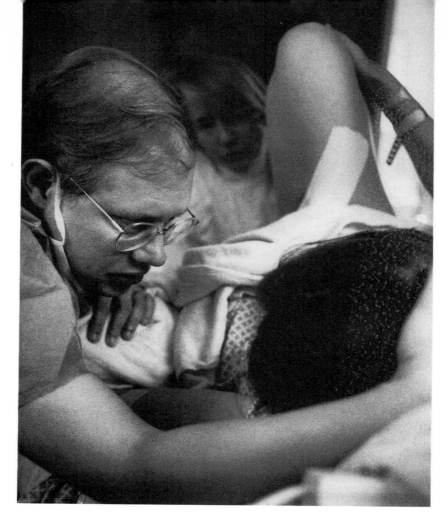

by you, the labor and delivery nurse, and your birth attendant. The doctor cannot give any drug or undertake any procedure without first adequately explaining how they work and receiving your and your birth attendant's approval. Doctors usually schedule an extra-long visit sometime toward the middle of the third trimester to discuss in detail which drugs will be available and how they are used. This might be a good visit for the coach to attend. Use this opportunity to ask questions. Natural-childbirth advocates sometimes make it seem that administering drugs during labor can cause learning problems in the baby. Most of the mothers of today's baby-boomers used many more drugs during their labor than will be available to you, and there did not seem to be an increase in learning disabilities among them. Neurotoxins such as lead and pesticides are much more likely to cause such problems than drugs carefully administered during labor.

After Professor Simpson introduced inhalation anesthesia during childbirth at the end of the nineteenth century, there followed a debate on the merits of its use. Clergymen insisted that if God had wanted labor to be painless, He would have made it so; Dr. Simpson responded by asking, "Should the fact that God gave us legs keep us from using a carriage?" Queen Victoria finally settled the issue when she decided to use the new method for the birth of Prince Leopold. Since then, many different drugs and a variety of techniques of application have been tried. After the epidural, which, by the way, can be used for a cesarean section too, the most popular form of pain relief for the dilatation stage is a morphine derivative injected intramuscularly or into a vein. For the expulsion stage, the preferred choices are a local anesthetic for the pudendal nerve, which supplies the area around the vagina with sensations; a pudendal block; or a local injected into the area between vagina and rectum to block the pain from an episiotomy and its repair. A spinal or a general anesthetic is generally reserved for emergencies or for specific situations, such as when there is no one available with the skill to administer an epidural.

Women's responses to pain-relieving drugs are another proof of the individuality of human chemistry. Some labors stop; others progress faster; some women push better; others need to let the epidural wear off and feel the urge before they can bring the baby down. Some women become nauseated when they use a morphine derivative to help them relax, while others feel so much better, their first question is "When can I have more?" Usually doctors prefer not to use drugs until labor is well established. Thus, self-help techniques remain important—first, to get to the point where drugs can be used; second, to help out when the use of drugs must be temporarily postponed; and, third, to give those whose bodies labor well a chance to do the job themselves.

I don't know why acupuncture and hypnosis, two drugless remedies that seem especially promising when combined, have not been tried more seriously. Acupuncture appears to be more effective in China, its country of origin, than here. It is not known why this is so; the difference may be dietary, a matter of belief systems, or genetic in origin. Perhaps it is all three. In China, major surgery, including cesarean sections, is frequently performed using acupuncture for pain relief. People recover faster, because they have no drugs in their system to slow them down. If you live in an urban area and this ancient form of pain relief and healing interests you, check if there is a pain-control clinic near you and call to see if they know someone who can do acupuncture for labor. If so, ask your birth attendant if it is acceptable that you invite this acupuncturist to attend your labor.

Both acupuncture and hypnosis suffer from the fact that it is difficult to separate the quacks from the competent practitioners. I had the privilege of being hypnotized a few times by the world-famous hypnotherapist Milton H. Erickson, M.D. From that experience I learned to trust the power of an altered state. However, since then I have tried many other hypnotherapists and never underwent anything close to what I experienced with Milton Erickson. If you are interested in trying hypnosis, your greatest challenge may well be finding a good hypnotherapist. Dr. Erickson, together with his pupil Ernest L. Rossi, Ph.D., has published numerous insightful books on the subject. There are many therapists who have been trained in Erickson's techniques, but the effectiveness of Dr. Erickson's treatment, like that of any good therapist, seemed to be more than a matter of technique.

Coping with Labor and Birth

THE ONSET AND
THE PROGRESS OF LABOR

Over the last twenty years—in the most unexpected locations, including the opera, the grocery store, and at parties—many people have told me about their labors. More often than not they end their account by saying, "So, you see, it was nothing like you said

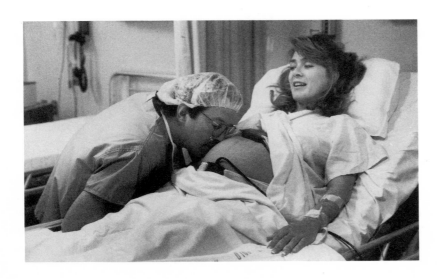

it would be. I was well prepared, but it started out differently from how I thought it would." Be prepared for that fact. Think of birth preparation as one of those treasure-hunting maps of old, the kind that noted landmarks by which to recognize the terrain, without removing the sense of adventure. Look for change during those last weeks of pregnancy: The baby may lower itself into the birth passage, the cervix may soften, contractions may become more frequent, the preoccupation with pregnancy may change to one with labor, and there may be a sudden urge to get the nest ready. Some women clean; some shop; others cook and freeze food. Sleeplessness usually increases, and especially at four in the morning this often causes anxieties about whether one has begun labor. During such a period, time the contractions that keep you awake by writing down the start and finish time of each. When the contractions begin to last longer, the time in between them grows shorter, and they feel stronger, it may be labor. If it is, other changes will follow: The gradually opening cervix will release the mucus that for nine months closed it off. This mucus rarely comes out as a plug; usually women describe a thick, pink, thready discharge.

Apart from contractions, which, if they feel like indigestion, may get ignored for a while, there may be a general feeling of malaise or change, similar to the onset of a flu. Some women complain of a steady lower-back ache with peaks of intensity—those peaks are contractions felt in the back. Some report fluid loss; the bladder sometimes keeps filling so rapidly that it is necessary to stay put on the toilet. Some experience diarrhea or a few loose bowel movements, and in some the sac that contains the amniotic fluid ruptures—"my water broke," women say. At this stage a leak in the sac surrounding the baby is natural. In fact, a break in this water bag is sometimes the first sign that the baby is on the way, and it can be a while before contractions catch up. How much water will escape depends on the size and location of the rupture. If there is a small tear way up high, the fluid will gradually seep out, and many women mistakenly believe that a strain on the bladder caused the slight wetness. When more fluid continues to seep out and does not smell like urine, women realize that they may have a so-called high leak. If the rupture is near the cervix, a cup or so of water may spill out at once. This can happen anytime, including during the night (which is why many women place a large flannelized-rubber sheet on their mattress toward the end of the last trimester).

When you call your midwife or doctor, undoubtedly you will be asked, "How far apart are the contractions?" This is the average time from the start of one contraction to the start of the next one. If they are still quite irregular, be sure to say so. The next questions are likely to be "How long do they last?" (the average time from the beginning to the end of a contraction) and "How strong are they?" To get an answer to the last question doctors sometimes wait on the phone until the woman gets another contraction; then they listen to how she responds. If she can continue to talk, they assume that it is still early. Unfortunately, if you choose a hospital birth, no professionally trained person will come to your residence to sit with you until it is time to leave or to help you decide when that time has come. Since early dilatation usually takes place at home, you may find yourself worrying about having the baby in the car if you stay home any longer. Call your health-care provider whenever you feel anxious and ask. Keep in mind that generally, as long as contractions are on the average five minutes apart, there is no risk of having the baby suddenly. The one exception is when the contractions are longer than sixty seconds each and very, very strong. Occasionally a woman will have her baby without ever experiencing contractions that come close together, but to do the work of opening the cervix, such contractions usually have to be very strong.

SIGNS AND SYMPTOMS OF PROBLEMS

The information that follows should serve to reassure you that labor is progressing safely for both mother and baby, and in the event of a difficulty, to help you to cooperate fully with the medical staff.

When contractions occur regularly and last on the average a minute, whether they dilate the cervix or not, they have the potential of hurting the baby. Therefore, all babies should be monitored for a while in early labor. This can be done at home with a stetho-

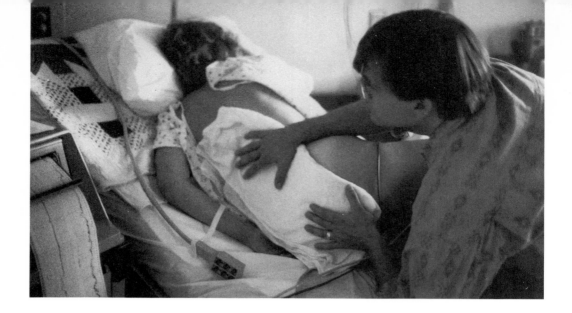

scope or in the hospital with a modern fetal-monitoring machine. In the case of a home birth, during early labor the midwife should be summoned to monitor the baby's heart and the mother's blood pressure. If both are fine, the midwife may leave for a while. When the contractions become much more intense or the membranes rupture, the baby should be checked again. If you have chosen to give birth in a hospital, the monitoring can be done there or at your doctor's office, and if all is well and labor is still mild, it might be fine to go home for a while.

If at any time during labor there is a sudden drop in the baby's heart rate, the nurse or midwife will ask the mother to change positions. If turning on the side does not bring the heart rate back up, the mother might be asked to get on her hands and knees with her buttocks held higher than her shoulders (the knee-chest position), and midwife or nurse might give the mother oxygen in an effort to get some to the baby. If signs of distress continue, the doctor will suggest more accurately monitoring the baby by placing a tiny spiral-tipped electrode in the skin. If this internal monitor also shows a reduced heart rate, the doctor may wish to take some blood from the baby and look at its oxygen/carbon dioxide ratio. If such fetal scalp sampling indicates that the baby is not getting enough oxygen, it may be necessary to perform a cesarean section.

Try not to get too worried at the first evidence of some fetal distress. It is often temporary, with unknown causes and no negative effect. Nurses who regularly monitor high-risk mothers who

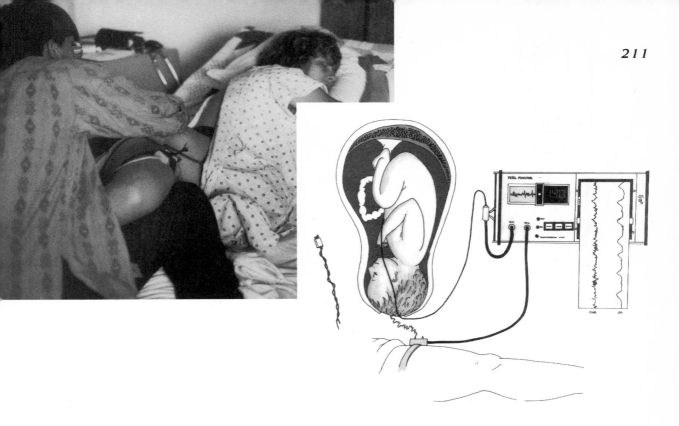

have been put on bed rest, say that even *without labor* some babies show sudden drops in the heart rate, and without treatment the heart returns to normal. Also, babies can withstand reduced oxygenation for a while; as long as steps are taken to treat the problem, the baby will most likely be fine. A drop in the baby's heart rate is quite common at the start of the expulsion stage. It is often the baby's response to the increased pressure on its head.

When the membranes rupture, try to ascertain whether your baby has dropped. If a baby has not entered its mother's pelvis when the sac breaks, the cord can slide along with the water and form a loop next to the baby's head (known as cord prolapse). There it might become pinched with each contraction. Call your birth attendant if you are not sure about your baby's position.

Very occasionally there is a long enough loop in the cord for it to slip all the way out; in this case it will appear, silvery and throbbing, at the vaginal opening. To keep the baby from blocking its own lifeline, the mother must get into the knee-chest position immediately. After calling the doctor, wash your hands and slide one hand inside the vagina and up along the cord until you feel the baby's head. Gently hold the head away from the cord. If this

The irregularity shown in the fetal heartrate (FHR) graph is a sign of vitality. The uterine activity (UA) graph shows contractions that last a minute with a minute to a minute and a half in between (these are called contractions about two minutes apart, and contractions in such rapid succession are considered very active labor). The probe floating next to the baby measures the strength of the contractions. It is used less often than the spiral-tipped electrode that measures the baby's heart rate. The latter is secured with a band placed around the mother's thigh.

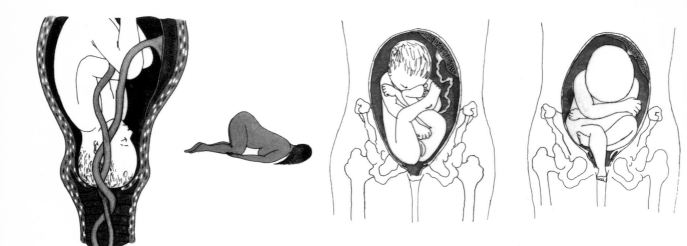

happens at home, an ambulance will take the mother to the hospital in this position, and there the baby will be lifted out of its precarious spot with a cesarean section. If it happens in the hospital, she will be taken into the operating room in this position.

Once a baby has dropped, it usually will not back out of the pelvic entrance. As long as a baby has not dropped, it can still turn. Thus, one that was head down at the last doctor's visit could turn its buttocks down, placing its feet just above the cervix. If the membranes rupture after a few centimeters of dilatation, a foot can slip out (foot prolapse). Don't push it back in or pull on it. Call your doctor and discuss how to get to the hospital. Ask if you should get into the knee-chest position. When a foot prolapses there is increased risk for cord prolapse too. Because of that, a so-called footling breech is usually delivered by cesarean section.

The amniotic fluid that escapes once the membranes have ruptured should be clear. It is okay if it contains little specks of white —those are bits of vernix caseosa, the greasy substance on a newborn's skin—but green fluid is a sign that the baby released some meconium, the accumulation of glandular material in its lower bowel. This can be a sign of distress. The baby's heart should be listened to as soon as possible, and at birth its air passage should be suctioned out carefully. Some doctors try to get some of the meconium out before the baby takes its first breath. In that case, during the expulsion contraction that will lead to the birth, the mother is asked to push the head out, then stop even though the shoulders are pressing to be delivered, and while the mother blows to keep from pushing, the doctor suctions the baby.

Once the membranes rupture or labor begins, someone should

keep an eye on the mother's temperature. At home, take her temperature every two hours or so, and report any rise of 0.5 degrees or more to your health-care provider. Dehydration can cause fever, so if a prolonged early labor phase occurs at home, the mother should be encouraged to take sips of cold water regularly. Cold water is absorbed by the membranes on the way to the stomach and thus produces less nausea and less gastric juice secretion. This is important because in an emergency the quickest way to provide pain relief is with general anesthesia, and the greatest danger of drug-induced sleep is that acidic secretions of the stomach can get into the lungs if the unconscious person starts to vomit. This is why many large labor and delivery departments allow the mother to ingest nothing but ice chips or the water she can suck out of a wet washcloth.

An infection will produce a fever too. Wash your hands well at the onset of labor and whenever you touch the inside of your nose or mouth. Be especially cautious once the membranes have ruptured; bacteria can get into the uterus and cause an infection in the baby. Nothing should enter the vagina. Keep the area between the legs clean by washing regularly with a clean cloth, stroking away from the vaginal opening to avoid bringing bacteria to this passage. Warmth and moisture provide ideal conditions for microorganisms. Wear a sanitary napkin only when up and about. While resting, catch the fluid with a pad or towel placed under the buttocks, and open the legs to allow for a free flow of air.

Some doctors feel that labor should be brought on if it does not start spontaneously within twelve hours after the membranes rupture. An induced labor is harder to handle than a naturally occurring one, perhaps because the contractions start out strong and so there is no time to get slowly accustomed to them. Also, women say, the contractions do not build, peak, and subside, but remain intense throughout their duration. When the membranes rupture in a woman whose cervix was ready to dilate, such induced labor stands a good chance of succeeding, but if the cervix is still long and firm, induction often fails to bring about dilatation, and a cesarean section results. For that reason some doctors prefer to wait until the mother's cervix ripens and her body starts labor naturally. Sometimes doctors try to speed the ripening of the cervix by applying a hormonal cream called prostaglandin. Which of these approaches is best depends on the mother's and the baby's health, the condition of the cervix, and the mother's preference, in that order.

Abdominal pain should wax and wane with the contractions. Back pain may stay strong between contractions, but powerful and constant pain in the abdomen can be a sign that the placenta is detaching. Mother and baby should be examined as soon as possible. Usually labor can proceed, but sometimes a cesarean section is necessary.

While some spotting is normal when the cervix begins to open up, bleeding is not—that is, a little bit of mucus mixed with blood is perfectly okay, but bright red blood in an amount that soaks a sanitary napkin or towel is not. This might mean that the placenta lies partially over the cervix, blocking the baby's exit. Call your health-care provider and go immediately to the hospital. Now a surgical exit through the abdomen is the baby's only road to life, and it is the safest way for the mother too.

If a woman complains of a throbbing headache or of dots floating in front of her eyes, and especially if her face looks swollen, call the doctor. These are symptoms of preeclampsia. For reasons unknown, perfectly healthy women sometimes experience this pregnancy complication near the due date or during labor. High blood pressure is a sign of preeclampsia too, but blood pressure can also go up when one is frightened. And once blood pressure is up, one is more easily agitated, which may cause a further rise. If the nurse at the hospital says, "Her blood pressure is high," try using relaxation techniques. Keep the room quiet, turn off the overhead lights, make the bed comfortable, and suggest that your partner turn on her left side to facilitate her blood circulation. As for the expectant mother, do not keep your fears inside. If you hear two professionals talking outside your room and you think it is about you, ask them what they discussed or tell them to hold their conversation elsewhere. Careful monitoring of mother and baby is essential when any of the signs of preeclampsia are present. Sometimes medication to relax the mother or to lower her blood pressure helps. Under the informed consent law, nothing can be administered to a patient without an explanation of what it is and what side effects it can have. Some nurses do this very well; others just confuse one more. Do not be embarrassed to ask for a clarification if something is not clear to you; anxiety will only make you feel worse. Preeclampsia, too, can make delivery by cesarean section necessary.

Remember that problems are exceptions. And while any of the complications described above can lead to a cesarean section, they are not the most frequent reasons for this now common operation. Most operative deliveries result from something called "failure to progress." This means that labor did not make sufficient progress in spite of hours of good contractions.

If you are planning a home birth, one of the above symptoms could necessitate a change in plans. Do not feel embarrassed if you discover that you cannot handle the pain, especially if your labor is long. Our ability to cope with pain seems to decrease the longer pain lasts. Also, a long labor increases the chance of bleeding after the delivery of the placenta. Thus, a labor that does not progress is a valid reason for transfer to a hospital.

HOSPITAL STAFF AND PROCEDURES

While it may feel like a disturbance to leave home, it can be rather nice to be surrounded by professionals and their equipment and to know that all their knowledge and experience is available at a moment's notice. Take with you whatever might make you more comfortable: bottled drinking water, an ionized-water spray, lip balm, mouthwash, a lotion with a relaxing smell, socks to keep your feet warm, comfortable slippers for when you walk around, a bathrobe to put over your hospital gown, your own favorite pillow (put it in a colorful pillowcase so that it won't get mixed up with the hospital pillows), some snacks for your coach, paper and pencil if you wish to keep a record of important events, a hot-water bottle to put against your back, some flowers or a plant to cheer up the room, and anything else that will help you feel surrounded with love and·life. Leave valuables, including jewelry, at home. Separate from the bag with articles for labor, pack a small suitcase for your·stay after the baby is born. Take what you would need for a weekend away, and if you are planning to nurse, be sure to choose gowns or shirts that open in the front or big T-shirts that you can lift up to expose your breasts. Leave this suitcase in the car during your labor; your coach can bring it to you after the baby is born. Unnecessary possessions can get in the way or be lost.

When you prepare this suitcase, preferably a few weeks before your due date, give some thought to what you and your baby might want to wear for the trip home. In general, a loose-fitting dress will be most comfortable for you, and for the baby a simple, comfortable outfit with a receiving blanket and an outer blanket is easier than a garment you will need to change when you get home.

It is fair for you to expect that during this phenomenal process the people in the labor and delivery department will tend to your needs with a sense of love and respect. If someone does not, be it nurse, resident, or intern, you can ask for the person in charge and explain that you need a different personality or someone with a better attitude. It is not necessary to work with someone you don't like, so don't let that worry add to your anxiety about the hospital.

The sounds of other women in labor can be quite disturbing. Try to see yourself and all the others as actors in a play. They have their parts; you have yours. Even though you have an effect on each other's performance, all you need do is play your own part as

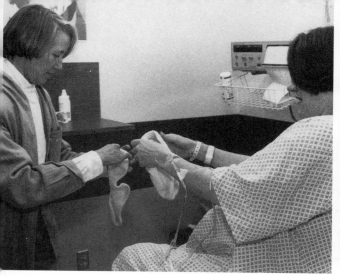
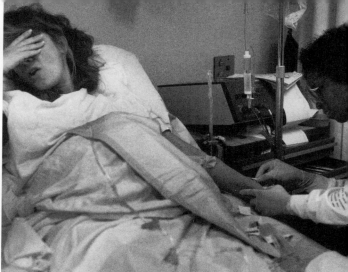

well as you can. As a coach, when you hear someone down the hall cry out in pain, don't hope your partner did not hear it. You might reassure her by saying, "Don't let that scare you. We don't know anything about her. If your labor gets too hard for you, you can get medication to help you." Statements that bring fear into the open are much more helpful than efforts to hush it up.

After about six to eight hours of hard labor (contractions past three centimeters dilatation), fatigue and/or dehydration can set in. Intravenous fluids can be helpful at this point, but they needn't be immobilizing. You should still be able to move around, stretch your legs, and get up to use the bathroom. Extra fluids do make the bladder fill up faster, and a full bladder makes labor more painful. If you find it too difficult to go to the bathroom, ask for a bedpan or just empty the bladder on the disposable pad placed under the buttocks to catch the amniotic fluid. The nurse will be happy to replace the pad and wash you off. Such a cleanup needs to be done regularly anyway; it cuts down on bacterial growth and makes you feel better. A sac that stays intact past five centimeters dilatation is usually ruptured by the birth attendant to speed up labor. There are no nerves in the membranes; it is a simple procedure, performed during a pelvic exam.

During a long labor, the intravenous may also be used to give the mother a drug to relax or to administer an epidural, and the longer labor lasts, the greater the chances that one or the other will be needed. When a relaxing drug is given through the intravenous, its effect is immediately seen and the dose adjusted accordingly. If it is injected into a muscle, the mother does not respond until about twenty minutes later, and since reaction to drugs is very individual, what was given might not be enough or might prove more than was necessary. Don't expect this type of drug to take the pain away. It is meant to help you relax and doze off between contractions so that you can cope better when a contraction comes. During a contraction your coach should help you focus on your breathing, because the drug may make concentrating a little more difficult.

It is safer to administer an epidural when the mother has been given some extra fluids first, because such a large part of the body becomes artificially relaxed that the blood pressure can drop— something the baby does not like at all—and the best way to prevent such a drop is by increasing the mother's circulating fluid. Thus, anesthesiologists usually give an epidural only after an intravenous is in place and the mother is well hydrated.

To receive the epidural, the mother lies on her side with her knees flexed toward her chest and her back rounded outward. A local anesthetic is given first, so the procedure is not painful. However, the position is uncomfortable during the next one or two contractions. After that, the epidural begins to take effect and the pain gradually subsides. It is not uncommon for women to get the shakes once their body relaxes. These get less or go away once the body becomes used to the drug and to the fact that the pain has left.

Administration of the epidural, and the relief once it takes effect

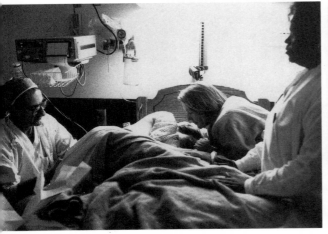
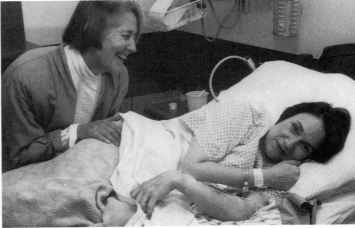

Sometimes an epidural stops the contractions. In this case, medication can be given to bring them on again. However, that medication—Pitocin, a synthetic form of the hormone the body secretes to make contractions—carries some risks for the baby, and careful monitoring of its heart rate becomes essential. Instead of listening with a receptor on the outside of the belly, doctors often prefer to attach a spiral-tipped electrode to the baby's skin to get a more accurate reading.

While an epidural sometimes stops contractions, in just as many or more women the relaxation it brings allows for quicker dilatation. Some women enter the expulsion stage within minutes after administration. If you should find yourself at the hospital on the night of a full moon—a guaranteed busy night, nurses say—or if you for any reason have to share your birth attendant and nurse with someone else, press the bell to call them as soon as you notice any of the signs that the dilatation stage is ending and the expulsion stage about to begin. These include rectal pressure, the appearance of some bright red blood at the vagina (when the cervix fully opens, a tiny blood vessel may rupture), a change in the pattern of the contractions (they usually occur further apart and are shorter), and a change in your mood. Some women suddenly feel that they can't go on any longer; others emerge from the very irritable state that often marks the last few centimeters of the dilatation stage. But the surest sign is an irrepressible urge to push.

The work of expulsion is very different from that of dilatation, and so are the accompanying physiology and psychology. Threats, doubts, insecurities, and fears can slow or stop dilatation, but they seem to speed expulsion. I often hear of women who were suddenly able to deliver after their doctors threatened to use forceps, or of those who were so frightened by a drop in their baby's heart rate that they forgot how tired they were and pushed the baby out in one contraction.

Even if you and your doctor agree that you will give birth in a delivery room, you will probably stay in the labor room until the baby's head remains visible between contractions. At that point, you will be moved, bed and all. Doctors who like to use a delivery room usually prefer the complete setup: a delivery table with stirrups and drapes for the mother; gown, gloves, mask, and cap for

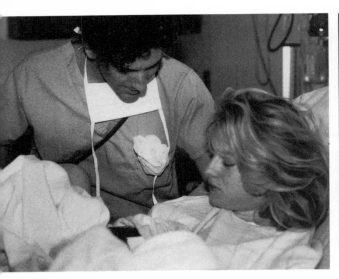

the doctor; and scrub suit, cap, mask, and protective boots for the coach.

Once in the delivery room, sometimes the mother can stay in the birthing bed. If not, the move from the bed onto the delivery table is usually easy. The table need not be uncomfortable. You can ask for a thin pillow to place under your back, and you can give the nurses feedback on how far apart and how high the stirrups should be for your comfort. Don't worry about losing the effect of gravity by lying flat on your back; it is unimportant now that the baby is already down. The coach's place is next to or behind the mother. Both can usually see the birth in a mirror hung for that purpose from the ceiling. Be prepared for this; it can be quite disconcerting to see your body from this angle, with a little bit of the baby's head showing at the vaginal opening. Realize that you see only part of the head; the part you can't see is what's making the area around your vagina bulge out. The skin on your baby's head can be of any hue from pink to purple; it may be loose and wrinkled, because the still-movable skull bones often get pressed together to fit through the birth passage, and it may have specks of blood on it from the cervix. Watching the head emerge is a most astonishing sight, comparable to watching the sun rise for the first time.

The doctor will sometimes invite the father to cut the umbilical cord. There are no nerves in the cord, so it does not hurt anyone. If the act of severing this physical tie to the mother does not attract you, don't feel embarrassed to say "No, thanks."

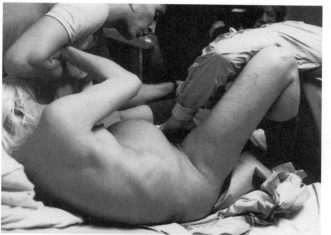

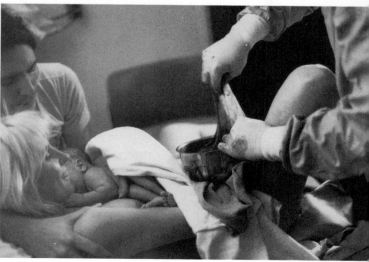

One reason why combined labor-delivery-recovery rooms became popular so quickly is that they allow the mother to stay in the room and the bed that have become familiar; they also make for a more relaxed setting after the baby is born. The atmosphere and structure of an old-fashioned delivery room are such that everyone feels like getting out as soon as the birth is over. It is harder to wait for the placenta and harder to enjoy the baby there. In a birthing bed or a regular bed, the woman can also move a little and perhaps sit up. Such movement sometimes helps the placenta detach. An eminent Dutch professor of obstetrics, Dr. G. J. Kloosterman, taught me that women should get into a squat if the placenta is slow in coming loose. Midwives used to recommend that; they would also try to make the mother sneeze. Today, in the rare event of a placenta that does not detach on its own, doctors reach in and remove it manually. The mother's pain is relieved during this procedure with an epidural or a general anesthetic. Some doctors like to check carefully inside the uterus to make sure the placenta came out intact, since even a very small piece left behind can cause bleeding a few days later. Such an examination is painful too, but it is usually over so quickly that anesthesia is not needed. Shortly after the delivery of the placenta, the doctor will say, "I am going to check you. Breathe; relax. It's done."

The birth attendant also checks the cervix, the lining of the vagina, and the area around the vagina for tears. If an episiotomy was performed or if there is a tear that requires more than one stitch, a bit of local anesthetic may be injected to numb the area. The repair is done with fine material that dissolves as the tissue heals, so the stitches do not need to be removed.

Close supervision of mother and baby is necessary for another couple of hours, even if all three stages of labor went smoothly, to make sure the uterus continues to contract and closes the blood vessels that once went to the placenta. Preferably this takes place in a room where mother and baby can get cleaned up and take a nap together. Sometimes the mother goes to a recovery room and the baby to a so-called stabilization nursery. The father feels torn in such a situation, worrying over who he should be with. The baby often wins out, in part because the mother would rather be alone than have her baby left by itself with strangers. If all is well, try to get reunited as soon as possible.

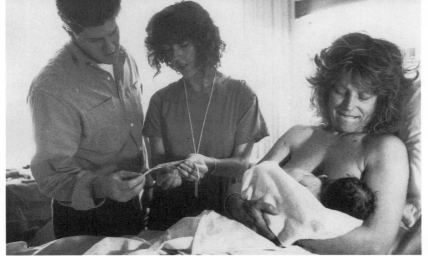

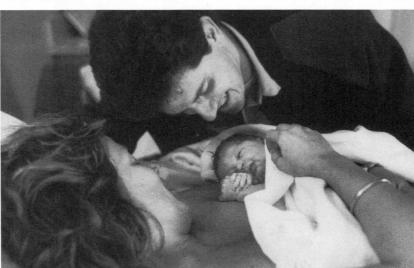

Before a baby leaves its mother's side, baby and mother each receive a wristband with an identical number. These numbers should be checked every time the baby is returned to its mother. For further identification nurses often take the baby's footprints.

ABOUT FORCEPS AND CESAREAN SECTIONS

The first humane solution to difficult birthing was tongs that could grasp the baby's head without harming it; doctors used them to turn the head to a better position or to pull the baby past a tight spot in the birth passage. Next came a suction cup that could be fastened to the baby's head to perform the same kind of manipulation. A few hundred years later, doctors learned how to open the mother's abdomen, lift the baby out, and close the window without serious consequences for mother or child. This operation, called cesarean section after an old Roman law (Lex Cesare) requiring that a baby be removed from its mother's body to be buried separately if the woman died, has become increasingly safe and common in the last twenty years. When the pelvis is truly tight, pulling the baby through is harder on both mother and baby than lifting it out. Thus, cesareans have come to replace forceps. Forceps and the vacuum extractor are still used to adjust a baby's head if it turns face up or to correct some other slight problem that impedes its passage. They are also tried when there is hope that a slight pull will bring a baby past a tight spot. But when delivery requires more than the mother's pushing, the application of some pressure to the uterus, and a bit of traction, a cesarean is probably a better choice. Thus it happens occasionally that a woman dilates, pushes, receives help with forceps or the vacuum extractor, and still ends up with a cesarean section.

For a time it was believed that all babies who were in a breech position would be more safely delivered through the abdomen. Lately some doctors have been returning to the practice of giving a woman with a breech baby a carefully monitored try at labor.

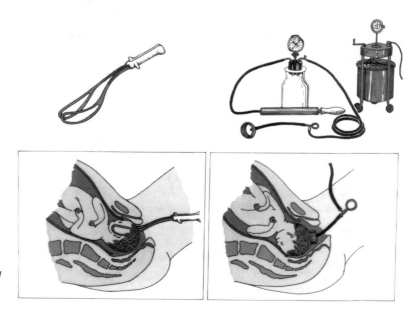

When the baby faces up, the mother often finds bearing down painful and in spite of excellent pushing, descent can be slow. Turning the baby's head may save mother and baby hours of hard labor.

Doctors have also revived an old technique called external version. If the baby is still in a breech position around two weeks before the due date, the chances that it will turn headfirst on its own are quite small. In this case, the mother may make an appointment in the labor and delivery department of a well-equipped hospital, where she will be given a muscle relaxant, and her doctor will massage her belly, using increasingly firm strokes, to try to nudge the baby into turning. The baby is watched on the ultrasound screen and its heart rate monitored, and if it shows any signs of discomfort, the procedure is stopped. Many babies can be turned, and they often stay in the head-down position. Some obstetricians advise women with breech babies to lie on a slanted board, with the head lower than the buttocks twice a day for about twenty minutes. The board should be at an angle of about 30 degrees, and your stomach should be empty. Once on the board, breathe slowly and deeply. Expand the abdomen and the rib cage, then the shoulders, as you inhale; let all tension flow out when you exhale. Picture the baby, its buttocks down, its head under your ribs, and think of it turning. Relax the muscles of your trunk as much as you can so that the baby has as much space as possible. I do know women whose babies turned with this method. Of course, we will never know whether they would have turned anyway.

If your baby is breech because the placenta is attached to the upper part of the uterus, it will probably stay in a breech position, because it fits better that way. Try not to get too frantic about wanting it to turn. Relax and be grateful for modern medicine—if need be you can have a cesarean section.

The head-down position is safer for the baby during birth because the head is the largest part and the malleable skull, whose bones are still movable, is ideally adapted for fitting through the birth passage in the process of coming down. When the buttocks are first, no such molding of the head takes place, and this can lead to difficulty delivering the head, especially if the baby is a little larger than expected or the birth passage is smaller. Recognizing the subtle signs of a discrepancy in size between mother and baby is a fine skill, acquired through years of training and practice. Many young doctors lack such training. If your doctor does not feel comfortable allowing you to try labor, do not pressure him/her. What is safe in the hands of one may not be safe in the hands of another, and respect between doctor and patient has to go both ways.

It has been known since ancient times that babies born in a breech position show more neurological problems than babies born headfirst. It was assumed that trauma received during delivery was responsible. It is now believed that this is not always the case. Some babies may stay in the breech position because they already have a problem. Birth can be traumatic, but it is not the sole cause of trouble for newborns. Genetic disorders and hardships such as toxins, drugs, or malnutrition during pregnancy are perhaps more frequent contributors than birth traumas.

This is a harsh reality for everyone. As long as we harbor the misconception that all imperfections are due to mismanagement of labor, we will have unnecessarily restrictive procedures and more cesarean sections than necessary. And while cesareans save lives, if they are done unnecessarily, they increase the risks for mother and baby, prolong the mother's recovery, and can lead to endometriosis (a disease of the uterine lining) or the formation of scar tissue in the mother later. That is why you and your doctor must be willing to try to let labor do its natural work.

Emotionally, women seem more able to accept the need for a surgical delivery after they have labored for a while and seen for themselves that they need help. Labor usually thins the lower segment of the uterus, making for less blood loss during surgery and better healing afterward. A bit of labor may be better for the baby too, because the changes brought on by labor prepare it further for beginning life on the outside. But this is not always possible. A mother with diabetes or high blood pressure may not be able to wait. If the mother has an outbreak of herpes, waiting may endanger the baby more than performing a scheduled cesarean before there is a chance of labor. In the case of a footling breech, going into labor may risk prolapse of the cord. A scheduled cesarean section also offers this advantage: You, the staff, and the room are already prepared, and this makes for a smoother procedure.

Of all the operations I·have seen (I was an operating-room nurse for eight years), a cesarean section is the most inspiring to watch. The moment when the doctor opens the uterus and lifts out the baby's head is different from but just as dramatic as the moment when the head appears at the vagina. Where possible, doctors give the mother an epidural or a spinal so that she can be awake and participate in the birth. Such anesthesia does relieve the pain completely, but the mother should expect to feel some pressure, especially just before the doctor lifts the baby out. Fathers and coaches are usually allowed to be present, and sometimes the mothers ask that the drape in front of them be lowered so that they too can see the baby right away. It is customary to have a pediatrician in the operating room to attend to the baby. This is because the obstetrician will be too busy closing the uterus, the muscles, and the skin, and the baby needs to be suctioned and checked. When that is done, it can be brought to the mother. If her hands were tied at the start of the surgery so that the anesthesiologist could take her blood pressure and regulate the intravenous, they can be loosened now so that she can hold her baby.

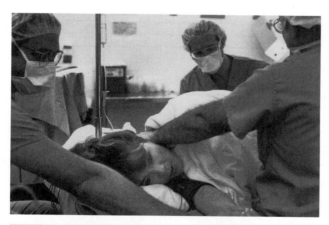

Administration of the epidural

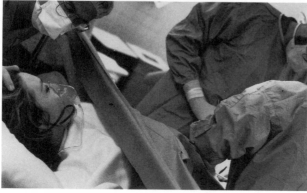

The set-up for a cesarean section with lowered drapes

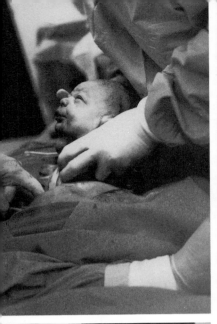
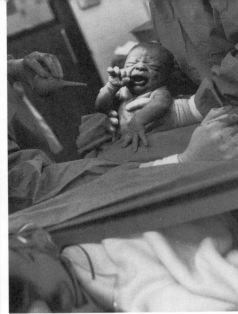
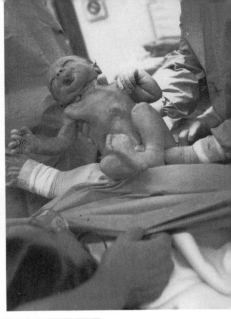
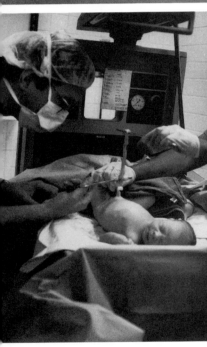
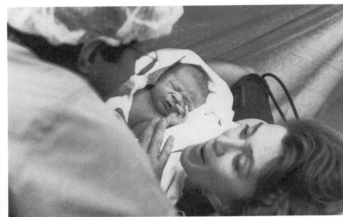
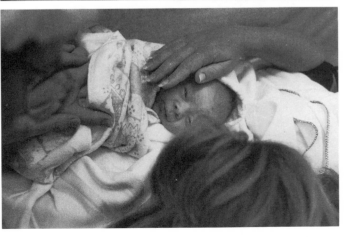

Shield your baby's eyes from the light and talk with it as if you were alone together. As a father, if you had hoped to give your baby a relaxing bath right after its birth, ask if you may do so in the operating room.

The operation usually lasts less than an hour. Most of that time is spent preparing the mother and closing the wound. The delivery of the baby generally takes no more than ten minutes. Once the placenta is detached, it is common for the mother to get the shakes, just as with a vaginal birth. Sometimes the anesthesiologist offers a bit of a relaxant. Take it if you feel that it will help you, but if you feel okay, you are better off without it. Anesthesiologists also often put a bit of morphine in the epidural. This cuts down tremendously on postoperative pain. Mothers given this pain relief often sit up and nurse in the recovery room within half an hour after the operation. There is a special beauty to realizing that your baby is alive and well because of the integrity of nature and the power of one of her great achievements, the human mind.

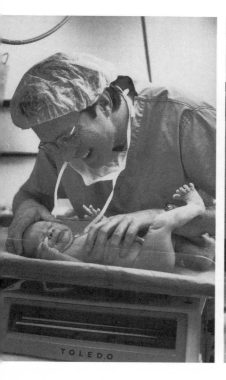
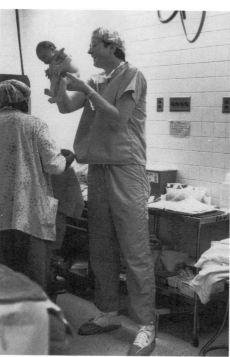
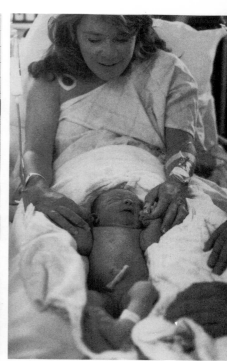

EMERGENCY CHILDBIRTH

While some babies are slow and or may need help negotiating the birth passage, others traverse it unusually fast. They surprise their parents at the side of the road or in their bedroom or bathroom. Fortunately, a birth this easy rarely poses a problem. Also, quick and easy births are not common. However, if one should happen to you you will feel less panicked by knowing what to do when all goes well and by having learned what to do in the rare event of a swift birth with a complication.

If sensations that you ascribed to the flu or to a spoiled dinner suddenly change into an overwhelming urge to bear down, look between your legs. If the vagina is still closed, and the area between the vagina and the rectum does not bulge out, notify your birth attendant immediately and discuss whether or not you have time to get to the hospital. If you do leave, drive safely or ask for a police car to help you through traffic. If you can see the baby's head, leave only if the hospital is less than five minutes away. It is easier to have the baby at home than in the car. Call your birth attendant for guidance and support.

No matter where you are, if the baby comes, don't try to keep it from coming by closing your legs and don't try to push it back in. Don't push hard to get it out either. Try to let the uterus do it while you blow, just as you practiced. Because the baby will be wet and slippery and may emerge with some force, don't rely on your or your partner's ability to catch it. Instead, position yourself so that, should it come flying out, it will not fall. Lie on the floor, on a bed, or on the car seat, if possible somewhat on your left side to ensure good circulation and the least amount of stress on the muscles around the vagina, and lift the top leg to make room for the baby. Babies born easily are usually expulsed within one contraction. Keep the buttocks relaxed, and blow. The head is the largest; the shoulders will pass more easily; once they are out, the hard part is over, and the baby slides or shoots out. With it will probably come quite a bit of water. Sometimes it is pink, because a corner of the placenta may have detached and spilled a bit of blood into the water.

If one of you—the birthing mother, the father, or a friend—can place your hands under the baby's arms and guide it toward the

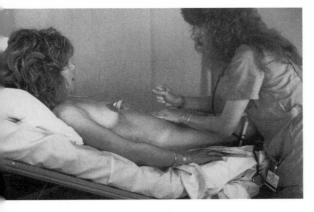

mother's abdomen, fine. If not, lift it immediately out of the puddle of water that came with the shoulders and place it on the mother's abdomen. Dry it off and cover it with something to keep it warm. The mother's bare belly is the natural place for a newborn. Breathing movements and rumblings are probably familiar, and the belly radiates warmth. Leave the cord intact and the baby on the belly until the placenta slides out, even if it takes forty minutes or more. Once the placenta is out, you can move the baby up to the chest, where it will enjoy some contact with the nipples. Catch the placenta in a basin or a towel and keep it close to the baby until a professional with sterile equipment arrives to clamp and cut the cord.

Some bleeding after the placenta comes out is normal. If there is a steady flow of blood, stimulate the nipples, preferably by sucking them. This makes the uterus contract and will cut down on the bleeding. If it continues, massage the uterus by kneading the lower abdomen, pressing toward the backbone rather than toward the vagina.

The only time you should cut the cord when birth takes place without professional help is if the baby is entangled in it. After the head has emerged, if it is around the neck, you may see what appears to be a silvery, shiny necklace. Take this necklace with the fingers of both hands. Pull on it to see if a loop large enough to slip over the baby's head can be made. If so, the baby is free. If

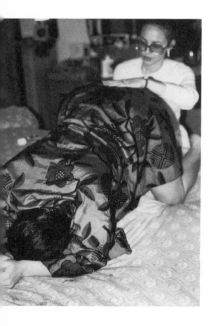

not, the cord is holding it back from being born. Sever it with whatever is available, if necessary the teeth. The cord has no nerves, so severing it does not hurt mother or child. Once the baby is born, its side of the cord should be clamped or tied as soon as possible; otherwise the baby will lose blood. Do this at the very end of the cord, away from the baby, and if you have nothing but your fingers, just hold it firmly doubled up between index finger and thumb. When professional help arrives, someone with sterile equipment can clamp it and cut it close to the navel.

If the head comes out and the shoulders do not follow, check around the neck for the cord, and if this is what is holding the baby back, sever it. If no cord can be felt, wait for the next contraction. These two or three minutes can seem like an eternity, especially if the baby's face is somewhat purple and motionless, which is normal but can be frightening to the inexperienced. If the next contraction fails to deliver the shoulders, the top shoulder may be stuck behind the pubic bone. The mother should push herself up into a squat, then roll forward on her hands and knees. Wait one contraction, and if this change in position fails to dislodge the shoulder and deliver the baby, slide an index finger into the vagina, toward the back of the baby's bottom shoulder, and hook it under the arm. Rotate toward the baby's face with a gentle outward pull. This will turn the shoulders to an oblique angle and release the top one from behind the pubic bone.

If the baby appears buttocks first, get in the knee-chest position and blow to keep from pushing until trained help arrives. A baby in the breech position often needs help with the delivery of its head. If the baby is coming no matter what, open your legs, push your upper body up, and let your baby slide out. If the head does not come, give a good push, then, if necessary, another one. If the baby's back is toward its mother's pubic bone and the belly faces her rectum, you can help by placing one hand on the baby's back and one on its chest. Slide three fingers of the hand on the chest into the back of the vagina, over the baby's face. Slip the middle finger into the baby's mouth, and place the outer two fingers on its cheekbones. Visualize that you are helping the baby keep its chin on its chest so that its head will fit better through the exit. Do not pull; just hold the baby in proper alignment. Have the mother press inward with one hand above the pubic bone while she pushes. If the body is positioned differently or if this simple

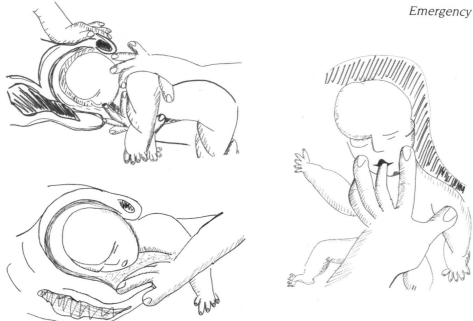

maneuver does not release the head, place your fingers near the baby's mouth and hold the vagina open to give the baby a little breathing hole. Keep the vagina open so that the baby can breathe, cover its body to keep it warm, and wait until professional help arrives.

No matter where or how it is delivered, a newborn baby must be kept warm, must be protected from harmful microorganisms, and must start breathing. Preventing a drop in body temperature is the most immediate of these needs; problems that arise from not breathing are magnified when the baby cools off. Even if the baby comes out purple, or white and unresponsive, first lift it out of its puddle of amniotic fluid, placing one hand under its buttocks and the other under its head and shoulders, and put it on its mother's belly. Dry it off and cover it with something soft and clean if possible; otherwise, use your sweater or jacket. Babies lose a lot of heat through their head, so if you have one handy, put on a soft wool cap; if not, cover the scalp with whatever you have that can do the job—a sock for instance.

A baby's color at birth is not as important as its color five minutes later. To assess the well-being of a baby after it is born, you try to determine how quickly it is progressing toward becoming a pink, kicking, responsive baby. A newborn need not cry, but crying right after birth sounds great (perhaps the only time it sounds that way), because it proves without a doubt that the baby is breathing.

If the baby does not start to breathe, turn it on its right side and place a folded handkerchief or a bunch of Kleenex under its shoulder—the right side is easier on the heart, and the slight stretch at the neck will prevent its tongue from obstructing the air passage. Gently suck, with your mouth or with a suction bulb, first at the baby's nose, then at its mouth. If you use a suction bulb, make sure that the tip does not touch the lining of the baby's nostril or cheek. Stimulate the baby by rubbing gently along its spine with your fingertips. Watch carefully for movement and for improvement in color. If this does not occur, give the baby mouth-to-mouth breathing. Place your mouth over the baby's nose and mouth. Make the breaths small—just the amount of air that comes when you puff up your cheeks—and measure one count in, one count out. Continue for about fifteen breaths. Then pause to

see if the baby has started breathing on its own. If not, continue mouth-to-nose-and-mouth breathing, pausing every minute or so for a few seconds to see if the baby has begun on its own, until help arrives.

Statistically, it is very unlikely that you will give birth to your baby away from professional help. And if you do, you almost certainly will not need any special techniques. Only 0.5 percent of babies have trouble with the shoulder against the pubic bone; only 4 or 5 percent of babies are breech, and most of those are detected before labor starts. So try not to dwell unnecessarily on the information in this section. See it in the same light as earthquake training: You learn what to do and then you store the information in case you might need it someday, but you hardly ever think about it.

GIVE WORDS TO FEAR AND SORROW

As you read this chapter with your child stirring inside you, you are probably thinking "I wish I had never read all this," and a moment later you find yourself poring over certain sections again. It is difficult information to digest. It helps explain why cultures without medical technology practiced rites such as the one on Sumatra, where, after seven months, the parents of a pregnant daughter would place a specially woven cloth around her shoulders during a family ceremony, uttering the words "We now present this garment, which is the enrichment of the soul force of our daughter. It brings coolness; it strengthens the stability of the soul; it is a garment in which sons and daughters may be carried by her." If you lived in such a setting, it would be much better not to mention the possibility of problems. Without remedies it is better not to know. But in a modern setting, it is dangerous to suggest that nature always knows best and working on inner strength is enough. It could set you up against medicine rather than prepare you to make graceful use of whatever you need to have a healthy baby and a good experience. When you reread this

Ceremonial cloth, ragi hidup (or long life), from Tarutung, North Sumatra

chapter, try to see the knowledge it gives you as the modern equivalent of the ceremonial birth cloth. Let it enhance your "soul force."

Talk about your fears, including the almost unmentionable one —that there could be something wrong with your baby. Fears have a much more negative effect when they are repressed. It is the same with sorrow. And in spite of all our tests, all our knowledge, and all our planning, sometimes babies do not live, or if they live, they are not always perfect. The feelings of a parent for a child go deep, beyond one's own existence. Don't ask "Why me?" but "What can I learn?" If used that way, sorrow, though still painful, makes one wiser and deeper.

A POEM TO EASE BIRTH

Once you have looked at birth and its still-unpredictable nature and, from that perspective, reevaluated the choices you have made with regard to your health care, allow yourself again to visualize the birth process, with thoughts that it will go well and that your baby will be healthy. As you can see from the ancient, anonymous Aztec "Poem to Ease Birth," women of all cultures and through the ages have practiced the art of positive thinking and visualizing what they wished:

In the house with the
tortoise chair
she will give birth to the
pearl
to the beautiful feather
in the house of the goddess
who sits on a tortoise
she will give birth to
the necklace of pearls
to the beautiful feathers we are

There she sits on the tortoise
swelling to give us birth
on your way on your way
child be on your way to
me here
you whom I made new
come here child come be
pearl
be beautiful feather

Ceramic effigy, Calima zone, Colombia, 100 B.C.–400 A.D.

THOSE VERY LAST DAYS

Gestation lasts, according to global observations, between thirty-seven and forty-two weeks. Anything in that range is normal. Only 10 percent of women give birth on their due date; 40 percent deliver between three days before and three days after. The other 50 percent will feel either that the baby came early or that labor is overdue.

Try to avoid focusing too much on the date your doctor gives you. Tell your family and friends a later rather than an earlier date, to avoid being asked, "Have you had it yet?" Don't cancel everything to sit and wait as soon as your doctor says, "Any time now; your cervix is getting ripe, and the baby has dropped." And don't take it as a certitude if your birth attendant, after examining you, says, "It is going to be another two weeks." You could go into labor that night.

If there are no indications that your or your baby's health is in jeopardy, try not to give in to the temptation to have labor induced. I know it is hard to leave the timetable up to nature, especially when you are quite uncomfortable and anxious to get labor over with and to hold your baby. If your cervix is effaced and somewhat dilated and you and your doctor are quite sure that your due date is correct, your doctor might try to bring labor on by "stripping the membranes." During a pelvic exam the care provider runs a finger around the cervix, gently separating cervix and sac. Some bleeding and cramping result, and sometimes the cramps change into labor contractions. The risk is that the sac can rupture, and early rupture of the membranes increases the risk of infection. Induction with Pitocin is often unsuccessful, especially with a first baby, and ends with a cesarean section. It also increases chances for jaundice in the newborn, which can cause problems with nursing.

If you go past the due date, your pregnancy health-care provider will want to keep a closer eye on both of you and schedule an ultrasound to make sure the fluid is not diminishing, and a non-stress test (listening to the baby's heart while the baby moves) to make sure the placenta is still an adequate nutrient provider, lung, and organ of excretion. Some doctors say that such an examination is especially important for first-time mothers past the age of thirty-five, because some of the intricate and complex mechanisms by which labor starts may be a little rusty, and the changes in the placenta that normally contribute to the onset of labor might not have the same result. Ask your doctor again to teach you how to watch your baby's movement patterns and to indicate what kind of changes would warrant a check.

Don't worry too much about the size of your baby. In spite of all medical knowledge and technology, neither the exact dimensions of the mother's birth passage, nor the exact weight of the baby is predictable. Estimates of both are often 20 percent off. Thus, if your doctor says, "Your baby is big, probaby nine to ten pounds, and I don't think you can deliver it," the baby could turn out to be only eight pounds, and your birth passage could be wider than estimated. The true test of the mother/baby fit is labor, especially with a first baby. Even though ripening of the cervix and the baby's dropping into the pelvic inlet are great indications that everything is proceeding well, the absence of either is not a sure sign that the birth process will not work. Induction before the baby has dropped, especially with a first pregnancy or if the first baby was born by cesarean section, is very often unsuccessful. Waiting it out means that the baby will grow bigger, but probably not that much. During those last days, babies often slow down the process of fat storage that made the mother's belly grow so fast for a while. Increase in size is one aspect of growth; the other is neurological maturation. Also, when labor starts naturally, the cervix is more ready to stretch open, and the baby is better prepared for the transition it has to make. True, a big baby can be hard to deliver, especially since in babies weighing over nine pounds the shoulders are larger than the head. But the decision to deliver it by cesarean can be made if labor does not progress. If you have doubts, consult with a reputable physician, such as the head of the department of maternal fetal medicine of a local hospital.

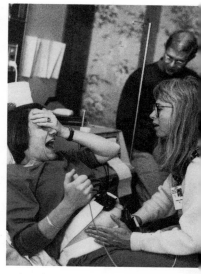

A loud noise, in this case an alarm held against the mother's belly, startles the baby into moving vigorously. The nurse will check for corresponding changes in the baby's heart rate to determine whether it is or is not under stress.

It is very hard for a doctor not to offer you help when he/she sees that you are anxious and uncomfortable. The emphasis in medical school and obstetric training is on what to do, not on how to sit back and wait. If you have a hard time waiting it out, and you and your doctor agree that you need not or cannot go on any longer, put yourself fully behind your decision. Should your attempt at labor end in a cesarean section, don't look back with regrets. You added up what you knew and made a choice. If you are faced with the possibility of having to forgo labor and deliver by cesarean section, it might help to tell yourself that the real miracle of birth is the baby, not how it comes out.

When you realize that neither this nor any other book or person has quite described your own situation, try to be relieved rather than disappointed. Not only are the circumstances of each and every person different, there is also more to everyone's inner life than anyone else knows, and what each of us is drawn to learn is different. Other people's experiences and insights are like a backdrop against which we create our own life. "Do not copy," says a sign painted by Elimo Njau, a painter from Nairobi, Kenya. "Copying puts God to sleep."

Recovery and the Recovery Workout

RECOVERY IN GENERAL

No other event in life forces you to move on the way a birth does. Once you have the baby, you have it twenty-four hours a day, seven days a week. Whether you have help or not, the responsibility for someone completely helpless whom you love more than yourself, is always with you. This, and the fact that in the beginning the mother has to recover and adjust to an abundance of new hormones, accounts as much as the physical work of taking care of the baby for the exhaustion and turmoil new parents everywhere describe.

The mother and baby department of modern hospitals is usually filled with joy and staffed with nurses who know that new mothers need a special sensitivity because they are in a special state. However, if any one of the nurses makes you feel as if she is lending you your baby or that she would make a better mother, don't look to her for guidance again. Turn instead to one who is a good teacher. If the postpartum care in the hospital is not what you had hoped for, and you and your baby are well, consider leaving sooner than planned. Once home, make your bed or some other comfortable spot in your house your headquarters, and place what you need for yourself (food and drink especially) and for your baby within reach. Treat the two or three of you as the most sensitive of

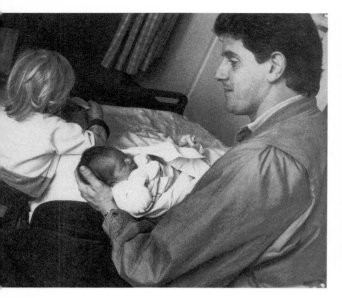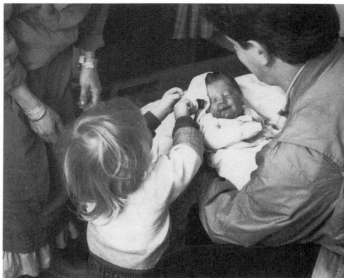

beings, and allow the tiny one exposure to what it likes and knows best: your face, voice, smell, skin, and breasts. Interestingly, many fathers say their baby also loved holding on to the hair on their chest.

If this is your second child, try to create an atmosphere that makes the first day home with your new baby fun for your other child or children. Some new toys, some great books to read, or time to watch a favorite video together will help. Don't expect prolonged interest in the baby. Children are quick and naturally self-centered. If your child is a little rough around the baby, ascribe it to nervous clumsiness rather than to jealousy. Protect your baby without making your child feel bad. New babies are quite sturdy, and they usually sleep well even in the midst of commotion.

Try to be selective about who visits at first. People who bring dinner without expecting to be entertained or who hold the baby while you take a shower are great. Those who are full of advice and stories of how they did it are not as helpful as those who respect you and admire the way you handle your baby. Grandparents are an exception: Their desire to meet the baby should be deferred to even if it means some emotional upheaval. If you consciously depart from the way they parented you, avoid making them feel that they did it all wrong. After all, knowledge of recovery and infant care is greater today, and this is a different era in other ways. Your child is growing up in a world unlike the one in which your parents raised you. For new parents, learning to listen to advice without feeling obliged to follow it or rejecting the person who gives it is almost as essential a skill as changing diapers. Your parents can be great teachers, even if from some of your memories you learned what you *don't* want to do as a parent yourself. Some grandmothers who did not nurse have a hard time trusting in the adequacy of mother's milk. They will eventually, when they see the baby flourish. Don't let them undermine your faith in your body. It did grow the baby you are holding.

Recovery, like growth, proceeds more in a spiral pattern than a straight line. After a good day, one may follow where you feel like doing nothing. Listen to your body and rest so that the next day can be better. Exhaustion sits on the heels of mild fatigue during convalescence, and exhaustion, especially at the start of the seemingly endless and often overwhelming task of new motherhood, makes you susceptible to depression and irritability. Also, a healing wound, whether in the abdomen or around the vagina, remains sensitive for a while, and with fatigue this sensitivity changes to pain. Try to respect the first signs of tiredness and make yourself rest.

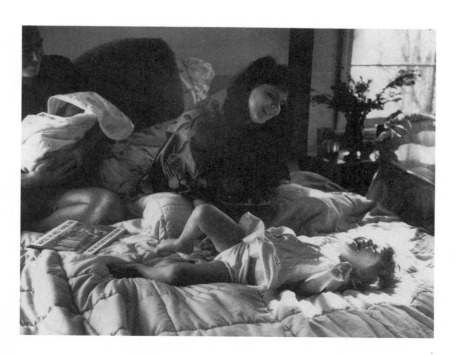

Tearfulness is common. A good cry is like a spring shower; it refreshes and softens the new and intense feelings of motherhood. Quite a few women experience night sweats or break out in a sweat while nursing, especially at first. Some complain of hair loss. Experts say these symptoms are a delayed reaction to changes caused by pregnancy rather than the result of hormonal changes from nursing. Nutritional remedies or costly hair tests are not necessary. The loss seems to stop just as well without treatment.

Whether birth was vaginal or by cesarean section, the healing process is similar. Nature wastes nothing: The enlarged uterus transforms into a small, solid one; the cells the mother no longer needs are broken down and used to make colostrum. The uterus repairs itself by contracting, and it contracts better when the mother nurses. Every time the baby suckles, the flow of wound fluid from the vagina increases. This fluid, called lochia, at first resembles blood. After a few days it begins to turn pink, and then it becomes white. The flow usually stops after three to five weeks. Lochia smells sweet, like the fluid secreted by healing cells, and a bit like menstrual flow. If color or smell differ from this, the physician or midwife should be consulted. New mothers can suddently start to bleed more, and such an increase should always be checked, or the wound inside the uterus can get infected, causing an unpleasant odor.

Nothing should enter the vagina while there is a discharge, so tampons and sexual intercourse must be avoided for a while. When the flow stops, wait one or two days to make sure the wound is healed. Do use contraception the first time you have sex. If you have vaginal intercourse before your first postpartum check-up, you can use an over-the-counter contraceptive. A suppository or sponge will probably work better than a condom, because the lining of the vagina tends to be dry and sensitive in nursing mothers. A lubricant can be helpful. Try a cream with aloe vera first or the white of an egg. If this does not relieve the discomfort, ask your doctor for a cream with estrace, a form of estrogen. Once you start ovulating, your own estrogen will relieve the problem. Even in women who delivered by cesarean, the muscles at the entrance to the vagina tend to be more lax than before from the pregnancy hormones, and since the nerve endings that make penetration feel good are in this muscle, intercourse at first produces fewer sen-

sations. It takes about six weeks for the effect of the pregnancy hormones to subside. The combination of nursing and pregnancy hormones tends to make women feel quite maternal; thoughts about the baby and their new role as a mother prevent many women from the passionate abandon that once was part of sex. Don't worry that it is gone forever. Eventually you will probably be more passionate than before. Most women become more sensual with age and maturity.

In some women, an orgasm stimulates milk secretion (the uterus and the breast respond to the same hormone), and some say this wakes up their baby. To stop the sudden flow of milk, press the palm of the hand (only if it is clean or if a bra is covering the nipple) flat on the breast over the nipple and areola and press toward the chest wall. Breasts full with milk are a sign of abundance. Don't let it make you feel unsexy.

In general, recovery is quicker after a vaginal birth than after a cesarean section. However, sometimes birth can be traumatic to the area around the vagina, and if you underwent a long and exhausting labor, a friend who had an uncomplicated cesarean section may well recuperate sooner. Once again, there are no hard-and-fast rules. In other cultures, not all women give birth in the fields and immediately return to harvesting, with the baby on their back. Ever since Pearl Buck popularized this image in *The Good Earth,* women in the United States have felt inferior by comparison. All over the world some women have easy labors and others do not. In the developed countries, more effective help is usually available if labor is difficult, but many other cultures take better care of new mothers. New mothers need a bit of mothering too.

AFTER A VAGINAL BIRTH

Many women report experiencing a new surge of energy and an inability to relax or sleep for a few hours immediately after giving birth. This wakefulness in the mother coincides with an alert state in the baby. In other mammals, the mother severs the umbilical cord, then stimulates her young by licking it and encouraging it to nurse. Human mothers in earlier times probably had to take care of infant, cord, and placenta too. Today the special alert state offers a nice opportunity for mother and newborn to enjoy each other's company.

During the first hour after birth, the bladder may fill up before the mother has regained her ability to empty it. A full bladder impedes the uterus from returning to its former position. The nurse can help out with a catheter; this is a very simple and painless procedure for women. Sometimes the womb is a little sluggish, causing more blood loss than necessary. The nurses check it regularly the first hour, and if they do not feel a firmly contracted, dome-shaped organ in the lower belly, they stimulate it with massaging and kneading. This usually need not hurt. If it does, tactfully request that the nurse do it more gently. Here, as always, you can ask for the person in charge if you feel that someone employed by the hospital is not sensitive to your needs.

Once the baby has had a try at exploring the breasts and nursing, you might like to doze off together for a bit. It can also feel great to get up and take a shower. If an epidural or a spinal anesthesia was used and getting up is not yet permitted, a sponge bath with a gentle massage might be an alternative.

It is not uncommon for the area between the legs to feel sore or to swell a bit. Applying an ice pack for a few hours will ease these symptoms. After that, heat-lamp treatments help the healing. If no heat lamp is available, the warmth from a sixty-watt light bulb, held close for about fifteen minutes a couple of times a day, will do just fine.

Stitches heal better when they are kept clean, dry, and exposed to air. This is a challenge in the case of vaginal sutures because of their location and the lochia. Rinse the area every time you go to the bathroom, then dry it with a clean towel or a hand-held hair dryer. (Do not aim the dryer at the vagina; air blown into the vagina might get to the placental site and enter the circulation, causing an air embolism.) Change sanitary napkins often and, when resting, place a pad or towel under the buttocks to catch the lochia and allow the area exposure to air some of the time. Don't be afraid to hold up a mirror and look at the stitches. They are of a material that will dissolve as the wound heals. The pain of the stitches is usually gone within a week, but occasionally women still feel pain after six weeks, especially during intercourse. Do not let your birth attendant make you feel that this is psychosomatic or abnormal. People have different sensibilities, different nerve distributions, and different rates of healing.

Hemorrhoids are not a sign that you pushed wrong. They happen as a natural result of the pressure put on the pelvic veins by the baby's head. They heal relatively fast, but they can be painful for a few days. If so, do not be embarrassed to ask for medication. Sitz baths with Epsom salts can speed the healing.

Stitches and hemorrhoids together can make sitting rather uncomfortable for a few days. It is okay to sit on a foam-rubber ring while nursing or during dinner, but not all the time, because the resulting localized pressure interferes with the circulation to the rectum and therefore slows the healing of hemorrhoids. It is better to lie on the side or the stomach.

If sitting causes pain in the area of the tailbone, check with an osteopath or a chiropractor. Misalignment here is not uncommon after a vaginal birth, especially if the baby was large, and it is usually easily corrected.

Avoid standing for long periods and lifting heavy objects or little people during the initial recovery period, while the uterus is still enlarged and the supporting pelvic muscles are stretched. Exercise the muscles between the legs as soon as you can by gently tightening, as if trying to stop urinating, and then releasing. Steadily increase the number of repetitions and the intensity with which you tighten the muscles until you are able to do twenty-four repetitions three times a day. Keep this habit for the rest of your life to prevent bladder problems.

AFTER A CESAREAN SECTION

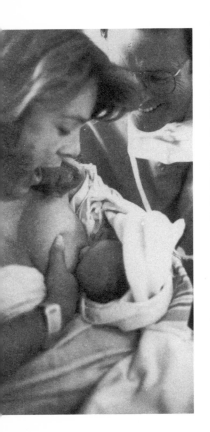

The human body never heals faster than in the period following birth, and so even recovery from this major surgery is amazingly speedy. Unless the anesthesiologist was able to place some morphine in the epidural after the surgery, the first day is usually quite painful, making drugs a must. Don't worry too much about the baby getting some. Relieving your pain is more important now, and the baby doesn't get that much from you the first day anyway. The second day is usually better, enabling you to cut down on the medication, but the third day is often plagued by a new kind of pain, that of gas. After that, recovery is well under way, and drugs are hardly needed anymore. Mother and baby often go home on day four, if not even earlier.

Getting up as soon as you can after delivery and walking a bit speeds healing in general, prevents blood clots from forming, and seems to lessen problems with gas. Sticking to a diet low in fiber for the first few days will also help prevent gas. If you do get gas pains, try lying on your side and pulling your knees as close to your chest as you can. If this does not help, ask the nurse for a Harris flush; this releases warm water into your bowels, and as the water flows out, some of the gas is taken along.

How one feels after a cesarean section depends in part on when and why the operation was done, as well as on one's resilience. Most women benefit from personalized care, especially the first

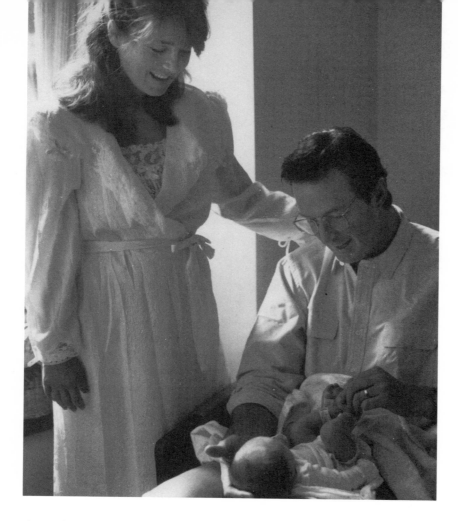

day. Check if a cot can be placed in the room for the coach or another family member or friend who is willing and able to help out. Some women like having the baby in the room with them while they have such help; others get more rest with the baby in the nursery. Delivery by cesarean section can have the benefit of increasing the father's role in taking care of the infant; many fathers who might have been less involved were they not needed thoroughly enjoy the resulting closeness with their infant. Another plus is the beautiful shape of the head of a baby that did not have to squeeze through the birth passage.

Watching a new baby and helping it find its mother's nipple reminds one that the true miracle of birth is not the physiological process of delivery but the phenomenon of a new being, familiar yet different, ready to take on a life of its own. Yet many mothers

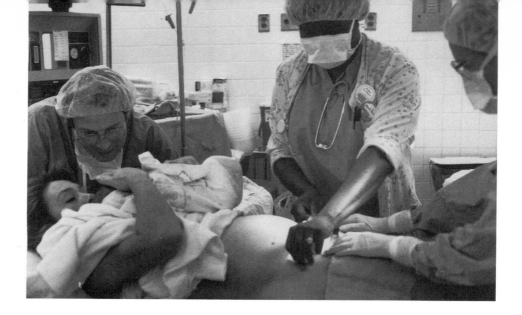

who are delivered by cesarean section nevertheless feel a sense of failure or disappointment. Sometimes this subsides a little once the baby begins to nurse. If not, allow yourself to cry. The psyche has it own healing to do after surgery. If fatigue or a medical condition dictates, nursing can be postponed for about twenty-four hours without impairing of the breasts' ability to produce milk.

It is a good idea to move the legs every once in a while and to take some deep breaths the day of the surgery. Ask the nurse to show you how. If you lie on your back, it will be more comfortable if the nurse places a pillow under your knees and/or flexes the bed there a bit. If you lie on your side, putting a pillow between your legs and one or two behind your back for support might help you relax. Don't be afraid of what you might see if you pull the blanket back and look at your belly. The wound is nicely covered with a dressing, and if you were to look underneath it, you would see that the skin is stitched so well that there is no bleeding at all and it is already beginning to heal. You would also see a catheter for your bladder. This usually stays in for a day or so. When the nurse comes to take it out, she will suggest that you get out of bed. That first time you will need her help. After that it gets easier. Try not to lean forward too much when you walk. Soften your knees, drop your tailbone, and lift your torso upright to place less pressure on your wound. It is okay to cup your hands over it at first. That kind of protective gesture seems to be very natural. Don't be afraid that moving will impair the healing; it actually seems to speed it up. It is quite normal to feel somewhat bloated for a day or two. In some women the ankles and fingers seem more swollen than they were during pregnancy. Fortunately this too goes away soon.

You don't have to defend the fact that you needed a surgical delivery. The natural-birth movement and the national concern over the high cesarean-section rate have made quite a few people respond to any cesarean section as if it were an unnecessary one. This can add to your feeling of failure over what probably was a lifesaving procedure. You also don't owe anyone an explanation of why you had a cesarean. Other people have no right to the details of your delivery. Because of the depth of the experience of becoming a parent and the special sensitivity that goes with it, be careful about whom you expose your feelings to those first days, especially if your own psyche is still healing from the fact that you were not able to give birth the way you had hoped. I always encourage my students to say yes to the question "Did you have a natural birth?" even if they used an epidural. Maybe they should say yes if they had a cesarean section too—it seems so natural to me to choose what is best for the baby.

Rest when you get home. If you have to go down stairs, try walking backward; it tends to be easier. If possible, sit down first and then let someone hand you the baby. Your abdominal muscles will need a few weeks to heal, and during this period your lower back is at increased risk for stress. If lower-back pain occurs, rest more and watch the way you move. If it persists, call a physical therapist for hints on posture, corrective exercises, and a deep-tissue massage.

CARE OF YOUR BREASTS

It is not necessary to wash your breasts before or after nursing, but washing your hands before handling your breasts is a good idea those first days, because while the breasts adjust to their new function, they are more prone to infections. Expect everyone who touches your breasts, including the nurse who helps you with your first try at nursing or the doctor who examines your breasts before you go home, to wash their hands. When you shower, avoid putting soap on the nipples. Air the breasts for about ten minutes after nursing before you close your bra. If the skin on your nipples is prone to soreness from friction, rest, with the breasts exposed, four times a day for twenty minutes under a sixty-watt light bulb or, if your breasts are used to sunlight, expose them a few times a day to the sun.

It is not uncommon for nursing to hurt a bit at first; the skin on the nipples is responding to friction and the connective tissue inside is being stretched. The soreness usually decreases every time the baby nurses. Women soon come to recognize the moment their breasts start to eject the milk in response to the baby's suckling (the let-down) by a kind of tingling or drawing sensation, and after a few days merely thinking of the baby triggers this reflex in some. Both breasts usually let down at the same time, but some women have, from the start, more milk in one breast than the other.

If a sensitive spot develops on one of your nipples, ask the nurse or the lactation consultant to look at it and at how your baby takes the nipple. Also, reread the section entitled "Nursing: The First Few Weeks" in Part Seven. Give the breast a little twist as the baby takes it to avoid friction on the spot that is already sore, and pull or push your baby quite firmly in toward your breast so that it will take more of the breast in its mouth and cause less friction on the nipple. A sore spot can make the initial latching-on of the baby quite painful, but the pain should quickly subside. If it doesn't, the baby has not latched on properly. Little sores heal fastest when you squirt a little colostrum or milk on them and gently blow them dry with a hair drier. If the sore gets worse, stroking it with an ice cube and then drying it with warm air sometimes speeds the healing. Let the baby take the nonsore breast first. Ointment is helpful only to prevent a small wound from adhering to clothes. Most ointments, especially aloe vera, taste bitter, and babies prefer a sweet taste. Placing a few drops of vitamin E on the nipples right after nursing is probably more beneficial, and it will not hurt the baby if done a while before you nurse again. Ask the nurse or lactation consultant for a breast shield made especially to keep clothes from rubbing against a sore nipple.

If your nipple becomes very sore, it might help to use a breast shield with a nipple for a few days. Don't use it longer than that, because the baby cannot get the fatter milk deep inside the breast as readily as when suckling your own nipple.

If after a few tries your baby does not nurse well (if it does you can see the baby swallow and usually can feel it inside your breasts), ask for advice from a lactation consultant. Some babies misuse their tongue, some have a receding lower jaw, and some have a very small mouth. Such babies need help learning how to suckle correctly. During this period of inadequate suckling, use a breast pump to regularly empty the breasts, or if no pump is available, use "manual expression" (explained on page 254) to prevent engorgement. Save the colostrum and/or milk you pump and, if it looks as if your baby has not gotten anything by nursing, try giving it your colostrum with the help of a Lact-Aid nursing trainer before using a bottle. A bottle can make getting the baby to nurse properly harder; resort to it only when it is necessary to prevent dehydration.

If engorgement does occur, it usually happens on the second or third day. The breasts may become quite large for twenty-four to

forty-eight hours, and they may throb and feel warm. Let the baby nurse as often as possible. If the breasts are so firm that the baby has a hard time getting hold of the nipples, soften them by applying a warm, wet washcloth to the breasts or by submerging them in a clean bowl of warm water. Gently massage the breast toward the nipple and, when it softens, try to squeeze out a little of the fluid behind the nipple. This is known as manual expression and is quite simple. Place your index and middle finger under and your thumb above the nipple just behind the areola and rhythmically squeeze and release the breast until drops of a yellowish fluid emerge from the nipple. Move your fingers back a little if nothing comes out. Once the pocket right behind the areola is a bit less full, try letting the baby latch on. Now, while the baby suckles, use a gentle fingertip massage to help the breast empty itself.

Don't panic and send your partner out to buy larger bras when your breasts get very large. Use warm wet compresses or a heating pad and take warm showers. If this does not relieve the pain, pack crushed ice around them after a feeding. Pumping cannot reduce engorged breasts, because engorgement is a swelling response of the breast tissue, not an overabundance of milk. If these simple remedies for the discomfort are not enough, ask your pediatrician what drug you can take. Medication ingested just before nursing will not get into the milk, and it can make the feeding better. And keep in mind that engorgement usually begins to subside within twenty-four hours.

Once most of the swelling is gone, check your breasts regularly for lumps. Localized hardness now usually means that a milk duct was not emptied. Make sure your bras support your breasts evenly, without cutting into them and impairing circulation. If you have large breasts, massage them toward the nipple while the baby nurses so that every part can get emptied. The next time you nurse, carefully massage any area that feels harder. Keep an eye on such spots. If one becomes tender, feels warm, or turns red, take your temperature and call your obstetrician. If it is a breast infection, you will most likely have to take an antibiotic for ten days. The kind of antibiotic you need depends on the type of infection. Check with your pediatrician to make sure that the one prescribed is the best one to cure the infection and will have a minimal effect on your baby. Pediatricians often know more about breast infections from the baby's point of view than obstetricians. Some obstetri-

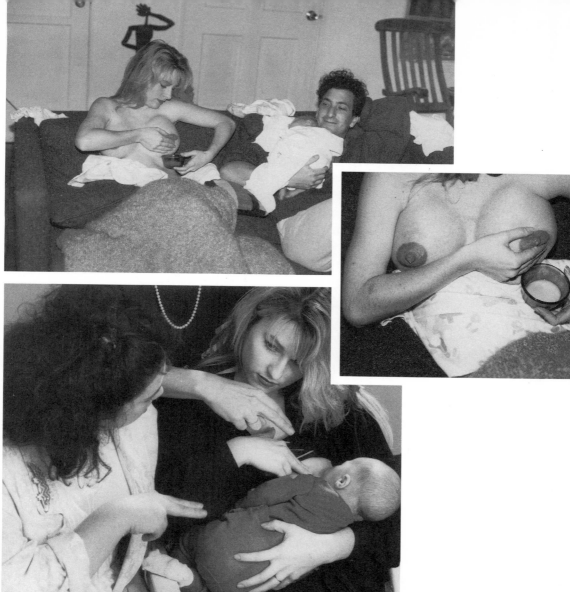

cians still tell women to discontinue nursing, yet infections usually clear up better when the mother nurses. Nurse the unaffected breast first so that the other one can let-down. Empty the affected side by pumping if feeding does not empty it. The above, combined with bed rest, plenty of fluids, ice or warm packs on the affected breast, and, if necessary, something for the pain, usually cures a breast infection without further problems. Yogurt helps the flora in the intestines stay fairly normal during antibiotic treatment.

After about ten days of nursing, the sensation of fullness in the breasts goes away. Don't worry—there will be enough milk; most of the milk is now produced while the baby nurses. One breast often produces more than another, and production varies from day to day. If your supply is a bit overabundant, it is best not to pump yet, because if you pump, your body will not learn that it should make less. Better to leak a little now and then. Adequate production continues to be mostly influenced by the baby's suckling and emptying of the breasts, but rest and nutrition contribute too.

NUTRITION AND WEIGHT LOSS

Nutrition is important for quantity as well as for quality of milk. The latter suffers first when a nursing mother's diet is not up to par. Her milk will have fewer water-soluble vitamins; then other substances will be affected, and eventually the amount of milk will decrease.

It takes about 900 calories to make a liter of milk. The baby may not need that much per day right away, but nursing a newborn does require at least 200 calories more than pregnancy, or 500 calories per day above regular intake. Nursing hormones increase one's metabolism and send more blood through the breasts. The breasts soon learn to make fat from carbohydrates. Some say that the ability of the breasts to synthesize fat determines whether or not mothers continue to nurse. Among women whose milk's fat content is under 20 grams, there is an 80 percent dropout rate; among those whose milk contains 20 grams or more of fat per feeding, breast-feeding is usually continued. It is not known how women can help their breasts accomplish fat production. The midday feeding seems highest in fat in many women. Is this the result of a good breakfast and some rest during the night, or is it some internal metabolic clock we do not know about? The type of fat a mother eats will affect the types of fats in her milk but not the amount. Vegetables and legumes produce less saturated fat. This will be especially important in families with a genetic predisposition to arteriosclerosis, the disease that often leads to heart attacks.

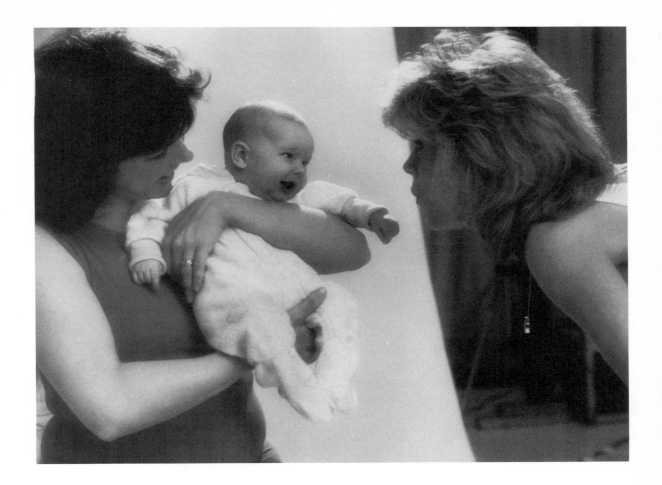

Proteins are passed on to the baby relatively unchanged, and this may well be a factor in the baby's inability to digest certain foods. Mothers with allergies on either side of the family should avoid dairy products and should be careful not to eat the same grain every day. Milk and wheat are the most common allergy-inducing nutrients. A good rule for nutrition during breast-feeding is to watch out for too much of any one food. A three-day rotational diet is a good idea. One day you can get your calcium from milk and cheese, the next day from dark green leafy vegetables and corn tortillas, and the next day from salmon or sardines canned with the bones. Figs and almonds are sources of calcium too. Sunshine provides calcium D3, which aids in the absorption of calcium from other sources. Don't worry too much about getting enough proteins; grains and vegetables combined with a little meat, an egg, fish, or legumes will give your body what it needs.

Rye, oats, and rice offer a tasty departure from wheat. Try to keep a variety of wholesome snacks handy, because the need for nutrients can come on suddenly and strong in nursing mothers.

It generally takes from two to six hours for something one eats to enter the milk, although vitamin C seems to be able to pass within half an hour, and alcohol can be very fast too. If a baby responds negatively to milk during nursing, it is more likely because of the taste than digestive upsets. The flavor of a substance can appear in the milk in twenty minutes. Indigestion usually appears after half an hour to two hours, and may take even longer.

While it is a good idea to be aware of your baby's response to what you eat, don't worry too much about it. Such responses are quite individual, so you have to experiment a little. You can have a beer or a glass of wine, and one piece of chocolate is most likely not going to hurt your baby, especially if you treat yourself during or right after nursing rather than an hour or so before.

The body learns to produce the right quantity of milk for a particular baby after about ten days of nursing; the quality stabilizes after two to four months. This usually coincides with a sense of confidence in the mother and with the baby's ability to show appreciation by smiling at mother and breast. If there are pounds to shed, this is a good time to start working on it, because all traces of pregnancy hormones have now disappeared, and as estrogen levels come back, weight loss is easier.

As always, weight loss is accomplished through dietary changes and aerobic activity. Don't cut down on variety; eat slightly less of each nutrient instead. Fat and alcohol are both high in calories, and neither is needed for milk production or for the mother's health. If you rely on a beer to relax you, see if you can accomplish the same with a walk. The baby will probably love to be carried in a front pack, and if you began the basic strengthening exercises a bit earlier, your body will be able to handle the extra weight, and the walking will help with the weight loss. To improve the fat-burning metabolism, aerobic activity needs to be at least fifteen minutes per day and five or six times a week. Walk crisply without stopping, while you hum a tune, describe the world to your baby, or talk with a friend; slow down when you can't do one or the other and you will be working at the correct intensity.

Don't be impatient. It is healthier not to lose the excess weight overnight. As you burn fat, the toxins stored in it are released into your bloodstream, and from there they enter your milk, so for both you and your baby it is better if you burn your fat off slowly. Work on it steadily and consistently. In most women, nursing helps to burn pregnancy fat, but it also keeps extra fluid in the body. Thus, women generally lose another five pounds or so when they stop nursing. Try not to stop sooner than you otherwise would just to get back into some of your favorite clothes. If possible, buy yourself some new outfits instead. Don't feel selfish buying clothes for yourself instead of toys and equipment for your baby. Your baby needs you in a good mood more than it needs material things at this early age. You will enjoy mothering more if it adds to your life instead of pushing you into unnecessary sacrifices. The desire to be beautiful is a universal one. Respect it, but realize that there is more to beauty than pounds and inches.

GETTING YOUR FIGURE BACK

Shortly after your baby's birth, your belly will feel astonishingly flat when you put your hand on it, but when you stand up, it might not look quite as flat as it feels. The pelvic tilt left over from pregnancy and muscles lax from their stretched condition combine to cause a still-pregnant look in many new mothers. Also, the breasts, heavy with engorgement or milk, tend to pull the upper back and shoulders forward. The resulting posture is not only unbecoming, it is hard on the upper and lower back. Try to become aware of the tilt in your pelvis and the tendency to slump forward, and correct it every time you think of it. Lift up on the pubic bone, drop the tailbone, soften the knees, lift the chest, relax the shoulders back and down, and reach up from the crown of your head. Increase your awareness of the position of your pelvis with the following simple exercises, which you can start as soon as you like after you give birth.

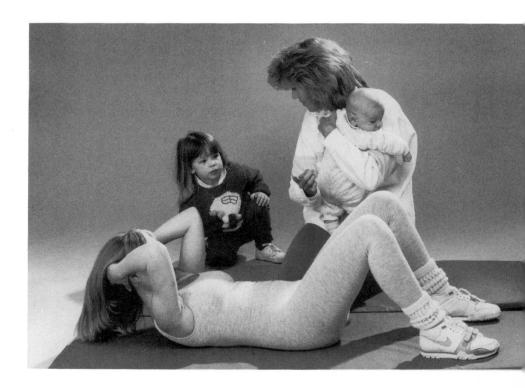

1. Abdomen Toner

1. Lie flat on your back on a firm surface, with your knees bent and feet hip distance apart, and place your hands on your abdomen.
2. Inhale and push your hands upward with your expanding belly.
3. Exhale and press your lower back into the floor. Feel your pelvis tilt, suck your belly in, and think of trying to bring the belly button to the backbone.
4. Inhale, release the tilt, and let your belly expand.
5. Exhale and repeat as often as feels comfortable. Steadily increase the number of repetitions until you can do 24.

Once your stitches and hemorrhoids have healed and you are able to do twenty-four repetitions of the first exercise, begin to add a modified curl-up. Doing curl-ups sooner than that may aggravate pelvic floor problems, because they cause pressure on that area. Wait three weeks or more if you had a cesarean section.

2. Curl-Ups

1. In the same supine position, inhale, tighten your abdomen, and press your back into the floor.
2. Keep your chin in and exhale as you lift your head.
3. Inhale and bring your head down. Work up to 24 repetitions.

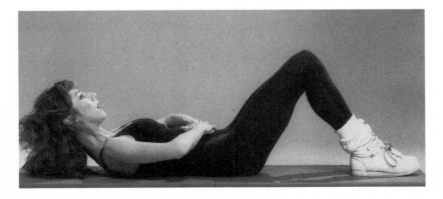

3. Curl-Ups, continued

1. Once you can do Exercise 2, place your hands crosswise over your chest and inhale.
2. Tighten the belly, press the lower back into the floor, and exhale as you lift your head.
3. Inhale and lie back. Work up to 24 repetitions and try lifting your head and shoulders instead of just your head. When that becomes easy, you can place a small weight on your chest. Mothers at the Workout often use their baby.

As the tone in your belly muscles returns and your awareness of the position of your pelvis increases, check yourself regularly in the mirror: Are your abdomen and chest lifted, and is your tailbone dropped? When you notice that your posture needs less and less correcting, your muscle tone and awareness have combined, and it is now safe to add other muscle-strengthening exercises.

The areas it is most important to work are the abdomen, buttocks, and thighs—both for looks and for strength—and the upper body, front and back. Upper-body strength is needed when the breasts are full and heavy and when a baby has to be carried in the arms. After you've worked your abdomen in the first three exercises, try the following:

4. *Buttocks Toner*

1. Turn on your abdomen, face turned to one side, arms next to you on the floor, one leg straight, the other bent in an 80-degree angle at the knee. Inhale.
2. Exhale and lift the thigh of the bent leg.
3. Inhale and bring the thigh down to the floor.
4. Exhale and lift it up. Don't change the angle at the knee. Work up to 24 repetitions for each leg.

5. *Modified Push-Ups*

1. Stay prone, bend your knees and cross your ankles in the air, and place your palms on the floor near your shoulders. Inhale.
2. Tighten your abdominal muscles and exhale with your mouth open while you push your body up by straightening your arms.
3. Inhale and lower your body to the floor.
4. Exhale and push yourself up. Always tighten your abdominal muscles while you push up, to protect your back, and exhale with the mouth open to avoid a sudden rise in blood pressure. Do not let your buttocks stick out. Work up to 24 repetitions.

6. Upper-Back Toner

1. Place a chair close to a sturdy door and swing a rubber band or an inner tube around the doorknob. Be sure it's on securely! Sit with your back straight and your feet firmly planted on the floor, one end of the rubber band in each hand. Inhale.

2. Exhale and bring your arms in, keeping your elbows shoulder high.

3. Inhale and let the rubber band pull your arms forward.

4. Exhale and pull back. Resist the return movement and do not arch your back when you pull your arms toward you. Work up to 24 repetitions.

7. Rowing

If you have time, add some rowing movements with the elbows bent down along the trunk. This will work your upper body differently to give you more overall strength and the kind of back and arms one likes to show off in a summer dress.

These simple exercises, combined with walking, will put you well on the road to recovery. Difficult as it may be to find time to do anything regularly, try to walk and do the abdominal exercises every day and the other exercises every other day. And don't forget the pelvic floor toners three times a day in groups of twenty-four.

You can do those while nursing. Once you have a little more time, you can do the stretches from the pregnancy workout, and if you feel up to it and want to tone buttocks and thighs more, you can add the squats and lunges. Squatting is good for the pelvic floor muscles as well as the buttocks and thighs. And small children like it when their mother squats down to look at them face-to-face, so the ability to get in and out of a squat should come in handy for a couple of years.

As soon as you feel up to it, and especially if the discipline to work out regularly on your own is hard to come by, join an exercise class. Recovery classes where you can bring your baby are great, provided they offer a good workout. Don't be afraid to join a regular exercise class. You don't have to do every repetition of every exercise right away. Many of our students, including mothers who had a cesarean section, return to the regular classes within two months of their baby's birth. If nutrition is good, exercise gives more rather than less energy, and it does not at all impair nursing.

GROWING INTO THE ROLE OF MOTHER

Recovery, coinciding as it does with your assuming the role of mother, can be rather difficult. Your own body needs care while you are caring for a helpless being whose needs never end. Your new responsibility, and the exhaustion it brings, may make you feel disorganized. Many new emotions may surge to the surface and at times throw you off balance. After the initial rapture at your child's perfection and the fear that neither you nor the world will be good enough, will come moments of despair when the baby keeps on crying in spite of your best efforts. You feel fatigued and weary during those first weeks, and may resent that being a mother is as difficult as it is, while feeling awe at the amount of love it will take to help this baby become the person it was meant to be. Some women profoundly doubt their ability to be a mother, and if they could, they would call it all off. Then, guilty that they could feel that way, they rush in to make sure their baby is still breathing. Some question their own place in the world. They yearn to do

something else, yet one look at their baby and they know they can't leave it. So many women experience depression, especially in the second and third weeks, that it seems a normal part of the transformation one has to make.

Don't be afraid of these baby blues; turmoil and a bit of depression often precede creation and growth.

The initial phase of motherhood seems most difficult for women who are used to an exciting career. The inability to "schedule" mothering produces a bit of culture shock, and at the end of the day a small baby cannot say, "Thank you, I could not have done it without you." It would if it could, and it will, with its smile, in just another week or two. By that time your hormones will have found more of a balance, your worst fatigue will be over, and you will find it hard to explain what it was that was so difficult about those first few weeks.

If, instead of subsiding, your crying spells become more frequent and last longer, or if a general feeling of apathy, of being overwhelmed or worthless sets in, reach out for help. Postpartum depression hits quite unexpectedly. It has nothing to do with how well adjusted one is or how much one loves one's infant. It is a hormonal imbalance, aggravated by fatigue and tension. Usually, all you need is someone to help you a bit, the company of other new mothers, and regular exercise. If not, expert help is essential. But in the midst of a depression, reaching out is very hard. Try to have someone in your life who will recognize the difference between baby blues and depression and help you get help. If depression persists, check with your doctor to see if you should have your thyroid checked. Low thyroid function is not uncommon after a pregnancy and it can make one feel depressed.

SHARING AS PARENTS

The phenomenal hormone change that follows birth does not entirely account for the increased sensitivity of new mothers, because fathers who are intimately involved in caring for their newborns often experience similar feelings. Some have a very hard time going back to activities that once seemed very important. Some feel envious and disappointed that the baby still seems closer to the mother, because she nurses or simply seems so naturally competent. Fathers can be as good as or better than mothers if they look after their baby with the same dedication to helping it flourish and be joyful. Moreover, from a very early age babies like change. If they have been with a woman for a while, they respond positively to a man's energy, and vice versa. Fathers and mothers interact and play differently with their babies, and the baby probably benefits from that natural fact.

A newborn tends to bring out everyone's more spontaneous and tender side. When you see your partner do something with your baby that truly touches you, express your appreciation. The best thing people can do for each other, as the philosopher Martin Buber said, is to acknowledge the other's finer self.

Some first-time parents have difficulty accepting the change that inevitably occurs in their own relationship. Even though they love their baby, they miss the intimacy just the two of them shared. Others find that the baby adds a window through which to understand and appreciate their relationship and life. Maybe new parenthood, like life itself, presents most people with a mixture of complex emotions, and happiness depends in part on which emotions are emphasized.

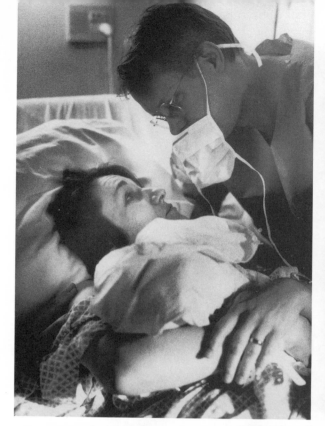

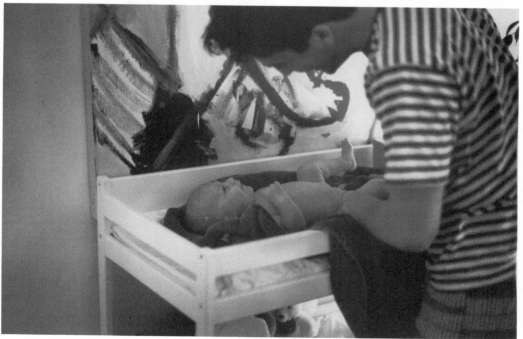

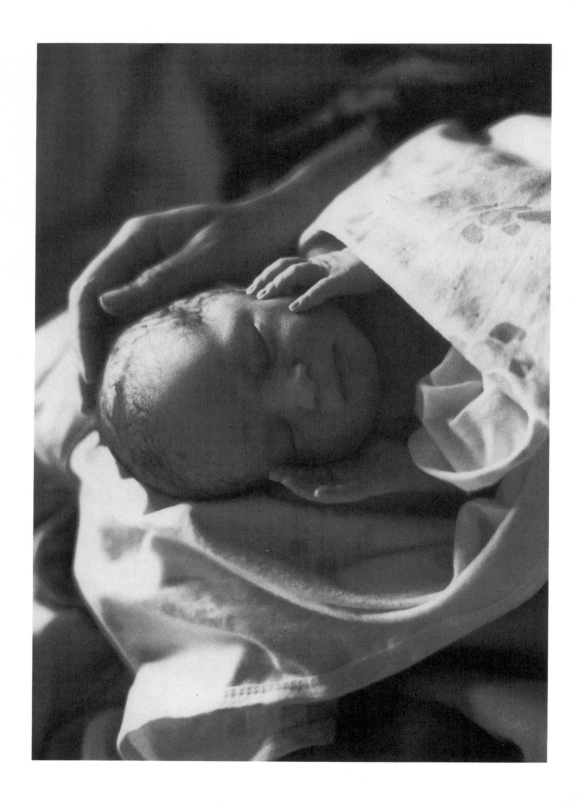

More About Babies

THE BABY AT BIRTH

Inside the womb, the baby—its spine rounded outward, its thighs against its belly—naps, kicks, and practices breathing movements with its chest muscles. It sucks its fingers or thumb, swallows the water in which it is submerged, and relies for oxygen, nutrition, and the elimination of waste on its mother. At birth the spine unfolds, the position of the diaphragm changes, and the infant responds to the sudden temperature and atmospheric change with the chest expansion rehearsed in the womb, sucking air into its lungs.

Until that first breath, enough blood went to the lungs to nourish them, but the major flow was diverted away by a duct near the heart. Now the full stream is dragged into the pulmonary vessels. This sudden change in the flow of blood causes pressure changes in the two sides of the heart and makes the umbilical arteries contract. The baby passes no more blood back to the placenta. The umbilical vein, less muscular than the arteries, closes more slowly, allowing the baby to get blood from the placenta for another minute before this flow too stops. As blood flow changes, certain ducts close and new ones open; organs wake up, and within half an hour after birth, the stomach secretes gastric juices, signaling hunger and making the baby interested in latching on to

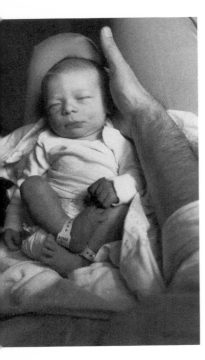

its mother's nipple. Before that point, babies often like seeing and nuzzling the breast, but now there is a need to suckle.

Some doctors encourage mothers to reach down after their baby's shoulders are delivered and lift the infant onto their belly themselves. The belly, which is naturally warm and moves with the familiar rhythm of the mother's breathing, seems a good place for the baby to catch its breath, and the umbilical cord is usually not long enough for it to go anywhere else. After a minute or so, once the baby has received most of the blood back from the placenta, the cord can be cut. Now the father can pick his baby up and, when the mother is ready, place it on her bare breasts. To pick up this finely formed, tiny person, place one hand under its buttocks and the other under its head and shoulders. If you would like to talk, bring your baby fairly close to your face. Your baby's gaze will become more intent, and crying often stops. If your baby looks at you, looks away, and then looks at your face again, perhaps, more than the inability to focus, it is because of the human characteristic of turning the eyes away temporarily during intense personal contact.

A newborn's skin has never touched anything but the inner lining of its mother's body. It is exquisitely soft. Cover it with something soft, warm, and clean (the nurses usually have a pre-

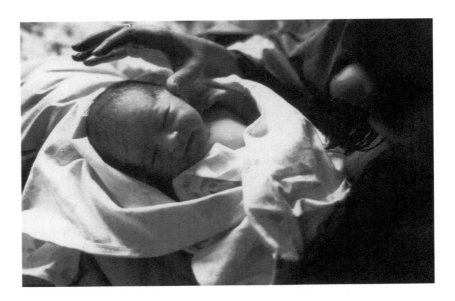

warmed receiving blanket ready), and put a soft cap on its head so that the baby stays warm.

Try not to panic if your baby does not breathe right away. Your birth attendant will probably suction the air passage and may tap the feet and give the baby some oxygen. This often starts a cry. Some babies take a minute or two. Inside the womb, the baby was used to less oxygen. The placenta is not as good at air exchange as the lungs, and to compensate, the molecules of hemoglobin for oxygen carriage in the fetus have a higher affinity for oxygen than adult hemoglobin. At birth a baby also has a greater number of hemoglobin molecules and a different metabolism, enabling it to go longer without oxygen than it will be able to later when its hemoglobin molecules have changed. This greater affinity for oxygen makes many newborns look rather red for a while after birth.

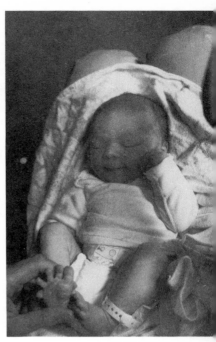

One minute after birth, and again five minutes later, birth attendants give the baby an Apgar score, named after pediatrician Virginia Apgar. Its heart rate, breathing, muscle tone, general responsiveness, and cry are each rated from zero to two. A combined score of ten may mean a biased assessor. A one-minute score of four to six means that the baby is in fair condition. Anything below that signifies that it needs help. More important than the one-minute score is the score five minutes later. If the first one was three and the second is seven, there is nothing to worry about. A baby who can recover like that has a lot of resilience. Gauging the rate of a baby's ability to recover is the best way to determine its well-being at birth. Don't boast about your baby's score at parties; it's worse than boasting about IQ scores. The Apgar score was devised to allow medical professionals to measure a baby's response to the birth process. It has been shown not to be a reliable indicator of future development.

The mother's estrogen, high during the last days of pregnancy, passes through the placenta to the baby, so that boys are born with a very full scrotum and baby girls have swollen labia and, occasionally, drops of blood at the vagina; sometimes a bit of milk ("witch's milk") will escape from the breasts of both boys and girls. Most babies are purplish at birth, and their hands and feet are slowest to turn pink. Their breathing is somewhat irregular the first couple of days—perhaps the need for oxygen is not as great as it will be later, when their hemoglobin molecules have become like ours. They sneeze to clear their nose, and they sometimes make grunting noises. Above all they cry. And their crying is painful to hear, especially for their parents.

Babies have been welcomed into many different worlds. Perhaps none was as alien to the human mammal as the·one that greeted newborns in the United States during the 1950s and '60s, when babies were whisked off to a constantly lit nursery, given sugar water, then put on a three- or four-hour formula schedule. Other cultures have had their share of strange practices: rubbing the cord with sheep dung (which, unknown to the people who did it routinely, is a sure way to increase the risk for tetanus); rubbing the baby's skin with salt; waiting for the mother's colostrum to change into milk before allowing the baby to nurse, for fear that colostrum was bad for the baby; or waiting to cut the cord until the father returned from the hunt, even if it took twenty-four hours. Smart and perceptive as we are, we have a hard time understanding someone not quite like us, and babies *are* different. However, even though they don't talk or think as we do, they have a way to express themselves, and they do hear, smell, taste, feel, listen, see, and remember. Like us, they are born with an inner potential, which will strive to be realized. From birth this makes them, to the observant eye, very much themselves and different from each other. But, like any other peer group, they do have certain things in common.

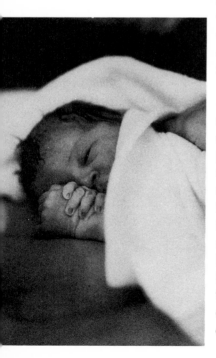

Their eyes focus best at the distance from the mother's breast to her face. They see contrasting colors best—dark and light, black and white. They prefer the configuration of a human face over other forms, and from birth they seem to be able to relate to pictures. They like to be spoken or sung to. But most of all they enjoy motion and being held close to a warm body. Their attention span is short, and when they are bored, scared, or uncomfortable, they choose one of three responses: look away, cry, or go to sleep. One of their most puzzling abilities is that of imitation. Researchers in Seattle and Edinburgh have again and again shown that babies will stick out their tongue, raise one eyebrow, or make other facial movements after the example of an adult. What does this teach us? Perhaps that we should trust that the expressions on our babies' faces are real. A smile is not gas, but an expression of contentment—not social yet, but blissful nonetheless.

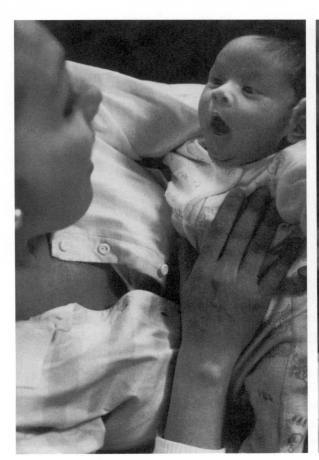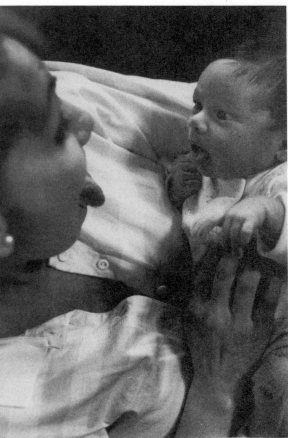

NURSING: THE FIRST FEW WEEKS

For a first try at nursing, it will help to position yourself so that you can see your baby and your breast. Most mothers choose to recline against a backrest, with their baby cradled in one arm. Let the baby roll against you tummy to tummy so that it faces your breast straight on. If you had a cesarean section or if your baby's chin recedes a little (until this corrects itself, it is harder for the baby to grasp the nipple), place the baby with its legs off to your side, its head right in front of your breast, and cradle the back of its head in your hand. This position, with the baby in the so-called

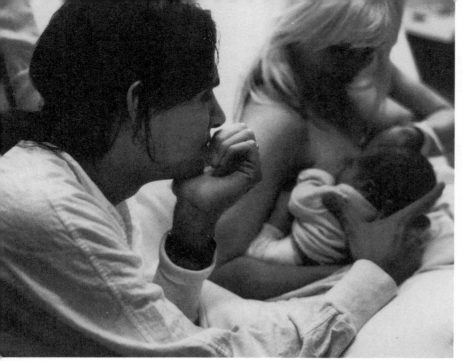
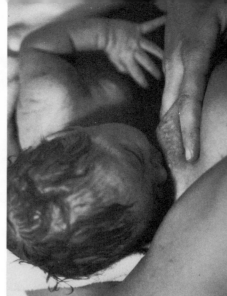

Some babies nurse better when they are skin to skin. Perhaps the cool air makes them suck more vigorously.

football hold, prevents pressure on the incision, and, because you have more control over your baby's head, it is easier to help if it has a hard time getting at the nipple properly. If neither position works for you, try lying on your side.

Hold your breast with four fingers placed below and thumb above the nipple and well behind the areola. Stroke the baby's lower lip with your nipple. If the baby is ready to nurse, it will open its mouth. Continue stroking until your baby opens wide; then quickly bring the baby's head to the breast to help it take the nipple in its mouth. The baby will suck the nipple into the back of its mouth and press part of the areola between its upper gum and tongue, which should be resting on its lower gum. The baby should slide its tongue back along the nipple toward its hard palate and forward to the gum again in a rhythmic fashion while it sucks. These two motions combined are called suckling, and when it is done well the mother can usually feel it inside her breast, because it sets off her let-down reflex. Some babies latch on at their first chance. Others have a hard time at first. Just keep trying—you are both learning, and there is no hurry. Sometimes it helps to slip a finger, (make sure that it is clean and that the nail is short) finger-tip up, well into the baby's mouth. As your baby tries to suckle your finger, have your breast ready. Take your finger out, stroke the baby's lower lip, and when its mouth opens, pull the baby close while you hold the nipple so that it can be grasped by the baby's open mouth. If your baby did not suck the nipple well back into its mouth and is now kind of chewing on it, slip a finger between the gums to break the suction, take your breast out, and start over. Don't worry if your baby gets a little upset. New mothers often fail to bring the baby's head firmly enough to their breast once the baby opens its mouth. Try a quick, firm pull toward you with the arm that holds the baby, or, if the father is trying to help, have him give a firm yet gentle push against the baby's head. Fathers are often good at this.

If your nipple is hard to grasp because it does not project, and if pumping for a minute or two does not seem to do it, use wet cold towels or ice to bring the nipple out. Be patient and tell your baby to do the same, and wear shields between feedings.

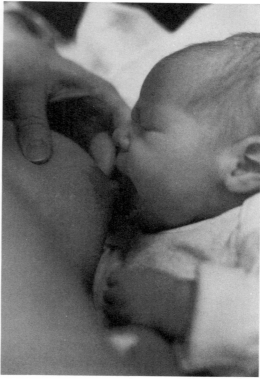

Apart from improper latching-on, what makes a nipple sore at first, experts say, is so-called nonnutritive sucking, which occurs when the baby, not hungry and almost asleep, lets the nipple almost slip out, then pulls it back in. When you notice this, break the suction if necessary, take the baby off the breast, and see if your baby needs to burp; then offer the other breast so that the baby gets used to both breasts from the start and both will receive equal stimulation. It is a rare newborn who will suckle more than ten minutes in one stretch so to prevent nipple soreness timing these first nursings is not as important as preventing too much nonnutritive sucking while your nipples are adjusting. Keep an eye on how your baby takes and holds your nipple those first few times. If your nipples get at all sore, ask one of the nurses, your baby doctor, or the lactation consultant to watch the two of you for any possible corrections in the latching-on technique.

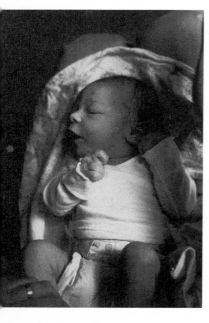

Don't be afraid of spoiling your baby by holding it in your arms a great deal. A baby likes closeness, especially with a body so thoroughly familiar. Try to take your cues from your baby about how often the two of you should nurse. It is not necessary to wait until your baby signals by crying. When a baby is awake and interested in the breast, its mouth resembles that of a little bird—the tongue moves in and out, and the head turns from side to side as if searching—and when you touch your baby's cheek, it turns toward the side you touched (that is the rooting reflex). Usually, frequent nursing is best. For you it may prevent or lessen engorgement. For the baby nursing is an essential physiological function. Premature babies keep a higher oxygen level and stay warmer while they nurse, and they don't lose weight from the work of nursing. If your baby has a hard time getting the technique right and you are worried about its not getting enough fluid those first days, ask your pediatrician whether or not the baby should have a little water. Try giving it through the Lact-Aid nursing trainer first. Most nursing experts say that if possible it is better to avoid giving a bottle, because some babies, when exposed to two kinds of nipples, prefer one over the other, and those who have a hard time with the breast tend to opt for the one on the bottle. If your baby cries inconsolably, does not have a wet diaper every two to three hours, or feels rather warm, water might be necessary. Try to be persevering and trusting of the nursing process without being fa-

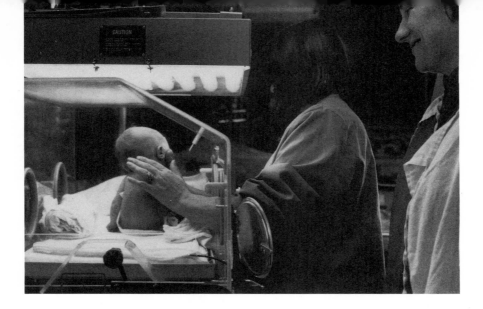

natical. Some babies need to mature a little before they can suck hard enough to get nourishment from the breasts. If the problem of weak sucking continues, see your baby doctor. A local breast-feeding expert and pediatrician says that babies who don't suck vigorously sometimes have a urinary-tract infection or some other minor health problem.

Each baby has its own rhythm of eating and resting. It is better not to hurry one that likes to take its time. There is a difference between what experts call "a gourmet eater"—a baby who tastes and thinks about every sip—and a baby who is sluggish due to an excess of bilirubin in its blood. Babies with the latter condition are usually jaundiced too, so you will be able to tell if there is a problem. A jaundiced baby needs as much colostrum and breast milk as it can take. Colostrum helps empty the bowels, and with the meconium goes some of the bilirubin. Bilirubin is released the first ten days or so when the baby breaks down the hemoglobin cells that are no longer of use. This accumulates if the liver is a little immature or overburdened. Light helps the liver function; placing your baby near a sunny window and letting it nurse as often as it wants might be enough. If the doctor says that the bilirubin is still too high, and the baby needs to be placed under a bilirubin light, ask if they are available for rent in your area. If not, and the baby needs to stay in the hospital for this treatment, you might prefer to stay with it. If the baby can't nurse, pump your breasts about as often as it would nurse. You or the nursery nurse can then feed it to your baby with a bottle.

Pediatricians vary widely in their approach to the treatment of bilirubin. Some are highly respectful of breast-feeding and believe that everything should be done to make it possible. Others are very casual about it. If you were hoping to breast-feed, and your doctor suggests that you stop because of the jaundice ("The baby needs more fluid, and it is easier to give it from a bottle," or "Your breast milk is causing it"), get a second opinion. If your baby needs more fluid, you can always offer some water after each nursing, and you can wake your baby up every two hours to nurse. Water helps prevent dehydration; it does not, like colostrum and breast milk, facilitate the evacuation of bilirubin. Very occasionally jaundice is associated with a substance in the mother's milk (breast-milk jaundice). This occurs after two to three weeks and is harmless. More often jaundice occurs because the baby is not feeding enough and is dehydrated (breast-feeding jaundice). This type of jaundice is common between the third and the tenth day. Very occasionally jaundice is a symptom of another health problem.

If your breasts did become engorged and you used a nipple shield, or if your baby was given a bottle during a bout with jaundice, afterward recheck the baby's latching-on technique and your way of presenting the breast. One of you may have picked up a bad habit while the breasts were so firm, or the baby may have forgotten how to take the breast. One of the common mistakes mothers make is placing their fingers too close to the areola. This does not leave the baby enough breast tissue to grasp. Babies often make the mistake of sucking on the nipple rather than suckling the breast. Support your baby well as it nurses so that the nipple does not partially slip out during a rest break.

After the rich colostrum, your milk might look quite watery, especially if you compare it with cow's milk. It is common to worry that the milk is not good enough or that there is too little, especially when the baby cries. It may be very tempting to give the baby some formula, and babies will almost always take some. This creates two risks: first, that the baby will find the bottle easier and will refuse to work harder at getting the milk from the breast; second, that less suckling at the breast, the inevitable result of giving a supplement, will tell the mother's body that it does not have to produce more milk. If the supply goes down, more formula

The tummy-to-tummy position prevents tension while nursing, and it lessens the swallowing of air; thus it can cut down the baby's discomfort after a feeding.

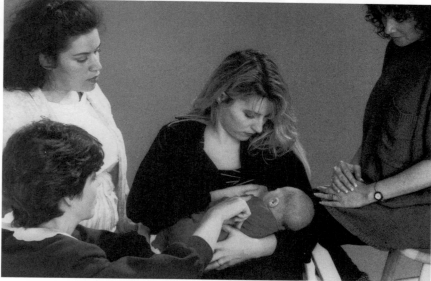

will be given, and breast-feeding will become more and more likely to fail. So say "no thank you" to the six-pack the formula companies place in your hands via the hospital nurse. Nursing mothers should treat formula like a prescription drug. This is what baby doctors who understand nursing will usually say.

Mother's milk can leave the baby's stomach within an hour, so babies who grow fast may want to nurse as often as every other hour. Try to nurse your baby someplace where you like to sit and where you can read, listen to music, or watch TV—anything you need to do to make the frequent and prolonged nursing spells nice for both of you. In general, a newborn may nurse twelve to

A footstool and a pillow can make prolonged nursing spells less tiring.

fourteen times in twenty-four hours, while a four-month-old may be down to six to eight times a day.

Natural and important for the baby as nursing may be, it is not always easy, especially at the beginning. For the mother it is learned rather than instinctual behavior, and that is why expert guidance is helpful. Genetic endowment plays quite a role too. Some mothers have a hard time producing enough milk; others have so much the baby can't swallow fast enough. If you fit into the latter category, don't be afraid that your baby will choke. Choking occurs only if the baby swallows something solid that obstructs the air passage, and milk cannot do so. If your baby gulps and coughs, perhaps some milk got into its air passage and caused the cough reflex (this is known as aspirating). Moreover, mother's milk is isotonic with plasma and therefore easily absorbed; even if a bit of milk were to get into the lungs, it would not cause pneumonia. Formula or cereal are different. This is another reason for postponing food other than breast milk where possible. Some women say that they can slow the flow of milk a little when they lie down while nursing and concentrate on relaxing.

If, in spite of expert advice and your own best efforts, you still are not able to nurse successfully, try not to feel that you have failed as a mother. We can only do our best. We don't have that

If lying on the side does not slow a rapid milk flow, do stop your baby every couple of minutes for a burp, especially if the baby is restless at the breast.

much control over the functions of our body. Your baby will still love you—babies love their mothers for reasons other than success at vaginal birth or at nursing.

ONCE THE MILK FLOW IS ESTABLISHED

After three weeks the breasts are usually producing a steady flow of milk and the baby is good at nursing. It is a good idea to introduce the bottle now. If you wait longer, the baby might refuse it and that would keep you completely tied down. If possible fill the bottle with your own milk rather than with formula. Manual expression is better for the breast, but an electric breast pump is faster, and the modern ones allow you to pump both breasts at the same time. If you are planning to return to work, renting one of these is your best bet. If you plan to pump only occasionally, a hand pump might be sufficient. The only good hand pump is the piston-and-cylinder type. Be careful with the amount of suction— too much, to the point where it is uncomfortable, can hurt your

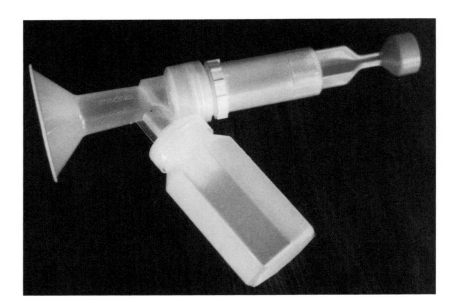

breasts. Pump between feedings, at the time of day when you usually have milk. Wash your hands and make sure all pump parts and the collection container are clean. Don't rush. Make yourself comfortable, think of your baby, stroke your nipples, manipulate them as the baby does, drink some water or juice, and then try to pump. If nothing comes, try placing warm wet towels against your breasts, or wait until your baby has brought on your let down. Some mothers say that their milk flows best while they relax in a warm bath. The flow will be slower than when the baby nurses, and you may collect only one ounce. Save it anyway. After a couple of days of pumping, you will have enough for one feeding. Perhaps your partner can feed the baby one night to allow you to catch up on some sleep.

Store your milk in glass or plastic containers, labeling each with the date and time. Mother's milk keeps in the refrigerator for forty-eight hours, in a refrigerator/freezer without a separate door for two weeks, in a freezer for three months, and in a deep freeze for six months (some say a year). You can add fresh milk to frozen milk if you chill the fresh milk first. Milk expands when it freezes, so do not fill a container all the way to the top.

Do not defrost milk in a microwave or over the stove, because doing so destroys many nutrients. The microwave also destroys the immune cells. Whenever possible, defrost frozen milk gradually in the refrigerator. Then warm it to room temperature inside a bottle placed in warm water. Shake the bottle well and test the temperature of the contents by squirting a few drops on the inside of your arm before you give it to your baby.

A baby needs to be held at an angle while drinking. This is especially important with the bottle because the milk tends to come out faster when the baby lies flat and the stream can hit the back of the throat and get into the connection between middle ear and throat, the eustachian tube; this increases chances for ear infections. The bottle should be held so that the nipple is filled with fluid. That way the baby will swallow less air. It might be a good idea to burp the baby a little more frequently when feeding it with a bottle. You can save what the baby leaves in the bottle and offer it again the next time, provided that you put it in the refrigerator in the interim and use it within forty-eight hours. Milk keeps at room temperature for about two hours. If you transport milk, pack it in ice, or keep it frozen and then defrost and warm it just before you need it.

A mother's milk supply is often most abundant in the early morning. Some mothers report that milk pumped late in the morning and given to the baby in the evening helped the baby sleep longer. This is perhaps because the supply tends to become low when the mother is tired, and the midday milk is usually the highest in fat. If the father gives the late-evening bottle, the mother can go to bed early and get a longer period of uninterrupted sleep before the baby wakes up for its first night feeding.

Wash pump parts and the bottle, bottle top, and nipple with soap and water, and scrub the screw-top with a brush to make sure no milk cells are left behind. Rinse well and leave to dry on a clean towel. Dishwashers sterilize quite well. It is not necessary to boil bottles, nipples, or pump parts unless you use a manual bulb-type pump. The bulbs are known to have caused infections because milk often gets lodged in them and spoils. Experts recommend that you do not use that type, since even boiling does not clean it well enough. Infant feeding equipment should be boiled when the water cannot be trusted to be free of disease-causing micro-organisms.

A stressful day, especially if it coincides with a growth spurt during which the baby wants to nurse all the time, can suddenly leave you with insufficient milk. In the case of a growth spurt, the baby will bring in more milk by nursing more often. If your supply does not return, ask your doctor if it is okay for you to make a tea with the herb fenugreek, available in health-food stores; some report that this herb is very helpful.

If doubts persist about the adequacy or quantity of your milk, see if the baby is producing at least six to eight wet diapers per day and preferably two dirty ones as well. If so, your milk supply is adequate. Also your baby's skin should look well filled out. If not, check with your baby doctor. One of the reasons the baby may appear hungry so much of the time, especially near the mother, is that she smells like milk, which stimulates the baby to root for the breast. This is why fathers can often calm a baby with gas pains more easily than nursing mothers.

If your baby's wanting to nurse all the time seems unrelated to hunger but is caused by the need to suckle, try a pacifier or see if you can help your baby find its thumb. Try not to deny him this simple satisfaction for fear that he won't give it up later. Generally, babies quite readily abandon what they no longer need. It is often the caretaker who, by continuing to reinforce a habit, keeps the baby from giving it up. Between the age of two and five weeks, babies go through a lot of growth spurts, and some days they want to nurse almost continuously. Don't worry about spoiling your baby by giving in; in another two months it will be much less interested in the breast, whether you impose limits now or not.

After three months of successful nursing, many mothers suddenly worry again about not having enough milk. Perhaps this is because around that time babies emerge out of the "fourth trimester" and, as they take on more of their own personality, their schedules and demands are confusing to the mother. If your baby is gaining weight and developing normally, you have enough milk and there is no need to add formula or cereal yet.

One of the first signs that the baby is ready to eat something other than breast milk is its interest in what you are eating. This often coincides with the ability to sit up and turn the head. Now the more developed neck muscles enable the baby to handle food given with a spoon. Most babies like and digest fruits and vegetables better than cereal at first. Making your own baby food is very

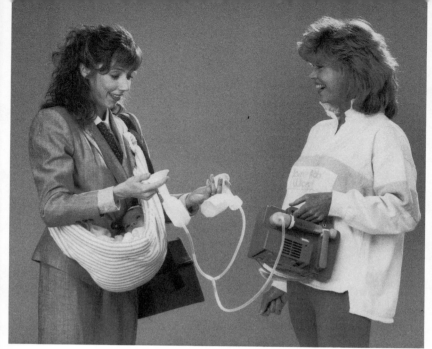
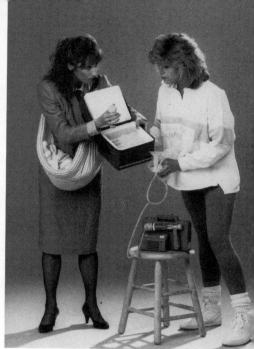

This portable electric breast pump, which also runs on rechargeable batteries, enables the mother to pump both breasts at the same time. The cold pack for milk storage, slung over the mother's shoulder, looks like a shoulder bag. This particular sling allows a baby to rest with a rounded spine, something many new babies like. Later, as the muscles along the spine develop, the baby can sit up and look out while being carried.

simple if you have a small electric food mill or a manual baby-food grinder. Freshly made food is better than canned food because it has more nutrients.

Going back to work does not have to bring an end to nursing. Mothers who work away from their babies often say that it makes them feel good to be able to nurse when they come home from work, during the night, and before they leave in the morning. Don't be surprised if a baby, after being without you most of the day, asks for more physical contact with you when you are home. Lie down skin to skin, or take a nap or sleep together, if everyone in the bed can sleep that way. Quite a few people enjoy a family bed.

Nursing mothers often pump their breasts at work and store the milk in a cold place, then take it home wrapped in ice. If this does not work out for you or if you cannot produce enough milk, keep in mind that when you add formula, the less the better—once in twenty-four hours gives the baby's body a chance to get it out of its system, and thus it is less likely to become an irritant. This is especially important if there are allergies in the family.

Experts say that it is beneficial to nurse a baby until its first birthday or longer, but not all babies—or all parents—are interested in that. When you decide that it is time to wean, the baby may well sense it and want to nurse more often. Reevaluate whether it is really necessary to take the breast away. If so, omit the least favorite feeding first, let a few days go by, and then omit the next one, continuing until only one, usually a night feeding, is left. Let someone else put your baby to bed for a few nights, bind your breasts close to your body, pack them with ice, and wait for your body to reabsorb the milk. This sometimes takes a while. When in doubt about lumps or a discharge, always call your doctor. When the decision to wean originates with your baby, it may surprise you. I have known a few babies who suddenly refused the breast altogether.

OTHER ASPECTS OF CARE

Ideally, your doctor or the nurse will examine your baby at your bedside and explain how to care for parts like the cord and the genitals. Circumcision does not enhance health or function; the ancient procedure is of value only if it has a symbolic meaning for you or if you are afraid that you will not like the way your baby boy

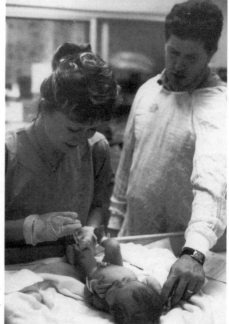

looks. Northern European boys do not have more bladder infections than their American peers and circumcision is almost unheard of in countries like Holland, Denmark, Norway, and Sweden.

Two important preventive measures are usually taken within an hour after birth: Vitamin K is administered, either in drops or by injection, and ointment or drops are placed in the eyes. Vitamin K helps a baby's blood-clotting factor mature, and the drops or ointment prevent eye infections from bacteria the baby may have encountered in the birth passage.

Doctors usually recommend that you don't submerge the baby in water until the cord has dried and fallen off. However, you may wish to give it a bath right after birth, a procedure made popular by Dr. Frederick Leboyer, who suggested that birth rooms be darkened just before the baby's delivery, that noise be kept at a minimum, and that the baby receive a warm bath soon after birth.

If you do this, or later, when you give your baby a sponge bath, keep in mind that cooling off is a threat to the baby's metabolism and that babies are very prone to it because of their large skin surface to weight ratio. They kick and cry in an effort to raise their temperature. First undress the baby's upper body, wash it, rinse it, dry it with a warm towel, and dress it (with prewarmed clothes on a cool day); then repeat the procedure with the lower body. Dry the skin well in the creases. If you choose to use talcum powder, apply it to your hands away from the baby so that it doesn't get into the air and thus into your baby's lungs. Read the label of anything you plan to use on your baby's skin. You may want to wash your baby's scalp with a little shampoo. If there are flakes on it, scrub it with a soft hairbrush. Be gentle but don't be afraid of the soft spot on top of the baby's head.

Your baby's eyes, ears, nose, and mouth do not need any special cleaning if all is well, but they need your awareness and ability to spot that something might not be right. It is not uncommon for a newborn's eyes to have a bit of a yellowish discharge. Wipe toward the baby's nose with a cotton ball while your other hand gently steadies its head; then squirt a drop of colostrum or mother's milk in the corner of the eye. If the discharge is worse the next day, contact your baby's doctor. If you notice that your baby always keeps one eye closed or displays some other pattern of preference for one eye over the other, give your doctor a call. Sometimes eye infections manifest themselves that way. Eye infections are not serious, but they need to be treated.

Clean the baby's ears and the area behind them well but gently. The ear canal cleans itself. It is safer just to let any wax fall out, because if you try to reach it, a sudden move of your baby's head could cause the swab to touch the eardrum. The nose cleans itself too. If you use a cotton swab to get something out, steady your baby's head, because babies usually try to get away from their parents' cleaning efforts. If you use a suction bulb, make sure the tip is not against the membrane of the nostril but faces straight inward instead.

A baby's mouth does not need any cleaning the first few months, but it is good to keep an eye out for cheesy specks of white on the mucous membranes inside the mouth. This can be an infection called thrush, and it will often give the mother sore nipples. Call your baby's doctor.

Babies do tend to scratch themselves with their nails. Some parents, afraid to trim the nails, wrap their baby's hands inside the sleeves of its nightgown. But babies like their hands free. Maybe one of you could hold the hand while the other uses a small nail scissor. The first time is the hardest. Some parents make a small cut and peel the rest instead of cutting all the way across.

When your baby is ready for a tub bath, usually on day ten or so, make sure the room is nice and warm, preheat the towel and

clothes, and check the water temperature with your elbow. If it feels pleasantly warm, the temperature is right. Babies don't need a bath every day, but if you and your baby enjoy it, it is a fine thing to do. You can also take your baby into the tub with you, if you don't mind having to change the water unexpectedly.

THE PUZZLE OF CRYING

It goes against most mothers' instinct to let their baby cry, even though experts say it airs the baby's lungs and relieves its tension. Trust your own feelings, and if you sense that you should offer your help, try to isolate the cause of the crying and see if you can find a solution. Your baby could be hungry, bothered by air or gas, too cold, too warm, wet, dirty, overtired, or in an uncomfortable position. Try to let go of the notion that a good baby is one that does not cry. A good baby lets you know when it needs something.

Small infants tend to wake up hungry. Because hunger feels like pain, they cry vigorously if they don't feel a nipple in their mouth soon after waking. You might find it easier to give your baby one breast before you change its diaper, unless of course the diaper is

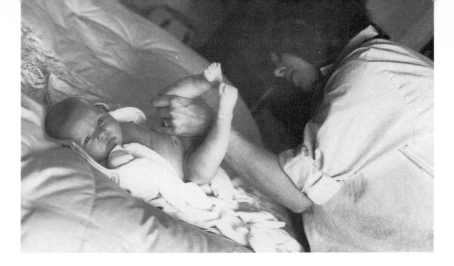

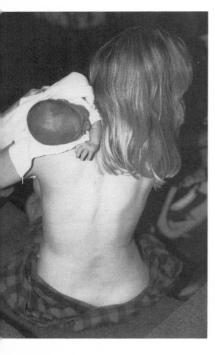

too much of a mess. Suckling relaxes the gut, and it is common for babies to have a bowel movement while at the breast. If you change your baby first, you will probably have to change it again after nursing.

A baby's diaper should be regularly changed. However, unless there is a rash in the area covered by the diaper, there is no need to change every time the diaper becomes a little wet. If your baby has a rash, a bare bottom is best, but that tends to be too messy. Change its diaper whenever it is wet, and rinse your baby's bottom with warm water, drying the skin gently but thoroughly. Rashes heal better with a bit of sun; expose the bare bottom for one or two minutes the first day and then increasingly longer, always protecting the baby's eyes and skull. Add a teaspoon of baking soda to the baby's bathwater to change the pH of its skin. Change diapers frequently, and do not use plastic or rubber pants. If the rash persists, change your diaper service or the way you wash the diapers. Sometimes boiling diapers or hanging them to dry in the sun a few times will do the trick. If you are using paper and plastic diapers, see if your baby does better with cotton. If these measures don't make a difference, ask your pediatrician which ointment you can use. If diaper rashes continue to occur, check with a pediatric allergist.

A lot of babies fuss when their diaper is dirty. It probably irritates their skin. Wash the bottom well, if necessary, with nonperfumed soap and rinse it off carefully. Oil can be applied occasionally, but it seems to clog the pores when used all the time. Commercial wipes are handy away from home, but for routine use water and nonperfumed soap are probably better.

Not all babies need help to bring up the air they swallow while

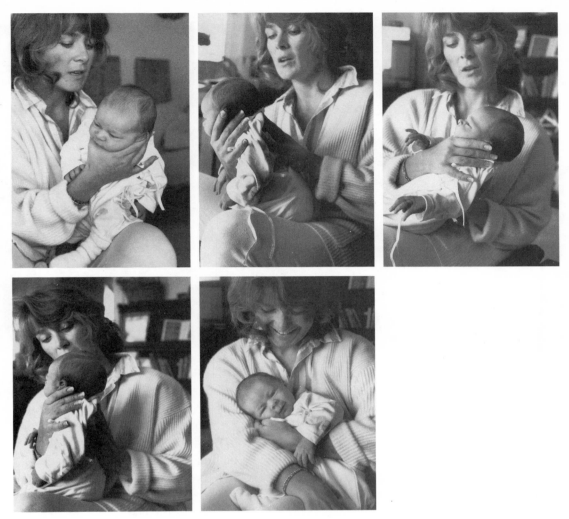

eating, but most seem to like a little encouragement at first. Holding the baby upright and gently rubbing its back at about stomach level usually works. If this does not bring the air up, some pressure on its stomach might. Place your baby a little higher, so that its belly is on your shoulder, and stroke its back again. It sometimes helps to swing the baby's upper body back and forth a few times before stroking its back.

Giving the baby a chance to burp will often relieve restlessness at the breast, as well as crying ten to twenty minutes after a feeding. It is often easier for the father to burp a baby who woke up crying; if the mother is nursing, she smells like milk, and the baby will root for the breast even if it actually needs to burp.

A baby will usually need to be burped during or within half an

hour after nursing. After that, the air may go down and possibly contribute to gas. A more likely cause of gas is indigestion brought on by food the mother ate. Dairy products are the most frequent offenders, especially in people not of northern European descent. Citrus fruit, wheat or eggs often cause gas, and spicy foods or onions can also cause havoc at first. Leave a suspected food out of your menu for a few days in order to determine whether it troubles your baby. Gas pains usually give themselves away by rather fierce and intermittent crying during which the legs may be drawn up and the belly may get hard. Try putting your baby over your shoulder. Fold one hand around its buttocks and rub its back in the area of the stomach with your other hand. Gently bounce the baby up and down, and if necessary walk back and forth too. After a few minutes the crying usually subsides somewhat. Don't panic if it does not. Speak to your baby in a reassuring voice. "It is nothing serious. It is just that you're growing so fast. It will get better." If you don't, you are likely to cry yourself, and when you feel bad and/or get tense, your baby may sense your distress and cry even more. Sometimes it helps to place your baby on your legs with its head facing your knees and its legs curled up against your belly. Grasp your baby's legs just above the knees and move them in, applying slight pressure to the belly as you do so, and out. After repeating this a few times, fold the legs up against the body

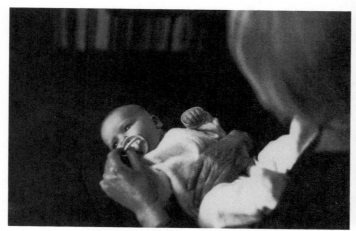

and press gently on the rectum. The baby will strain and possibly release some gas. If it experiences another cramp, cover its belly with your hand and let the weight and relaxing warmth of your hand sooth its belly. Offer your baby a pacifier (sucking relaxes the gut) and/or rub its shoulders while talking calmly and lovingly. Placing the baby's tummy over your thigh also can relieve gas pains. Some say that a warm wet compress soaked in water with some oil of chamomile helped their baby, and some pediatricians suggest that the baby be encouraged to take some chamomile tea from a bottle. Once the worst is over, it may help to wrap the baby in a receiving blanket with its thighs close to its belly.

Although it may be hard to believe, it seems to be true that babies too can become so tired they are unable to relax. Whenever your baby is fretful and you can think of no reason, try what Work-out students call the "flying baby rock." It works for a combination of reasons. The outward-rounded spine is reminiscent of the baby's position in the womb, and the warm hand on its belly has a soothing effect. Longitudinal rocking, especially with the baby's head higher than the buttocks, is more relaxing than rocking from side to side. Perhaps it helps the cerebral spinal fluid move and/ or is a craved stimulation to the vestibular system, the fine mechanism in the inner ears by which we sense our position and find our balance.

The "Flying Baby Rock"

Lay your baby facedown. Slide one hand under the baby between his legs and open that hand under his belly. Place your other hand under his chest in such a way that you support his head as well.

Rock the baby, swinging your arms forward and up, then down and back. When the baby begins to relax, allow his spine to round outward slightly. Shift your weight back and forth as you rock your baby.

To help your baby stay asleep after it dozes off in your hands, continue the rocking a little longer, until your baby enters into deep sleep. Preheat its bed by placing a hot-water bottle over a couple of rolled-up diapers. Remove the bottle when you put your baby down, and place its belly on the preheated roll. Turn its head to one side and let the thighs stay close to the belly. Keeping the thighs in this position, along with the warmth and the rounded spine, often helps a baby stay asleep. It can also relieve gas pains that are too severe.

When babies are awake, they like approximately the same temperatures we do, but if the room is on the cool side, it might be better to cover the baby's arms and legs. When a baby is asleep or trying to fall asleep, a light blanket may promote relaxation. Too much warmth may not only cause fussing but also produce a bit of a rash. Don't get too upset when your baby's skin breaks out; you learn as you go along. Not all rashes are due to heat. Babies also tend to get little pimples, which pediatricians say are similar to the skin reactions of puberty.

Since babies can't change their position very well at first, they will fuss less if you change it for them every once in a while. Most babies like variety, not only in how they are positioned but also in what they look at. Some parents draw different designs, with a black marker on white paper plates, and they put those nearby so that the baby can see them. Babies are from an early age quite intriqued with objects. Once babies can see a greater distance (usually after two to six weeks), they like to watch the patterns sunlight makes on a wall—for instance, the shadows of leaves moving with the wind. When they get a little bigger still, they like looking directly at the trees. Babies used to sleep part of the day outside, even if the weather was quite cool. Remember the pram, with a hood for sun and rain? Parents believed that fresh air was good for the baby and helped it sleep better at night. It is probably true. Try it if you can find a safe place away from too much traffic or other air-polluting elements. Just bundle your baby up a little when the weather is cool and avoid too much direct sunlight.

From about seven days to three months of age, babies are very often fretful and demanding in the late afternoon and/or evening. Numerous solutions have been put forward: The mother should eat pickles or sauerkraut for lunch to help the baby's digestion; she should pump her breasts and have someone else, who is not

tired from caring for her baby all day, give it the bottle; someone should take the baby for a drive. Some say that the late afternoon is a special time for all of us and that babies too find it hard to cope with the change from day to evening.

Most puzzling, to anyone who has lived with one, is a baby who cries all or most of the time. While it is often attributed to colic, such crying may or may not be caused by the bowels. Some babies get better when a chiropractor or osteopath with special training in infants gently adjusts or treats them. It may seem strange that babies should need an adjustment, yet they are sometimes born with a nose made crooked by pressure or a foot turned toward the inside of the leg. In such cases the doctor usually recommends regularly stroking the affected area toward the proper position. Why, then, might the bones of the head or one of the vertebrae not be out of alignment? Some babies, especially after a difficult delivery, refuse to nurse on one side. While preference for one or the other breast is often associated with the mother's handling one breast more easily than the other, if the baby absolutely refuses one of the breasts, it may be because there is something wrong—for instance, there may be no milk, the nipple may be too difficult to grasp, or it may hurt the baby to turn its head toward that side. A baby who does not like to lie on its stomach with its head turned to the side may also have a problem. Experts say that parents can tell by holding their baby upside down by the feet. If the head pulls to one side or the other, the baby will benefit from an adjustment. If no adjustment is made, the body will eventually correct the problem on its own; seeing a trained expert might save some crying.

Astonishing as such persistent crying is, equally astonishing is the baby's personality when it suddenly stops. Such babies show no signs of remembering their suffering, and they are filled with delight and curiosity. Until such time, relieve each other and hire help even if you can barely afford it. Caring for a crying baby is very stressful. Also, experiment with harmless remedies such as placing the baby, carefully strapped in its infant seat, on top of a turned-on drier for a while. Like a car ride, this often puts a baby to sleep. If a car ride is the only thing that quiets your baby and you are tired of taking a spin at four in the morning, there is a contraption—devised by a father in a similar situation, who received a grant from the National Institutes of Health—that can be hooked to the crib and creates the noise, shaking, and other characteristics of a car ride. It does seem to work. Try your local baby store. One baby I know could be quieted only by his father. He held his baby to his chest, danced up and down, and made sounds he had learned from an Indian healing ceremony. He was a prom-

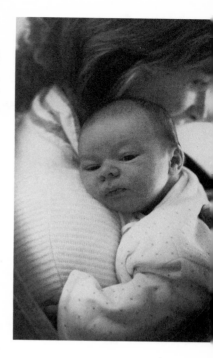

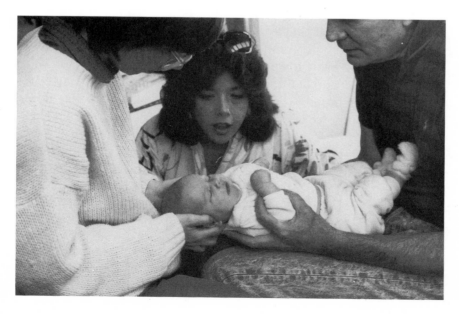

A gentle treatment by an osteopath

inent labor attorney, but he rushed home to help his son—and his wife—whenever he could.

As you get to know your baby better, you soon learn which crying it needs to do and which you should help it with. Some babies do seem to have to cry a minute or two to get to sleep. The Omaha Indians of eastern Nebraska held that some people were more gifted in understanding the sounds made by a baby than others, and in the case of persistent crying such a person was called upon for help. Occasionally the interpretation was that the baby did not like its name, and the name would be changed. I don't know whether it ended the crying.

ABOUT SCHEDULES AND SLEEP

One of the most perplexing differences between babies lies in how readily they adjust to the rhythm of their parents' life. Sleeping through the night is one of the more popular topics among mothers at the Workout, and after listening for years, I have come to believe that getting your baby to sleep through the night requires a degree of maturity in the baby and sensitivity on the part of the baby's caretakers to its signals.

Almost all babies need so many calories at first that they can get enough only if they eat every couple of hours. Hunger causes pain, and when they surface from sleep into semiwakefulness, which they do every couple of hours, hunger will make them wake up all the way and call for food. As a baby's metabolism matures, the need for around-the-clock feedings subsides. At that point, when they stir from deeper sleep, if there are no discomforts bothering them, they can often get back to sleep on their own. Some babies accomplish this suddenly, and the mother runs to the crib at six in the morning, anxious to see if her baby is all right. Some do it one night but call for help the next. Don't be in too much of a hurry to feed your baby now; go see if your baby is okay, stroke its back a little, talk softly or sing, and offer it some water. If the crying becomes rather desperate, offer your breast or a bottle, but don't encourage your baby to take a lot. You are trying to help the stomach get over the need to be filled during the night.

Some babies sleep better close to something that smells like

their mother, such as a bra or some other intimate item. Others sleep better away from their mother's smell and the sound of her breathing. A nighttime routine—for instance, a bath, a massage, a feeding, and then bed—often helps too. An easily overstimulated or tense baby probably has a harder time getting back to sleep than a more placid one. Some babies continue to need the relaxation that comes with suckling even though they tried repeatedly to give it up. Experts say that it is better to try to wean a baby from falling asleep at the breast or with a bottle before or around four months of age, because when a baby's only way of getting to sleep is while feeding, it will ask for it when it wakes up during the night too. Don't let your baby fall asleep with a bottle of juice, since the juice stays in the mouth, which is very bad for the teeth. Take cues from your baby and continue to watch carefully for signs that it is ready to adjust to your needs a little. Babies like to please their parents.

There is nothing wrong with continuing night feedings and/or letting the baby sleep with you some or all of the night, unless this interferes with your own needs. If getting up twice a night to care for a plump and healthy four-month-old is beginning to exhaust and annoy you, your feelings of resentment are probably more confusing for your baby than a limit set by you would be. A good rule for child-rearing is: Encourage your baby to do for itself what it can, help it with what it cannot yet do, and don't let it get away with something you truly disapprove of.

Most parents are surprised to discover how little their baby sleeps during the day and to learn that their baby actually seems to get bored and run out of things to do. Most small babies like to be bounced on a variety of knees and be sung to by different voices. Anxiety in the presence of strangers does not develop until later. Babies also like to be carried in a sling. This must have been one of woman's earliest inventions; it seems so indispensable, and babies have such a natural affinity for being toted about that way. A baby swing can also be fun. Before you buy one, try it out in the store and make sure your baby likes it.

BABY MASSAGE

Many parents enjoy giving their baby a massage. Some babies are ready for it right away; others don't like it until they are a few weeks old. Try it every once in a while and stop when your baby lets you know that it has had enough. A massage is a stimulating experience for a small baby (premature babies grow better when regularly massaged), and as their senses get aroused, many desire to nurse. With babies under three months of age, immediately after massaging, wrap the baby in a blanket and offer your breast. You can dress the baby once it has satisfied the urge to nurse.

Position yourself so that you can touch your baby without strain. At the Workout, the mothers usually sit on the floor with their babies on a blanket between their open legs. Relax and warm your hands by rubbing them together vigorously; then shake them out.

Place your hands in the middle of your baby's chest, index fingers touching,

and, with just the weight of your relaxed hands, stroke the chest just as you would stroke the pages of a new book to keep it open. Repeat once or twice.

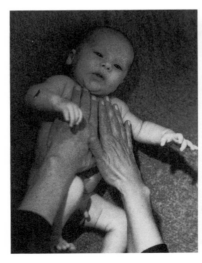
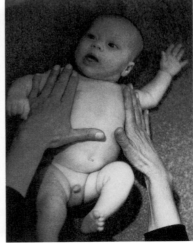

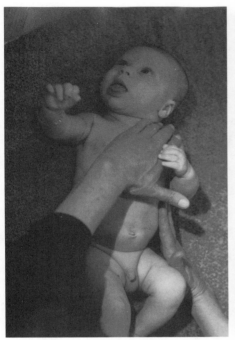

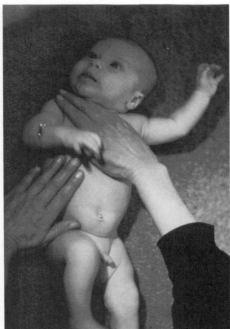

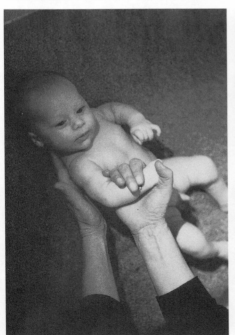

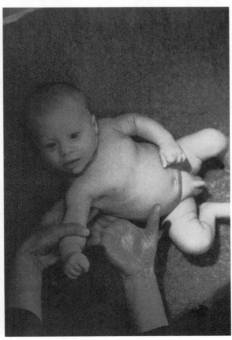

Next, slide your right hand down to the baby's left hip and place your left hand on his left shoulder.

Slide your left hand down to the baby's right hip, then slide the right hand up to the right shoulder. Repeat these strokes crosswise over the baby's chest, from hip to opposite shoulder, a few times in a rhythmic fashion.

Turn your baby so that his right arm is toward you. Take this arm in your right hand and lift your baby's shoulder a little, then slide your left hand from the top of his shoulder to the upper right arm. Fold your hand around the arm and slide it down to the wrist while imagining you are gently lengthening the arm.

Hold on to his right wrist with your left hand and place your right hand under the baby's back, then slide it toward the arm.

Circle the arm with your right hand, then slide this hand down to the wrist as if gently lengthening the arm. Repeat these strokes rhythmically a few times with your right and left hand.

Gently circle your fingers on top of the baby's wrist.

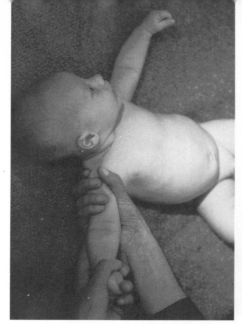

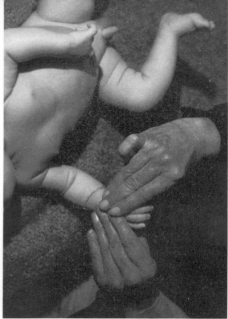

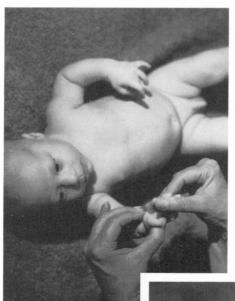

Then stroke the palms of his hand with your thumb. Don't pry the hand open; just gently see if your baby will let you open his fist.

Turn your baby so that his right arm is toward you and repeat the arm strokes.

Turn your baby so that his legs are toward you. Take the right leg in your right hand and lift the right buttocks slightly. Slide your left hand under the buttocks, then bring it to the top of the right thigh.

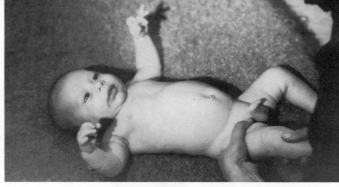

Hold the thigh in your hand and stroke down toward the foot, imagining that you are lengthening the leg.

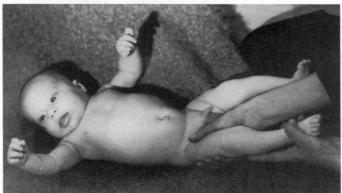

Hold on to the ankle with your left hand and place your right hand around the upper thigh. Stroke downward with this hand; repeat once with your left and then with your right hand.

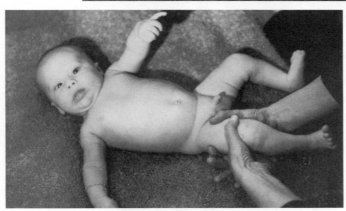

Place both hands close together around the thigh and move them downward in a twisting motion, much like the Indian burn you may have learned in grade school but more gently. Think of breaking up the tension in these long muscles as you twist your hands in opposite directions while sliding them down toward the ankle. Finish with one more long stroke with each hand.

Stroke the sole of your baby's foot, heel to toe, with your thumbs a few times.

Repeat all the leg strokes on the left leg. If your baby likes the twisting strokes, consider incorporating them into the arm strokes next time.

Place your baby crosswise over your legs. Place both hands, parallel to each other, on your baby's back. Move your hands simultaneously but in opposite directions (one hand away from you and one toward you, then the reverse) across the baby's back as you slide them steadily down toward the buttocks.

When your right hand reaches your baby's buttocks, cup the buttocks in this hand, then move your left hand up to just below the neck.

Hold on to the buttocks with slight pressure while you slide your left hand down your baby's back. When your hands meet, move your left hand up to the neck again, then slide it down in a caressing fashion.

When you feel your baby's back relax, slide your right hand down the legs, place your index finger in between and your thumb and middle finger around his ankles and gently straighten both legs. Place your left hand at the base of the skull.

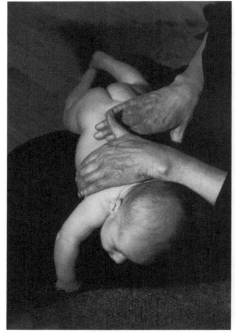

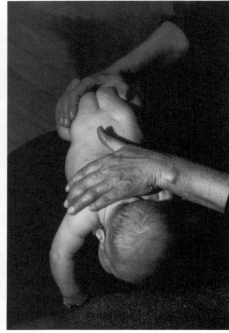

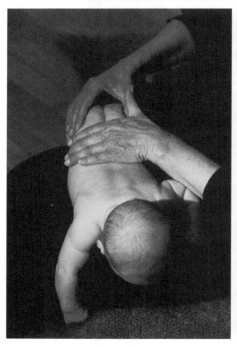

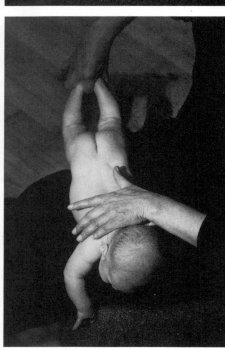

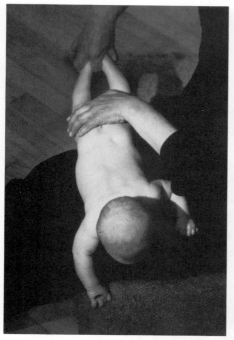

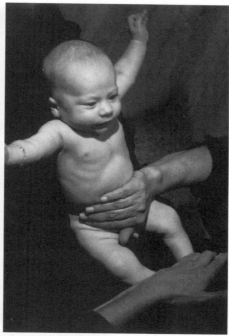

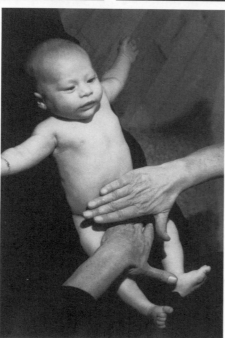

Now stroke down the neck, the back, the buttocks, and the legs all the way to the feet. Repeat these long back strokes a few times.

Next place your baby so that his head is near your knees and his legs curl up against your body. Gently place your right hand on your baby's belly. Think of enclosing the belly in your hand and let the warmth and weight of your hand soothe his belly. Hold still for a few moments.

Stroke downward over the belly to the thighs with your right and then your left hand. Repeat a few times. If your baby is still having problems with gas, take the thighs in your hand and move the legs in, putting pressure on the belly, then out a few times. Fold the legs up against your baby's body and, with your free hand, press against your baby's rectum gently. Your baby will strain and probably release some gas.

THE MYSTERY OF GROWTH

Human beings born in this century in a so-called developed country grow taller, reach sexual maturity sooner, and live longer than those born in earlier times or in third world countries. This phenomenon is called "secular drift" among experts, and speculations as to its cause abound. What is certain is that in babies and children growth is a sign of good health. Thus, babies are measured and put on the scale on a regular basis. Those that do not gain according to the norm are often suspected of not getting enough food. This is not always the case; some babies just grow at a different rate. If your doctor suggests formula supplements but your baby has six to eight wet diapers, has regular bowel movements, sleeps, eats, and does not cry a lot, get a second opinion before you decide.

The trouble with statistics is that 50 percent of babies will fall below the median. Some babies never crawl, but they walk at eight months. Some don't walk until they are fourteen months old. Don't expect your baby to fit into a statistical mold or to meet some notion of perfection. Babies born with a problem often turn what was initially a disadvantage into a strong point. We thrive better when we are helped to face a challenge than when everything is perfect and easy.

Babies with a black heritage usually develop physically faster than all others. They tend to have greater muscle strength and coordination than their age mates from other genetic backgrounds. Quite a few babies like to be held so that they can stand on their own two feet. Don't fear that this will make your baby bowlegged; you will both sense when it has had enough. Some babies enjoy looking at picture books very early, especially when the pages are flipped by rather fast, and many babies are fascinated with television. Ours must be a remarkable time to be born; so much can be done with the touch of a button that the world seems a more magical place than ever before. Babies who are shown their mother's face on a screen together with someone else's voice look puzzled. When it is their mother's face and voice, they look for a longer time.

THE KEY TO INJURY PREVENTION

One of the reasons why babies are so much fun is that they so often come up with surprises, or they suddenly do things their parents did not think they could. Be aware of that in terms of safety. Babies do scoot to the edge of the bed or turn over on the changing table unexpectedly. Being conscious that babies are capable of the unexpected, and realizing that, until age three, children cannot control their impulses and therefore should not be trusted without adult supervision, will do more for your child's safety than all the locks, gates, and other devices combined. Do learn how to make your house more childproof, though; it makes living with a small child a lot easier. A good place to start is by asking your pediatrician to go over safety issues with you at your well-baby visits. When your baby begins to eat solids and is getting ready to crawl, be sure to ask what you can do to prevent choking. And remember this rule, which I learned from one of our mothers: While driving do not give babies or small children any-

thing they could choke on; a sudden stop seems to increase the chance that the baby will get what was in its mouth into its air passage. A bottle is okay, but don't let your baby chew on a frozen bagel or a pear, and later on, no hard candies in the car.

If you hear your baby crying, make sure that it is not ill or in trouble and that the crib is safe. If you use plastic diapers, cover the plastic, because a baby can pick off a little piece, inhale it, and choke. When the crying stops, check to make sure that it has stopped for a good reason.

The American Academy of Pediatrics publishes lists to help pediatricians make parents more aware of which injuries at what age a child is at greatest risk for. While learning to prevent is much better than learning to cure, you might also ask your doctor for the first-aid chart published by the academy. And maybe you should take a CPR class for infants and toddlers at your local Red Cross. Since it is hard to remember those techniques because learning them can be so stressful, I have illustrated them here but use my instructions as a reminder rather than as a substitute for classes.

HOW TO REMEMBER CPR

Make the relatively simple CPR skills less overwhelming by dividing them into two separate categories: what to do if you see your baby choke and what to do if you have to help an unconscious child maintain oxygenation until professionals can take over.

In the case of choking, remember that a baby's cough reflex is more effective in evicting an obstruction than any external techniques. Therefore, if your baby turns red in the face and coughs, calmly encourage him or her and watch. If your baby cannot make a sound, if her eyes bulge out, if her color changes to purple, or if her muscles become limp, call for help. If there is someone in the house, call for them; if you are alone, telephone the emergency squad. Usually, dialing the number and leaving the phone off the hook and talking while attending to your baby will bring them to your door.

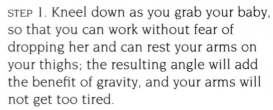

STEP 1. Kneel down as you grab your baby, so that you can work without fear of dropping her and can rest your arms on your thighs; the resulting angle will add the benefit of gravity, and your arms will not get too tired.

STEP 2. Sandwich the baby between your arms with one hand supporting her head at the back and the other at the face.

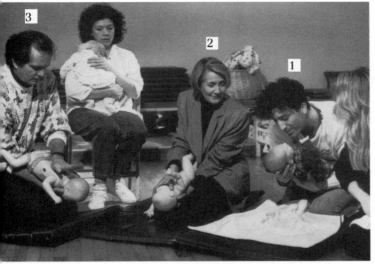

STEP 3. Turn your baby facedown, and with the hand that was at the back of her head give four thrusting blows to the baby's back, right beneath the shoulder blades. Then return the hand to the back of her head, support head and body in alignment, and turn your baby over so that she is face up and resting on your hand and arm.

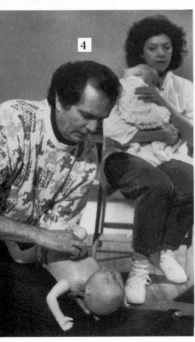

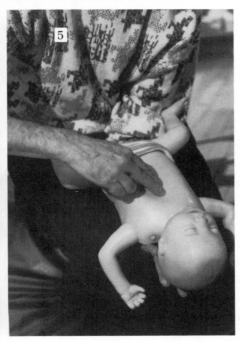

STEP 4. Take your hand from the baby's face and place your index and middle fingers on your baby's chest so that the top one is right underneath the nipple. Slide your fingers to the middle of her chest.

STEP 5. With your fingers thus carefully placed (in the middle of the chest and at the right height to avoid injury to the liver or spleen), and without letting your fingers leave the skin, make four thrusting movements strong enough to compress the chest inward about half an inch. Return your hand to the baby's face, and turn the baby over to do the back blows again. Repeat these front and back blows a few times.

You can usually hear and see when the object is released because the baby gasps for air and cries or her color improves. Carefully remove the object from your baby's mouth if it did not come flying out. If, after turning the baby from front to back a few times, nothing comes out and you see none of the changes mentioned, put the baby down on her back in front of you, place one hand on her forehead, open the airway by lifting the chin, and perform mouth-to-mouth breathing as shown and described on pages 314 and 315. If the air does not go in, repeat the sandwiching with front and back thrusts. If the air goes in, continue mouth-to-mouth breathing until the baby starts to breathe on her own or until professional help arrives.

Note: Do not practice the front and back thrusts on a baby or a child. They can cause harm and therefore should be done only in a situation where the benefits outweigh the risks. It is perhaps a good idea to practice the sandwiching a few times. Your baby will not mind if you make a game out of it and support her head well.

Wait until your baby is a few months old. Before then there is not much risk of choking, because, as you know, babies don't choke on milk or water. But remember that anything you give a baby goes into the mouth, so be careful what you let your baby play with. When your child begins to explore the world and hold food, be especially careful with grapes, a teaspoon of peanut butter, a piece of hot dog, toys from an older child, and articles made of plastic. Never tie a balloon (or anything else, because a string is dangerous too) to a crib.

The following CPR skills should be used when you find a child unconscious without knowing what caused it: choking, drowning, poisoning, sudden infant death syndrome, an injury, etc. To learn how to proceed in such a case, imagine you are at a gathering of people and children, and you see a small child lying on the ground in a way that makes you suspicious. Don't panic. Go to the baby and look at the environment around it for clues to what might have happened. If it does not look like a fall with a neck injury, turn the baby onto its back while asking, "Are you okay?" If there is no answer, tap the soles of the feet. If this meets with no response, call for help. If you were at home alone, you would telephone the rescue squad.

STEP 1. Stabilize the baby's head with one hand and open the baby's airway with the other by lifting her chin. Bring your face close so that you can look at the chest to see if it rises and falls, listen for the sound of breathing, and feel for any air current on your cheek.

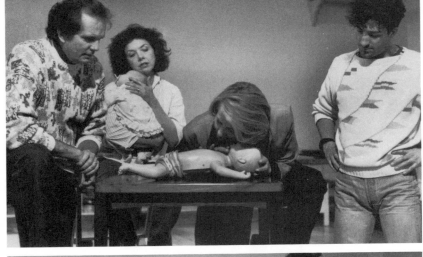

STEP 2. If none of these signs of breathing are present, place your mouth over the baby's mouth and nose (or pinch his nose closed with one hand), keep the airway open, and give a few short breaths.

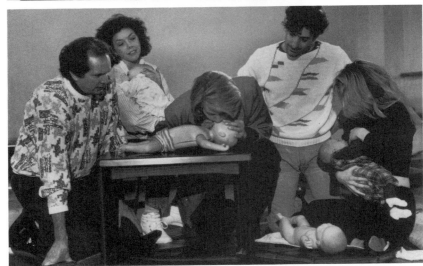

STEP 3. If the air does not go in, check the position of the baby's head. If it is tilted quite far back, lessen the angle; too much of a tilt can close the air passage. Make sure her chin is lifted and try again. If still no air goes in, try the choking techniques described and shown above. If air does go in, give a few quick short breaths.

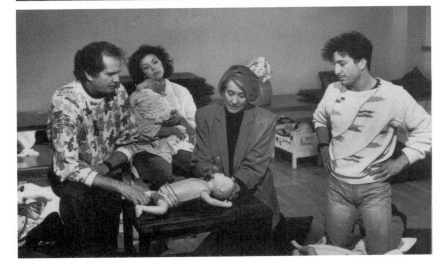

STEP 4. Open the hand that is holding the baby's head and fit it around the face, lifting the chin with the fingertips of this hand. Place the fingertips (not the thumb, because you could mistake your own pulse for the baby's) of the other hand on the inside of the baby's upper arm and feel for a pulse while you look, listen, and feel for breathing. If you feel and see the baby breathe, her heart is beating too, and you can stop feeling for a pulse. Keep the baby warm, talk with her and make sure the breathing continues.

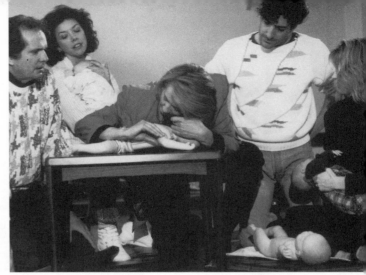

STEP 5. If you do not notice any breathing but you feel a pulse, give the baby oxygen and her heart will pump it to the brain. Give mouth-to-mouth breathing at a rate of about twenty breaths per minute. (A simple way to get the right tempo is by saying, "One, one thousand; two, one thousand" between breaths.) The breaths should be short puffs of air, about the amount that you can hold in puffed-up cheeks. Continue for about a minute and a half, then pause to look, listen, and feel for breathing and to check for a pulse. If the baby has started to breathe, keep her warm and under close supervision. If you continue to feel a pulse but there is no breathing, go back to mouth-to-mouth breathing. If there is no pulse this time, carefully double-check before you conclude that the heart has stopped beating. Move your fingers around a bit before you go on to cardiac massage.

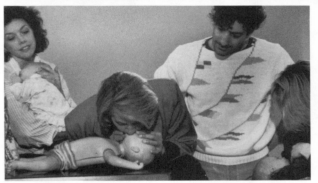

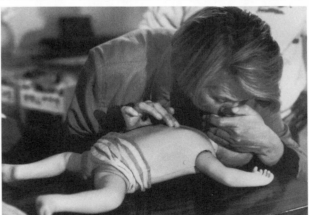

When there is no pulse and no breathing, the baby needs not only oxygen but also help to get the oxygen to the brain, because the heart is not pumping the blood through the arteries.

STEP 1. Hold the baby's airway open with one hand, place the fingertips of the other hand in the middle of the chest with the top finger just below nipple level (yes, cardiac massage is the same technique as the chest thrusts for choking), and give a short breath.

STEP 2. Keep your face close, do five rapid chest thrusts without letting your fingers leave the skin, give a short breath, repeat five chest thrusts, and so on. Keep your face close so that you don't lose too much time between giving oxygen and helping the heart get the oxygen to the brain. Continue for a minute and a half, then stop to look, listen, and feel for a pulse. Return to cardiac massage and mouth-to-mouth breathing if there is no pulse and no breathing. If there is a pulse but no breathing, give mouth-to-mouth breathing. If you notice that the baby has started to breathe, stop all CPR techniques and keep the baby comfortable and under close supervision until professional help arrives.

Note: Do not practice mouth-to-mouth breathing and or cardiac massage on a baby or a child. These techniques can interfere with the heart's rhythm and cause injury. Use them only when they are clearly necessary, and then observe good technique. Position the fingers carefully, open the airway with a chin lift, and keep your breaths small.

It is a good idea to practice looking, feeling, and listening for breathing as well as to learn how to feel your baby's pulse. If you cannot find the pulse, ask your doctor to show you how. Discuss with your doctor what you should do in case of accidental poisoning and what you should have in your first-aid kit. Also ask your doctor or the nurse in the office to show you how to take your baby's temperature. Whenever a baby has a fever and seems lethargic, take her temperature regularly; call your doctor if it continues to rise.

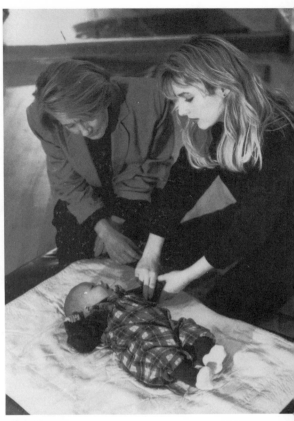

MEASURES FOR A LONG LIFE

Babies are vulnerable to all environmental diseases, those that are contagious and those that are caused by toxins. Combine that with the fact that they have a tremendous need to explore and no foresight or reasoning power, and we have to marvel that so many babies reach adulthood unscathed. Of all the classes I teach, the one that touches me most is one called Safety First, because I see in my students' faces how much they care. This uniquely human ability to care for others as much or more than we care for ourselves seems to get born with our babies.

People of all cultures and times have looked for ways to protect their vulnerable offspring from harm. Among the Omaha Indians it was customary to give a small child moccasins with a little hole in them so that if the Great Spirit called, the baby could say, "I can't travel now; my moccasins are worn out." Today we use immunization, nutrition, and sanitation to protect our babies. Immunizations save many lives, but they can harm an occasional individual one. To make it as safe as possible for your baby, ask your doctor to explain the pros and cons of early versus later administration of DPT (diphtheria, pertussis, and tetanus) shots. Mention any allergies in your family. If you and your doctor decide to go ahead and start the shots, make sure your baby does not have a cold or any other illness. Also, ask your doctor to list the

signs of an overreaction. Babies who react adversely to the first dose of the pertussis vaccine are better off without the second one until later.

Keep a record not only of your baby's immunizations but also of major events such as the first smile, first turning over, and first tooth, and jot down symptoms of illnesses and when they occurred. The Academy of Pediatrics publishes a booklet called "Child Health Record" to help parents with the task. Such information facilitates the diagnosis of any illness, and on a trip or in an emergency, it helps to have such data on hand. Moreover, keeping a record makes your doctor a consultant rather than an authority, and it makes changing pediatricians less frightening.

If you have not cut down on indoor pollution yet, now is a good time to take a look at how to get rid of some of the toxins in your house. Don't let the seemingly overwhelming nature of the task frighten you. Reread the "Improving Your Nest" section of Part One. Decide what you should tackle first, and use the resource guide at the end of the book to get started. Getting rid of pollution is a bit like good parenting, I think. It starts at home; then, as one's awareness of the importance of clean water and air grows, one begins to influence one's circle of friends and the world at large. Parenting, too, starts at home as a very private function. But as your child matures and begins to venture out into the world, you realize that caring for your child means caring about other children and about the world.

ABOUT THE PEOPLE IN
THE PHOTOGRAPHS

The common denominator that linked the fifteen women who helped me illustrate this book was pregnancy. Their lives otherwise are as divergent as most women's lives are in a modern metropolitan area. Some worked throughout their pregnancy—Cola Smith, a textile designer; Sandi Wildman Padnos, a public-relations executive, and Kathryn Gimbel, a hair colorist, for example. Some worked part-time while taking care of a first child—Teri Herron, who works in a stationery store; Janie Gates, who works with the handicapped; and Monica May, who makes pottery. Some were out of work because of their pregnancy—for instance, actress Kirsten Frantzich found it hard to get parts—and some, like musician Pia Vai and actress Anne-Marie Crighton, decided to take time off from career demands. Dedication to fitness ranged from the disciplined approach of actress-dancer Jillie Mack, who never missed a class, to the sporadic attendance of Monica May. Actresses Wendie Jo Sperber and Beth Collins, both second-time mothers, liked the program so much that they decided to learn how to teach it.

Thirteen babies (four girls and nine boys) have been born at this time. The course of their mothers' labors, while as diverse as their lives, was not predictable from their fitness, age, or appearance.

For example, Jillie Mack, whose fine control over her body inspired everyone in our pregnancy exercise class and who handled hours of strong contractions beautifully, did not dilate past three centimeters, while Monica May's labor lasted only four hours. This was Monica's second baby and she chose a midwife-attended home birth this time. She spent most of her labor in the bathtub and she handled her contractions with admirable control. She walked to her bed when she was ready to deliver and she had her baby fifteen minutes later. Beth Collins's first baby was delivered by cesarean because she stayed breech in spite of efforts to turn her. Her second baby, but first full labor, lasted all night without any dilatation. Then, at six in the morning her cervix began to open up and she was completely dilated two hours later. She pushed her baby out in about half an hour and she had no need of an episiotomy. Her husband, who had gone home to have breakfast with two-year-old Hanna, missed the birth. Kirsten and Pia, both first-time mothers, did not use any drugs for their labors either, but both needed an episiotomy. In Pia's case, it was given just as the

baby's head emerged and she did not feel it; Kirsten received a local anesthetic just before. Second-time mother Teri Herron delivered a nine-pound eleven-ounce baby boy without any drugs, without an episiotomy or even a small tear. Under her doctor's guidance, she changed positions between the delivery of the head and the shoulders, to help the baby's large shoulders emerge. First-time mothers Martha Coolidge, Sandi Wildman Padnos, and Cola Smith were induced with Pitocin after their membranes ruptured. Martha and Sandi used an epidural once labor was on the way. Both were able to push their babies out just fine. In Cola the Pitocin failed to bring on contractions and she was delivered by a cesarean section. First-time mother Elaine Balden dilated rather rapidly, but she could not bring her baby down and after two hours of pushing she too was delivered by cesarean section. Sandra Macat and Anne-Marie Crighton went way past their due dates without signs that their bodies were ready for labor: their babies were still high and there was no effacement or dilatation of the cervix. Both took their doctors' advice to forgo induction and they delivered healthy babies by cesarean section. And, finally, the story of Hunter Gimbel's birth should be told. After an uneventful labor, suddenly, while he was coming down nicely with his mother's pushing, his heart rate dropped almost to zero and did not come back up when her contraction was over. He was quickly delivered with forceps. After a bit of assistance with oxygen and some suctioning of his air passages, he started to breathe on his own. When he was handed to his mother he broke out in a smile.

Everyone was successful with breast-feeding. Here I especially admired Martha Coolidge, because her baby, Preston, was born with a cleft lip. Martha's patience and dedication helped him nurse, and he flourished on her milk. His lip has since been repaired and he is a rather dashing baby boy.

The first-time mothers all found new motherhood more overwhelming and consuming than they expected. The second-time mothers found it much easier, but the two whose children came in close succession to each other, Monica and Beth, did discover that having two small children leaves a mother with no time or energy for anything else for a while.

All the fathers were active participants. I thank them and all fifteen women for giving so much love and creativity to this project.

Resources for New Parents

CUTTING DOWN ON TOXINS

For free information on how to create a toxin-free home environment, check with the U.S. Government Printing Office, which has pamphlets on ventilation, insulation, alternative energy sources, indoor pollution, etc. Write S. James, Consumer Information Center—Y, Pueblo CO 81009 for a free copy of the catalogue called *U.S. Government Books*.

For general home pollution questions, call your state health department, the regional office of the Environmental Protection Agency, or the Consumer Product Safety Commission at (800) 638-2772. To test the air or the water in your home, contact the American Council of Independent Laboratories, 1725 K Street N.W., Washington, DC 20006, (202) 887-5872, for names of accredited labs in your area. To test the water in your home for lead, ask your municipal water company if they can do it for you free of charge. You can also ask to see the latest municipal water test report. For questions about this report, about home water filtration or about how to use water softeners safely, call the EPA Safe Drinking-Water Hotline at (800) 426-4791. For a good overview of home water filtering systems see *Is Your Water Safe to Drink?*, by Raymond Gabler, Consumer Reports Books, Feb. 1988 (available in bookstores).

Below is a list of chemicals commonly found in households, including information on what you can do to learn more about their detection and impact on health.

• **Radon,** the colorless and odorless radioactive gas that seeps out of the ground and out of some building materials into the house as uranium disintegrates, is estimated to be present in unhealthy concentrations in perhaps one third of American homes. It is a potent carcinogen. If your house has not been tested, do it now. Testing kits are available from Air Check, P.O. Box 2000, Arden, NC 28704, (800) CK-Radon. If you have questions, call your county or state health department and ask for the section dealing with radiation, or call the EPA radon information number at (202) 475-9605.

• **Asbestos** is best left alone unless it is disintegrating and releasing microscopic fibers into the air. When removal is necessary, it should be done only by trained people with professional equipment. Asbestos is fairly common in buildings erected between 1930 and 1950, when it was used as an insulating material; it was also used to cover pipes and in furnace ducts, oven linings, floor and ceiling tiles, shingles and sidings, and hair driers. For information, call the EPA at (202) 382-3949. The Consumer Product Safety Commission and the Environmental Protection Agency have published a guide, "Asbestos in the Home." For a copy write to Superintendent of Documents, U.S. Government Printing Office, Washington, DC 20402, or call (202) 783-3238.

• **Formaldehyde** is another pollutant primarily associated with insulation. Energy-efficient homes often have a urea- or phenol-formaldehyde foam sprayed between indoor and outdoor walls. Formaldehyde is also used in carpets and drapes, pressed wood (including wood used for baby furniture), wrinkle-proof sheets and clothing, deodorants, shampoos, and cosmetics, as well as in mothballs. It causes eye and upper-respiratory irritation, dizziness, and fatigue, and is believed to be a carcinogen. For a copy of the pamphlet "Formaldehyde: Everything You Wanted to Know but Were Afraid to Ask," send a self-addressed stamped envelope to Consumer Federation of America, 1424 16th Street, N.W., Washington, DC 20036. Some state health departments will test a house at no cost.

• **Cigarette smoke** makes everyone who inhales it more vulnerable to toxins from other sources. Babies exposed to cigarette smoke have a greater risk of being born premature or underweight; of dying of sudden infant death syndrome, and of suffering upper-respiratory and ear infections. For the name of a self-help group that will assist you in giving up smoking, contact the March of Dimes, 1275 Mamaroneck Avenue, White Plains, NY 10605, (914) 428-7100. For written material on how to quit, write to the Department of Health and Human Services, Office on Smoking and Health, Center for Health Promotion and Education, Centers for Disease Control, 5600 Fishers Lane, Rockville, MD 20852.

• **Pesticides** are made to kill, yet there is no skull-and-crossbones sign on the aisles where they are displayed, and most people use them without the precautions their toxicity warrants. Products banned for agricultural applications because of their toxicity are readily available for home and garden use to people who may not read the instructions. They do cause temporary illnesses and serious chronic diseases, and, especially when misused, they can cause death. Their incorrect use and the careless way in which people dispose of them has had serious consequences for many small children. Exposure to home and garden pesticides has been associated with increased incidence of brain cancer in children. To learn about less toxic ways to control pests, including roaches and fleas, or weeds, or how to buy professional pest-control services that are safe, send $1.00 for a publications catalogue to Bio-Integral

Resource Center, P.O. Box 7414, Berkeley, CA 94707. The EPA has funded a national pesticide telecommunications network through the Department of Preventive Medicine at Texas Tech University at (800) 858-7378. Call them with questions about the safety of a specific pesticide, or call the National Coalition Against the Misuse of Pesticides, 530 Seventh Street, S.E., Washington, DC 20003, (202) 543-5450. Also, avoid permanently mothproofed clothing, as it may place a toxic pesticide such as dieldrin very close to the skin.

- **Dry-cleaning fluids** evaporate from clothes for about a week after they leave the cleaners. The vapors from tetrachloroethylene and other halogenated hydrocarbon solvents are irritating to the skin, the eyes, and the upper-respiratory tract. Together with their cousins, the hydrocarbon pesticides, they are stored in the fatty tissue, including women's breasts. They cause cancer in laboratory animals, and toxicologists believe that people may be more sensitive to these solvents than animals. Hydrocarbon solvents are frequently linked to birth defects. They enter the house through dry-cleaned clothes (if you have a garment that must be dry-cleaned, afterward hang it outside for a few days if possible), through cleaning products, and, in many parts of the country, in minute but consistent amounts, through the tap water.

- **Cleaning products** can be among the most toxic substances found in the home. As heavy-duty chemicals they are regulated by the Federal Hazardous Substances Act, and they are labeled DANGER, WARNING, or CAU-TION to indicate whether a few drops, a teaspoon, or a tablespoon may cause death when swallowed or incorrectly used. Their long-term effects on health, through the fumes they emit even when correctly used, is not mentioned. The exact ingredients of most cleaning products are not listed, because they are protected as a trade secret. Most of them can be replaced with soap and a nonchlorinated scouring paste. To learn more about the potential toxicity of commonly used products such as latex paints (some contain mercury, which can stay in the air for as long as a week after painting at five times the level considered safe) and laundry detergents (today's detergents are much more caustic than the ones that contained phosphates), consult *The Product Safety Book, The Ultimate Consumer Guide to Product Hazards*, by Stephen Brobeck and Anne C. Averyt, E. P. Dutton, New York, 1983. Another excellent source of practical remedies is the *Household Pollutants Guide* from the Center for Science in the Public Interest, Anchor Press/Doubleday, 1978.

- **Lead** is a more serious problem than even the most alarming newspaper articles have told us. Lead was made mobile when it was added to gasoline. Since then the lead content of the oceans has multiplied by five and the lead content of soil, especially near freeways and heavily trafficked areas, has reached an alarming level—particularly for children who play on the ground. Now that the amount that can be added to gasoline has been controlled, the most worrisome sources of exposure are food and water. Probably the most widespread source of lead in the U.S. today is drinking water. The extent of the problem was hidden for decades because of a national failure to test water at the tap. Almost all the contamination comes from plumbing, not from the water source. You should have your water tested. If levels exceed ten parts per billion, look for lead in your pipes. Lead pipes are dullish grey, quite distinct from the orange-brown of copper or from galvanized metal pipes, which often appear corroded. More difficult to detect is lead solder, which was used in plumbing until 1986. (Although lead solder was restricted in 1986, *do* request unleaded solder if you are having any plumbing done because lead solder can still be sold). Canned food, too, is a source of lead because lead solder is still used in canning. Some cans are labeled "lead free." Cans that do not have a visible solder line are also lead free. Be cautious with all other and particularly with imported canned foods. Avoid cans that are not labeled "lead free" and that contain acidic food such as tomatoes or sauerkraut and foods preserved with vinegar or citric acid. Paint is another source of lead. Any paint made before 1976 is likely to contain lead. Removal of such paint should be done only with professional equipment to avoid inhalation. Dr. Ellen Silbergeld, a toxicologist with the Environmental Defense Fund, has made it her mission to help people reduce their exposure to lead. She can be contacted through the EDF, at 1616 P Street N.W., Washington, DC 20036.

• **Oxides of nitrogen** are an old member of the diverse family of indoor pollutants. They get into the air through incomplete combustion in home furnaces, stoves, and heaters. If you suspect faulty operations or leakage, call the gas utility company. Pilot lights on gas ranges should be blue-tipped, not yellow. If there is no vent above a gas stove, partially open a kitchen window whenever the stove is in use. "Air Pollution in Your Home," a pamphlet published by the American Lung Association, gives tips on the problems of incomplete combustion and other indoor air pollutants. Contact your local office or the national office at 1740 Broadway, New York, NY 10019, (212) 315-8700.

• **Aerosol propellants** are highly flammable (propane) or toxic (nitrous oxide or methylene chloride, for example). Propellants, along with the fluid they are designed to disperse, enter the air in very fine droplets that make their way deep into the lungs. Aerosol propellants always cause irritation of the respiratory tract; other effects will depend on what is being propelled. Paint-strippers and polishing agents will disperse more methylene chloride, a central-nervous-system irritant, and air fresheners and cosmetics will add formaldehyde. Infants and small children are especially susceptible to the toxins dispersed by aerosol sprays.

• **Cosmetics** that warrant close scrutiny are hair dyes, nail products, deodorants, and hair sprays. I know of no book or organization that specifically addresses itself to these products, but they are discussed in the books listed under "cleaning products." Hair dye is known to cause chromosomal changes. Most nail products contain hydrocarbon solvents. Some products to remove press-on nails contain acetonitrile, which is converted by the body into hydrogen cyanide, a deadly poison for a crawling toddler. Antiperspirants contain aluminum. Perspiring is more severe in pregnancy, and it is not necessary to go without a deodorant. Health-food stores and some drugstores usually offer safe alternatives.

• **Art supplies** can release hazardous pollutants. Information on the toxicity of artists' materials, including such commonly used supplies as glue and ink, can be obtained by contacting the Center for Safety in the Arts, 5 Beekman Street, New York, NY 10038, (212) 227-6220.

If you are thinking of buying a house, consider its location. A busy intersection with gas stations will add many pollutants to the air. So will living downwind from a freeway or near an airport. Power lines close to the house create an electrical soup that has been found to increase the occurrence of leukemia in children; it seems to interfere with the body's magnetic field. Some say that it is better for the same reason not to sleep under electric blankets, especially when they are turned off. For further information concerning the magnetic field and electrical interference contact Child Health Alert, a monthly survey of current developments affecting child health, P.O. Box 338, Newton Highlands, MA 02161, and ask for the August '88 issue. Keep this newsletter in mind when you become parents. You might also request a list of their publications, so that when a health or safety question comes up, you will know where to turn. The July '87 issue of the Brain Mind Bulletin

(P.O. Box 42211, Los Angeles, CA 90042) had an interesting article on electric fields. The latter is a wonderful newsletter for surviving the difficulties of the modern era because it inspires confidence in the human brain and mind.

For questions about workplace safety, contact the National Institute for Occupational Safety and Health, Division of Standards Development and Technology Transfer, 4676 Columbia Parkway, Cincinnati, OH 45226, (513) 533-8326. An excellent source of information, including a newsletter and a list of work-related publications, is Columbia University Women's Occupational Health Resource Center, 117 St. John's Place, Brooklyn, NY 11217, (718) 230-8820. The organizer of this center, Jeanne M. Stellman, a doctor of chemistry, has written numerous informative books on health hazards in the workplace, what you can do to make simple changes, and what your legal rights are. If your health-care provider does not seem very interested in helping you evaluate your work record, and you feel that such an evaluation is in order, contact the March of Dimes, 1275 Mamaroneck Ave., White Plains, NY 10605, (914) 428-7100. Someone there can refer you to a local branch, where they will have names of occupational-health nurses or geneticists in your area. The March of Dimes can also provide a form to make it easier to keep family health records. A work record and a family health record are important when questions about one's health and fertility arise.

If you have reason to believe that you have been exposed to a lot of toxins (for instance, if you lived near fields that were regularly sprayed with pesticides or worked with insulating material) check with your doctor or with the local Public Health Department. Ask if your state has a teratogen information hotline. Or call 1-800-858-7378 and ask for the teratogen hotline nearest you for information on whether or not you need a special detoxification program. To quit the cigarette habit, the U.S. Department of Health and Human Services publishes pamphlets with advice on quitting and where to obtain help. Write to the Department of Health and Human Services, Office on Smoking and Health, 5600 Fishers Lane, Rockville, MD 20852, (301) 443-1575. Your local office of the March of Dimes can also be of help. If the problem is alcohol or recreational drugs—drinking in pregnancy is a major cause of mental retardation—consider Alcoholics Anonymous. The camaraderie of people getting together to overcome the same problem has a healing effect. Meetings are free, and every city and town has a chapter.

The Center for Science in the Public In-terest publishes a newsletter called *Nutrition Action*. It is filled with tips on how to get quality food products, including fast foods, and it has many simple-to-make, healthy recipes. For membership in CSPI, which includes a subscription to *Nutrition Action*, send $19.95 to CSPI, 1501 16th Street, N.W., Washington, DC 20036, or call (202) 332-9110. CSPI also publishes a guide to help identify suppliers of safe meat and poultry. The Natural Resources Defense Council also regularly publishes information on food; among their publications is an article entitled "Pesticides in Food, What the Public Needs to Know" and a pamphlet called "Hidden Hazards in Meat and Poultry, a Consumer Guide." For information, contact the NRDC, 40 West 20th Street, New York, NY 10011, (212) 727-2700. An organization called National Foods Associates, at P.O. Box 210, Atlanta, TX 75551, (214) 796-3612, can help you locate mail-order organic-food suppliers.

HEALTH-CARE REFERRAL ORGANIZATIONS

American College of Obstetricians and Gynecologists, 409 Twelfth Street, Washington, DC 20024-2188, (800) 533-8811

American College of Nurse-Midwives, 1522 K Street, N.W., Suite 1000, Washington, DC 20005, (202) 289-0171

American Academy of Pediatrics, 141 Northwest Point Road, P.O. Box 927, Elk Grove Village, IL 60007, (800) 433-9016, ext. 7943

American Academy of Family Physicians, 8880 Ward Parkway, Kansas City, MS 64114-2797, (800) 274-2237

Asthma and Allergy Foundation of America, 111 North Wabash Avenue, Chicago, IL 60602, (312) 346-0745

International Childbirth Education Organization, P.O. Box 20048, Minneapolis, MN 55420, (612) 854-8660

American International Perinatal Health, Inc. (for questions about pre-conception planning or for referrals to appropriate healthcare), (916) 783-5200

PARENTING ISSUES

To assist parents in need of child care, many countries have a state-funded referral service that provides names of, as well as information on how to interview and evaluate, child-care providers. Check your local listings for headings like "Child Day-Care Licensing," "Family and Children's Services," and "Human Resources." There are private services that will find someone for a fee, and you can check with local churches and community centers. The National Association for the Education of Young Children, 1834 Connecticut Avenue, N.W., Washington, DC 20009, publishes up-to-date information on child care. For breast-feeding information, contact the 24-hour hotline of La Leche League, P.O. Box 1209, Franklin Park, IL 60131-8209, (708) 455-7730. For quality breast-feeding equipment or for a lactation consultant near you, contact Medela, 6711 Sands Road, Crystal Lake, IL 60014, (800) 435-8316 or Ameda-Egnell, 765 Industrial Drive, Cary, IL 60013, (800) 323-8750. For questions on car safety, call the National Highway Traffic Safety Administration at (800) 424-9393. For other product-safety questions, contact the Consumer Product Safety Commission, Washington, DC 20207 (800) 638-2772. For more information on the diapering dilemma, write for a free copy of the "Natural Diapering Handbook" to the Natural Baby Company, R.D. 1, Box 160 S, Titusville, NJ 08560, (609) 737-2895, or look in your local directory under "Diaper Service." To order biodegradable disposable diapers, contact Eco-Matrix, 124 Harvard Street, Brookline, MA 02146, (617) 730-8450, or Tendercare, 200 Apollo Road, Montrose, CO 81401, (800) 344-6379. For cotton clothing at affordable prices, write for a catalogue to Hanna Anderson, 1010 N.W. Flanders, Portland, OR 97209. *Mothering* magazine lists numerous reasonably priced mail-order companies; for a subscription, write to P.O. Box 1690, Santa Fe, NM 87504, or call (505) 984-8116. The National Organization of Mothers of Twins Club, Inc., 12404 Princess Jeanne, N.E., Albuquerque, NM 87112-4640, (505) 275-0955, can help you find experienced parents who are willing to share their knowledge. For more information on having one's children present at birth, contact Pennypress, 1100 23rd Avenue East, Seattle, WA 98112, (206) 325-1419. For child-abuse prevention programs, contact the National Committee for the Prevention of Child Abuse, 332 South Michigan Avenue, Suite 950, Chicago, IL 60604, (312) 663-3520. For information on Sudden Infant Death Syndrome (SIDS), contact the National Center for the Prevention of SIDS, 330 North Charles Street, Baltimore, MD 21201, (800) 638-7437. For government-printed information on issues related to pregnancy and new parenthood, contact the National Maternal and Child Health Clearing House, 38 R Street, N.W., Washington, DC 20057, ((202) 625-8410. Also at this address is a comprehensive information service that can link individuals with a particular problem or question with relevant professionals or organizations. It is the National Center for Education in Maternal Child Health, (202) 625-8400.

Index